Abstracts of the
TESTAMENTARY PROCEEDINGS
of the
PREROGATIVE COURT OF MARYLAND

Volume V: 1682–1686

Liber: 13 (Folios 1–432)

by
V. L. Skinner, Jr.

CLEARFIELD

Printed for
Clearfield Company, Inc., by
Genealogical Publishing Co., Inc.
Baltimore, Maryland
2006

International Standard Book Number: 0-8063-5300-7

Made in the United States of America

INTRODUCTION

Purpose of the Prerogative Court.

The Prerogative Court was the central point for probate for Provincial Maryland. It was mirrored after the Prerogative Court of Canterbury. There was a judge as well as clerk(s) of the court. Initially, all probate was brought directly to the Prerogative Court, located in the Provincial Capital. As the Province became more populous, all documents were still to be filed with the Prerogative Court; however, administration of probate was delegated to the various county courts. Even so, there are documents only in the Prerogative Court and not in the appropriate county, and vice versa.

Documents filed in the Prerogative Court.

The following documents were filed in the Prerogative Court: administration bond, will, inventory, administration accounts, and final balances. The testamentary proceedings contain the administration bond and the docket for the court. If the administrator is lax in filing documents, then a summons is also recorded.

Equity Court

The Prerogative Court was also the court for equity cases--resolution of disputes over the settlement and distribution of an estate. The case was brought before the judge and could take several years to resolve. Often depositions were taken and recorded in the minutes.

Notes on the Abstraction.

1. The left hand column contains the liber/folio number. The folio numbers are presented just as they appear in the actual document, e.g., 32a, 78½.

2. The right hand column contains the abstraction text.

3. Various libers specify a particular session for the Prerogative Court, e.g., 1678; or, September Court 1742. This information is presented as "Court Session:" followed by the

appropriate session. Should no session have been specified, then the phrase "no date" is used.

4. An ellipsis (...) is used to indicate a continuation of the previous information, but no relevant genealogical information is present.

5. The following symbols are used in the abstraction:
```
?       difficult to read.
#       pounds of tobacco.
!       [sic].
```

Abbreviations.

The following abbreviations have been used throughout this abstraction:

AA — Anne Arundel Co.
ACC — Accomac Co.
BA — Baltimore Co.
CE — Cecil Co.
CH — Charles Co.
CR — Caroline Co.
CV — Calvert Co.
dbn — de bonis non
DE — Delaware
DO — Dorchester Co.
ENG — England
FR — Frederick Co.
g — gentleman
HA — Harford Co.
IRE — Ireland
KE — Kent Co. MD
KEDE — Kent Co. DE
LaC — letters ad
    colligendum (for
    temporary
    collection &
    preservation of
    assets)

LoA — letters of
    administration
MA — Massachusetts
MD — Maryland
MO — Montgomery Co.
NE — New England
NY — New York
NYC — New York City
p — planter
PA — Pennsylvania
PG — Prince George's
    Co.
PoA — power of
    attorney
QA — Queen Anne's Co.
SM — St. Mary's Co.
SMC — St. Mary's City
SO — Somerset Co.
TA — Talbot Co.
VA — Virginia
WA — Washington Co.
WO — Worcester Co.

This is a continuation of the series, covering 1682-1686.

13:1 26 January. Arnold Elzey (SO) exhibited letter from his mother Sarah relict & administratrix of Charles Ballard (SO) & now wife of Stephen Luffe (merchant, SO). Mentions: Sarah's hard fortune to marry said Luffe, brothers & sisters of her eldest son Arnold Elzey. Said Elzey also exhibited letter from Henry Smith (g, SO), stating that Sarah Ballard was granted administration on estate of Charles Ballard last September. Said Sarah married Stephen Luffe 4 days after taking oath. Said Luffe has alienated himself from the county & not returned. Said Sarah purchased the plantation that she lives on, to be conveyed to her youngest son Gervais Ballard. Date: 15 January 1682/3.

13:2 Former administration to said Sarah is recalled. Said Elzey was granted administration. Appraisers: Capt. David Browne, Roger Woolford. Henry Smith (g, SO) to administer oath. Sheriff (SO) to summon said Luffe to render accounts.

27 January. Richard Gardiner (g, SM) exhibited the nuncupative will of Colline Mackensye (SM), proved before Clement Hill (g, SM). Said will was judged valid for goods & chattel, but void for land. Said Gardiner was granted administration. Appraisers: John Bullock, Joseph Fowler. Said Hill to administer oath.

Richard Gardiner (g, SM) exhibited that Colline Mackensye (dec'd, SM) had LoA on Richard Craines (SM). Said Gardiner was granted administration. Appraisers: John Bullock, Joseph Fowler. Clement Hill (g) to administer oath.

13:3 1 February. Michaell Taney (CV) exhibited will of Ambrose Sanderson (CV), constituting said Taney & Abell Browne (AA) executors. Said Browne renounced administration. Mentions: Mr. Parker, said Browne is brother of said Sanderson, Capt. Ladd, Maj. Nicholas Gassaway. Date: 8 December 1682. Said Taney was granted administration. Said

will was proved before Thomas Grunwin by
Eduard Molins & Joseph Recant.
Appraisers: Thomas Tasker, Richard
Smith. Roger Brooke (g, CV) to
administer oath.

5 February. Inventory of Charles
Ballard (SO) was exhibited, by
appraisers David Browne & Roger
Woolford.

Col. William Burges (AA) exhibited
accounts of Mary Williams (AA) relict &
executrix of John Robinson (AA), sworn
16 January last.

13:4 John Greene (p, SM) son of Elisabeth
Potter (alias Greene) exhibited her
will, constituting her son-in-law Thomas
Dixon (SO) executor. Said Dixon has
renounced administration on 30 January,
by depositions of Thomas Doxey (SM) &
Eduard Chester (SO). Said John Greene
was granted administration. Appraisers:
Thomas Doxey, Eduard Chester. Richard
Lloyd (g, SM) to prove said will.

6 February. Clement Hill (g, SM)
exhibited oath of John Bullock & Joseph
Fowler, appraisers of Colline Mackensye
(SM), sworn 4 February 1682. Also
exhibited was oath of said Bullock &
Fowler, appraisers of Richard Craine
(SM), sworn same day.
13:5 Also exhibited was bond of said Gardiner
administrator of Richard Craine.
Sureties: John Gardiner, Luck Gardiner.

Sarah Hooper (BA) widow of Richard
Hooper was granted administration on his
estate. Appraisers: William Yorke,
James Collyer. Col. George Wells (BA)
to administer oath.

Mary Stansby (BA) widow of Capt. John
Stansby (BA) was granted administration
on his estate. Appraisers: William
Yorke, Thomas Hodge. Maj. Thomas Long
to administer oath.

12 February. Col. George Wells (BA)
exhibited oath of James Phillips (BA)

administrator of John Dunston (alias
John Gaskell, BA). Sureties: Thomas
Jones, John Johnson. Also exhibited was
oath of William Croshaw & William
Osborne, appraisers. Also exhibited was
inventory.

William Robson (DO) administrator of
John Taylor (DO) exhibited accounts.
Distribution: orphan.

13:6   13 February. Sheriff (DO) to summon
said orphan.

Kenelme Chiseldyne (g, SM) was granted
administration on estate of William
Berief, as principle creditor.
Appraisers: John Adisson, Francis Hill.
William Hatton (g) to administer oath.

Eduard Swetnam (KE) exhibited that Mary
Evans relict & administratrix of Richard
Pether (KE) is infirm & very weak, &
cannot travel to Office. Phillip Connor
(g, KE) to examine & administer oath.

17 February. James Thompson (BA)
exhibited will of John Scott (BA). Maj.
Thomas Long to prove said will.

19 February. John Thompson (clerk, CE)
exhibited letter to Commissioners of CE,
regarding
13:7   William Asbey administrator of John
Murwent & Joseph Spernon & William
Syncklers administrators of William
Porter. Said Asbey is not fit to
administer & is not able to find
security. Said Thompson to provide
bond. Signed: Eustachius Turin (clerk).
Exhibited was bond of William Synckler
administrator, with sureties: Thomas
Skelton, Samuell Wheeler. Also
exhibited was bond of Richard Roberts
administrator of William Murwent, with
sureties: Thomas Skelton, Richard Leake.
Said Synckler was granted administration
on said Porter. Appraisers: Thomas
Hinton, John Cambell. Henry Ward (CE)
to administer oath. Richard Roberts was
granted administration on William
Murwent. Appraisers: Richard Edmonds,

Thomas Skelton. Henry Ward to administer oath.

20 February. Thomas James (BA) who married Sarah relict & administratrix of Giles Steevens (BA) exhibited accounts. Discharge was granted.

13:8   23 February. James Pattisson (Crosse Mannor, SM) who married Anne relict & administratrix of Pope Alvey (SM) was granted discharge.

John Cox (CE) for Katherine Linsey relict of Robert Morrice (CE) was granted administration. Appraisers: said Cox, Andrew Peterson. Nathaniell Garrett (CE) to administer oath.

26 February. Robert Doyne (CH) exhibited that Robert Thompson was granted LoA on John Wright as next of kin, & said Thompson is neither kin or any other way concerned with said estate. Said Doyne is principle creditor. Said Thompson summoned.

Jane Calvert widow of Phillip Calvert (Chancellor & Chief Judge) was granted administration on his estate. Appraisers: John Llewellin (g), James Patisson. Bond by: Maj. Nicholas Sewell.

13:9   Stephen Luff (SO) who married Sarah relict of Charles Ballard (SO) exhibited a bill of Jacob Jones received of Henry Hooper, bill of John Gouldsmith, bill of Laurence Gary (carpenter). Before: Henry Darnall, William Digges.

28 February. Richard Holland (TA) who married Hanna relict & executrix of Thomas Alexander (TA) exhibited accounts & oath of said Hanna, sworn before Eduard Man (g, TA). Discharge was granted.

3 March. George Parker (g, Clifts, CV) petitioned for Capt. Richard Hill (AA) to prove will of Alexander Gardner (AA). Appraisers: Richard Beard, William

Trevile. Said Hill to administer oath.

13:10 Maj. John Welsh (g, AA) exhibited accounts & oath of John Sollars executor of John Shrigley (AA).

Exhibited was LoA to Barbara Bell (Southfeilds, Durham, ENG) administratrix of Dr. Thomas Bell (Durham), granted by Bishop of Durham Richard Lloyd Miles. [Paragraph in Latin.] Signed: Gabriel Newhouse, Ed. Kirkby. Also exhibited was PoA from said Barbara to Henry Saddler (taylor, New Castle, ENG) to recover of William Hemsley (p, TA) & from Richard Marix (MD).

13:11 Date: last September 1680. Witnesses: Eduard Soulsby, Francis Robinson, Da. Whealas, Henry Winship. Affirmed by said Soulsby & Robinson before Philemon Lloyd. Date: 14 February 1682. Said Saddler was granted administration. Appraisers: Griffith Jones, Richard Mirax. Col. Philemon Lloyd (g, TA) to administer oath.

John Heathcott (g, AA) exhibited LoA from Archbishop of Canterbury: [Paragraph in Latin].

13:12 Mentions: Samuel Heathcott, Elisabeth Heathcott. Date: 7 July 1682. Said John exhibited his accounts of Nathaniell Heathcott (AA).

5 March. John Gallwith (CV) was granted administration on Richard Barton (CV), who died in said Gallwith's house, having no relations in this country, as principle creditor. Appraisers: Thomas Robinson, John Sawell. Roger Brooke to administer oath.

13:13 12 March. Samuell Hatton & his wife Elisabeth relict of Richard Gorsuch (TA) petitioned that Eduard Roe (TA, dec'd) bequeathed to Anne Gorsuch (one of the children of said Richard & Elisabeth the petitioner) & the remainder of the children of said Richard. Said Roe died shortly afterwards, constituting his wife Mary, daughter Elisabeth, Phil.

Court Session: 1682

Lloyd, Peter Sawyer, & Richard Gorsuch executors. Mary Roe & William Combes who married Elisabeth (daughter) were granted administration; the others renounced administration. Said Anne died before she married. Said Richard Gorsuch had at the time of the death of said Roe 4 more children: Mary, Richard, Elisabeth, Sarah. Said executors paid 1 share to Richard Keene who married Mary (one of daughters). Petition for residue. Said Combes appeared & is to pay next year.

13:14 William Combes (TA) exhibited oath of MM Eduard Man & George Robotham, appraisers of Walter Dickenson (TA), sworn 14 November 1682. Also exhibited was inventory.

Exhibited was will of William Hamstead (TA), proved by Jos. Atkins, William Wintersell, & James Colland. Also exhibited was oath of Walter Quinton & William Wintersell, appraisers, sworn 1 January 1682. Also exhibited was inventory.

13 March. Exhibited was inventory of Henry Stockett (AA), by appraisers Maj. Nicholas Gassaway & Capt. Thomas Francis.

13:15 Thomas Claggett executor of James Pennington (CV) exhibited accounts, proved before Col. Henry Darnall (CV).

14 March. Col. Thomas Taylor (AA) exhibited oath of John Watkins, Jr. administrator of John Watkins (AA). Surety: Woolfran Hunt. Also exhibited was inventory, by appraisers Maj. John Welsh & Capt. Thomas Francis.

Exhibited was will of John Hillens (AA), proved by Richard Wigg, John Custis, Eduard Talbit, & Richard Arnold before Col. Thomas Taylor.

Thomas Clagget (CV) administrator of James Pennington (CV) was granted discharge.

Court Session: 1682

Court Session: 1683

13:16 26 March. Samuell Bourne (CV) exhibited oath of Sarah Barnes administratrix of Henry Barnes (CV), now wife of Thomas Simpers. Surety: Thomas Viney. Also exhibited was inventory, by appraisers Basill Warren & Charles Bathurst.

Exhibited was will of Richard Custins (AA), proved by Robert Eades, John Mayhew, Richard Barewell, & Thomas Pratt before Col. Thomas Taylor.

Exhibited was inventory of John Hillen (AA), by appraisers John Welsh & Woolfran Hunt.

Exhibited was will of Mathew Silly (AA), proved by Timothy Thorold & John Alford before Maj. John Welsh. Also exhibited was inventory, by appraisers Nicholas Painter & Walter Carr.

Robert Thompson (CH) administrator of William Wright (CH) was granted continuance to answer Robert Doyne.

13:17 Elisabeth Fooke (CV) widow of Francis Fooke (CV) exhibited his will, constituting her executrix, proved by Francis Higham, William Crud, & John Page. Said Elisabeth was granted administration. Appraisers: James Veetch, James Cobb.

27 March. John Barecroft (g, SM) was granted administration on estate of Peer Hipkes (SM), as principle creditor. Surety: Robert Doyne (CH). Appraisers: Clement Heyley, Garrett Roules. Joseph Piles (SM) to administer oath.

Robert Doyne (CH) & Robert Thompson (CH) appeared. Robert Thompson, Sr. deposed that William Wright (now dec'd), overseer for Mr. Robert Doyne, was related in blood to Robert Thompson the younger, the father of William Wright & the mother of Robert Thompson were brother & sister's children. Date: 15

Court Session: 1683

March 1682, before Ri. Boughton.
Ruling: for said Thompson.

28 March. Capt. Richard Hill (AA)
exhibited oath of Rachell Meeke
administratrix of Guy Meeke (AA).
Sureties: Thomas Browne, Charles
Stephens.

13:18   Capt. Richard Hill (AA) exhibited oath
of Adam Shipley & Henry Peirpoint,
appraisers of Guy Meeke (AA). Also
exhibited was inventory.

Exhibited was inventory of Robert
Francklin (AA), by appraisers Nicholas
Painter, Walter Car, Henry Hanslap, &
John Gray.

Exhibited that George Scarve (CV) died a
year ago, leaving a widow Mary & an
orphan. Said Mary did not administer
the estate, & has since married one who
embezzled the estate of the dec'd. Mary
White the relict was summoned.

Providence Rennolds (AA) executrix of
Robert Davidge (AA) petitioned for
Richard Hill (AA) to examine the
accounts & take her oath.

Sarah Fletcher (AA) administratrix of
Robert Gudgeon (AA) is unable to travel
to Office & petitioned for Eduard Dorsey
(AA) to examine the accounts & take his
oath.

John Willmoth (CV) exhibited will of
Richard Millson (CV), constituting his
wife Anne executrix. Francis Hutchins
to prove the will. Appraisers: William
Howes, John Willmott. Said Hutchins to
administer oath.

13:19   29 March. Exhibited was bond of William
Finny (TA) administrator of Walter
Riddall (TA). Surety: Moyses Harris.
Also exhibited was inventory, by
appraisers Thomas Emerson & David
Johnson.

31 March. Exhibited were accounts of Henry Simons, Jr. administrator of Henry Simons, proved before Samuell Bourne (CV).

Samuell Bourne (CV) exhibited accounts of Sarah Harrison relict & administratrix of Henry Harrison (CV).

William Hopkins grandfather & guardian for William & Henry Lewis (AA), orphans of Henry Lewis (AA), petitioned that their father Henry made Elisabeth Lewis his executrix, who married John Bird. Said petitioner sued before the Chancellor for their filial portions, but the Chancellor died before issuing a decree. Said John & Elisabeth Bird were summoned.

13:20   Henry Smith (SO) exhibited oath of Arnold Elzey, sworn 5 March 1682. Sureties: Richard Whitty, Richard Crockett. Also exhibited was inventory of said (N) Ballard, by appraisers David Browne & Roger Woolford.

2 April. George Parker (Clifts, CV) exhibited regarding the will of Thomas Cosden. Thomas Cosden (under age 21) is constituted executor, & Mr. Hunton, Mr. Parker, & Capt. Bourne overseers. The chattel is to be sold to maintain the widow, children, & servants. Anne (relict) has renounced administration & desires Mordecai Hunton, George Parker, & Samuell Bourne to administrate. Date: 23 February 1682. Witnesses: Charles Boteler, Mich. Taney. George Parker & Mordecai Hunton were granted administration. Appraisers: Richard Smith, Xopher Banes. Capt. Richard Ladd (CV) to administer oath.

13:21   James Phillips (BA) administrator of Thomas Jones (BA) exhibited accounts.

Inventory of William Berief (SM) was exhibited, by appraisers John Addison & Francis Hill. Kenelme Chiseldyne administrator was granted continuance.

Col. Philemon Lloyd (TA) exhibited oath of Henry Saddler (TA) administrator of Thomas Poell (Smithfeilds, Durham, ENG). Sureties: Richard Everax, Griffith Jones. Also exhibited was oath of Richard Merare & Griffith Jones, appraisers.

Mich. Miller for Hanna Gibson (KE) widow of Isaak Gibson exhibited his will, constituting her executrix. Said Miller to prove said will. Appraisers: Thomas Boone, Richard Lowder. Said Miller to administer oath.

3 March [sic]. George Parker (Clifts, CV) exhibited that James Maxwell died about 12 years ago & Mary his relict married Patrick Hall (AA) who administered the estate & exhibited an inventory. Said Hall died before accounts were exhibited. Said Mary then married John Spencer (AA) who survives said Mary, but no accounting has been done. Sheriff (AA) to summon said Spencer.

13:22   3 April. Inventory of George Johnson (Annamessix, SO) was exhibited.

Bond of Elisabeth Dix (DO) administratrix of Robert Dix (DO) was exhibited. Sureties: Peter Stocks, Gournay Crow. Also exhibited was inventory, by appraisers Alexander Fisher & Eduard Pindar.

Mary Howell (CE) was granted administration on estate of John Howell (CE). Joseph Hopkins (CE) to administer oath.

Samuel Bagby (CV) exhibited renunciation of Levina Dickson (Patuxent River, CV) widow of Andrew Dickson (d. 20 March 1682/3, CV) & appointed her son said Bagby administrator. Date: 24 March 1682/3. Witnesses: Mary Rouce, William Hewes, Jr. Said Bagby was granted administration.

13:23   Appraisers: Thomas Hillary, George Ardesty. George Lingham. to administer

oath.

Ebenezar Blackiston (CE) exhibited that
his brother John Blackiston (KE) died in
1679 & his widow Sarah did not
administer his estate & is since dec'd,
leaving an orphan. Said Ebenezar was
granted administration. Appraisers:
Richard Lowder, Daniell Heathcott.
Mich. Miller (KE) to administer oath.

John Rousby (TA) exhibited will of Simon
Warford (d. 1676, KE), which is still
unproved. Petition to William Laurence
(KE) to prove said will, by oath of John
Rogers.

Inventory of Richard Jackson (TA) was
exhibited, by appraisers Richard Jones &
John Offley.

4 April. Exhibited was will of Robert
Richardson (SO), proved by Col. William
Stevens (SO). Said Stevens to
administer oath to Susanna relict.

James Phillips (BA) administrator of
William Hill &
13:24   administrator of John Dunstone (alias
Gaskell) was granted continuance.

John Watson (SM) appeared, per summons
requested by Robert Graham & his wife
Jane (SM), to render accounts of George
Mackaall (SM) & petitioned for summons
to send Graham to render accounts.
Ruling: granted.

Inventory of James Wildgoose (KE) was
exhibited, by appraisers Robert Griffith
& Bennett Staires.

Inventory of Robert Craine (SM) was
exhibited, by appraisers John Bullock &
Joseph Fowler.

Inventory of Colline Mackensie (SM) was
exhibited, by appraisers John Bullock &
Joseph Fouler.

5 April. Robert Carvile (SM) procurator
for Robert Graham (SM) who married

relict & executrix of George Mackaall
(SM) exhibited accounts, with an account
between said Mackaall & Robert Williams
& Bryan Rogers (merchants, Falmouth,
ENG). Mentions: schooling of Jane
Mackaall, bills of Bryan Rogers & Robert
Williams & Bryan Thompson (merchants,
Falmouth).

13:25 Also exhibited was libel by Robert
Graham & his wife Anne (relict) vs.
John Watson & his wife Jane
administrators dbn. Said George by his
will gave to his daughter Jane
(defendant) his plantation at Pyny Point
& Negro Tony & Negro Kate (girl), to his
daughter Hanna Negro William & Negro
Rose, to his daughter Sarah Negro
Phillip & Negro Jane, to his daughter
400 a. on Sassafras River & Negro
Charles, to his wife Anne chattel. Said
Anne was constituted executrix. If
daughter Jane dies without issue, then
land to daughter Hanna. Overseers: John
Whahob, John Cambell, orator, Henry
Williams.

13:26 Said Mackaall was commanded into service
against the Susquehanna Indians. After
returning, said Mackaall sold Negro
William & Negro Rose. Said Mackaall
then died on 28 January 1675. Said Anne
Mackaall proved his will on 3 February,
& exhibited an inventory in May 1676.
She married the orator on 24 June 1676.
Said Anne Mackaall gave birth to a
posthumous son, now since dec'd.

13:27 Mentions: bill from George Phenix,
accounts of Bryan Rogers & Robert
Williams & Bryan Thompson (merchants,
Falmouth, ENG),

13:28 Jane Williams (widow, eldest daughter of
said Mackaall) who married John Watson
(merchant, ENG) shortly after October
1681. Said John took possession of
plantation at Pyny Point.

13:29-30 ...

13:31 Amount of inventory: #70850. Accounts:
Payments to: Dominick Bodkin, Samuell
Hall, John Winne (chirurgeon), Marmaduck
Seems, Stephen Murty, James Beamont
attorney for Joshua Winson (Liverpoole),
Joshua Guybert attorney for George Pile,
John Baker, George Dundasse paid to

Court Session: 1683

Henry Phipps, Robert Carvile executor of
Richard Moy,
13:32   John Watson, Robert Bagnall (merchant,
Bristoll) paid to Thomas Spinke, Robert
Williams (merchant, Falmouth) for
schooling Jane Mackaall wife of John
Watson, Capt. Gerrard Slye attorney for
Samuell Cockes (London), George Phenix.
Amount of accounts: #57487. Date: 14
March 1682/3. Account of debits &
credits between George Mackaall (MD) &
Robert Williams & Bryan Rogers
(merchants, Falmouth).
13:33   Debits: Joseph Hext, Capt. Cooper, Mr.
Hinson by Joseph Hext, John Heard by
Joseph Hext. Amount: #219254. Credits:
John Morecroft, George Deacon, Capt.
Smith. Amount: 141431.
13:34   Further accounts: Received from: Bryan
Thompson (merchant, Falmouth). Payments
to: George Robins, Garrett Vansweringen,
John Boweth, Nathaniell Fisher, Thomas
Griffin, Robert Doyne, William Turvile,
John Ellitt, Robert Simons, John
Rycroft, Edward Jollye, Jonathon
Squires, Joseph Baker, Joseph Walker,
Thomas Simonds, Mathew Ward, Randall
Hinson, Eduard Clerk, Phillip Calvert,
Esq., Daniell Smith, John Warren,
Richard Moy, John Jordain, John Wade,
Francis Sowerton, Eduard Morgan, John
Browne, John Hepworth, William Pitts,
William Kannady, Bryan Daley, Henry
Ryder, John Wahob, John Baker, John
Doxey, John Cambell, Peter Mills, Eduard
Clarke, Leonard Greene, Eduard Horne,
Thomas Price, Thomas Courtney, Robert
Ridgely on Clement Hill, John Winn,
Patrick Forrest, Henry Phipps, Mr.
Chiseldyne on Mr. Ward, Mr. Chiseldyne
on Mr. Tilghman, James Greene, John
Newton, Thomas Hatton, Thomas Dent,
Robert Cager, William Baker. Amount:
#88579.
13:35   Inventory at Pyny Point when John Watson
took possession: Amount: #75448.

17 April. Petition of Hugh Manning (SM)
that Eduard Size (SM) died intestate,
but deposed that Cornelius Manning (son
of petitioner) should be his heir. Said
Hugh petitioned for administration.

Page 13

13:36   Bryan Daley (SM) who has right was
         summoned.

         19 April. Joseph Bullett (CH) exhibited
         will of Peter Carr, constituting James
         Tyer executor. Said Tyer is unable to
         travel to Office. Appraisers: Robert
         Henley, Thomas Clipsham. Capt.
         Humphrey Warren to administer oath.

         Bond of Anne Randall (KE) administratrix
         of Benjamin Randall (KE) was exhibited.
         Sureties: Joseph Weeks, Mich. Miller.
         Inventory was exhibited, by appraisers
         Mich. Miller & Thomas Warrin.

         23 April. Robert Reede (CV) & Anne
         Armstrong (CV) exhibited will of Robert
         Andrews, bequeathing to said Reede, said
         Armstrong, & Richard King. No executor
         was constituted. Said Reede & said
         Armstrong were granted administration.
         Appraisers: Eduard Blackburne, Francis
         Higham. Capt. Richard Ladd to
         administer oath.

         Capt. Richard Hill (AA) exhibited oath
         of Mary Gardner executrix of Alexander
         Gardner (AA). Also exhibited was oath
         of William Jones & William Treaveale,
         appraisers. Also exhibited was will,
         proved.

13:37   Exhibited was inventory of Elisabeth
         Greene (SM), by appraisers Thomas Doxey
         & Eduard Chester.

         24 April. Brian Daley & Hugh Manning,
         were summoned regarding the estate of
         Eduard Size (SM). Owen Guyther deposed
         that Anne St. George (daughter of
         dec'd's late wife) was to have all &
         said Daley was to be the guardian.
         James Mackglavin deposed that he was at
         the house of Hugh Manning the day before
         Eduard Size died, when said Size said
         that Daley was to have all for the girl.
         Hugh Manning was granted continuance.

         Petition of Stephen Luffe (SO)
13:38   that his wife Sarah conspired with Henry
         Smith (SO), regarding the estate of

Court Session: 1683

Charles Ballard. Administration was
granted to Arnold Elzey. Petitioner
requests that said administration be
revoked. Said Sarah was summoned.

28 April. Lydia Newman (GH) widow of
George Newman (CH) exhibited her
renunciation, desiring that her son
George Newman be granted administration.
Said George was granted administration.
Appraisers: Thomas Gibson, Ralph Smith.
Capt. Humphrey Warren to administer
oath.

1 May. Hugh Manning (SM) appeared,
regarding the estate of Eduard Size.
Sarah Pinke, age 30, deposed that a
month before he died, Eduard Size
declared Cornelius son of Hugh Manning
as his heir.
13:39   Ellinor Chester, age 40, deposed the
same. Ruling: Daley has more right &
was granted administration on behalf of
said Anne. Bondsmen: Thomas Keyting,
Owen Guyther. Appraisers: said Keyting,
said Guyther.

Dennis Hurley (SM) exhibited will of
Derby Donnovan (SM), constituting said
Hurley, Cornelius Donnavan, & Perce Wall
executors. Said Cornelius Donnavan was
a servant to the dec'd. Said Hurley &
said Wall were granted administration.
Appraisers: John Hilton, Eduard Maddock.
Joseph Piles to administer oath.

2 May. John Spencer (AA) exhibited that
Patrick Hall had married the widow of
James Maxwell (AA) who died intestate.
Shortly after, said Hall died intestate,
& petitioner married Mary widow of said
Hall. Said Mary died afterwards,
leaving a son James Maxwell & a daughter
Mary Hall.
13:40   Said James will be of age in November, &
said Mary Hall married Henry Everitt
(AA). Per George Parker (g), said
Spencer was summoned to render accounts
of said James Maxwell & said Patrick
Hall.

Court Session: 1683

Exhibited were accounts of Robert Davidg
(AA) by Providence executrix, proved
before Richard Hall (g, AA).

8 May. Henry Howard (AA) exhibited will
of Rowland Nance (AA), constituting
Henry Constable (BA) executor. Eduard
Dorsey (AA) to prove said will.
Appraisers: Nicholas Greenbery (AA),
Richard Gwin (BA). Said Dorsey to
administer oath.

Miles Gibson (BA) exhibited that Mary
Stanesby widow of Capt. John Stanesby
(BA) has not found security.
Continuance was granted.

13:41   10 May. Col. George Wells (BA)
exhibited oath of Sarah Hooper
administratrix of George Hooper (BA).
Sureties: James Collyer, William Yorke.
Also exhibited was inventory, by
appraisers James Collyer & William
Yorke.

11 May. John Willymott (CV) exhibited
will of William House (CV), constituting
Anne House executrix. Francis Hutchins
(CV) to prove said will. Appraisers:
Timothy Hunton, Thomas Eduards. Said
Hutchins to administer oath.

Exhibited was will of Richard Millson
(CV), proved before Francis Hutchins
(g). Also exhibited was inventory, by
appraisers William House & John
Willymott.

Exhibited was bond of Samuell Bagby (CV)
administrator of Andrew Dickenson.
Sureties: William Wadsworth, John Jaman.
Also exhibited was oath of Thomas Hillay
& George Ardesty, appraisers sworn by
George Lingham. Also exhibited was
inventory.

17 May. William Combes (TA) exhibited
will of George Reade (TA), proved before
him.
13:42   Also exhibited was oath of Samuell
Abbott & Thomas Martin, appraisers sworn
on 23 March 1682/3. Also exhibited was

Page 16

inventory.

19 May. Stephen Murty (SM) exhibited
will of Edmond Dermott (SM),
constituting said Murty executor.
Clement Hill (g, SM) to prove said will
by witnesses: Thomas Clarke, Dennes
Loade, Timothy Hess. Appraisers: John
Bullock, John Taylor. Said Hill to
administer oath.

22 May. Petition of Johanna Goldsmith
(BA) widow & relict of Maj. Samuell
Goldsmith that said Samuell devised to
petitioner & to George Wells (g) who
married eldest daughter of said Samuell
& said Johanna. Said Johanna left the
management of the estate to said Wells.
Residue
13:43 is far greater than reported by said
Wells. Also the petitioner has not been
allowed her share. Said Wells was
summoned.

Robert Carvile for Nicholas Scudamore
who married Anne (CH) relict of Joseph
Brough (p, SM) petitioned that said
Brough died in August 1674 & while said
Anne was absent, George Marshall (SM)
was granted administration, as principle
creditor. Per said Marshall, the estate
was overpaid; several items were
omitted. Petitioner has recently
arrived in the Province, & is inquiring
about said Brough's estate. Said
Marshall is dec'd, & his estate & that
of said Brough are gone & wasted. Said
Marshall had sureties Thomas Doxey (SM)
& Henry Smith (SM), & bond remains in
the Office.
13:44 Petition that said Doxey & Smith pay
amount of estate of said Brough.
Exceptions cited to inventory of said
Brough. Mentions: bill of Robert Large
(p, SM), 2 servants. Sheriff (SM) to
summon Thomas Doxey & Henry Smith.

13:45 Robert Carvile (g, SM) petitioned that
Joshua Doyne (sheriff, SM) summon
Gerrard Slye administrator of Richard
Chilman (SM).

John Salisbury administrator of William
Salisbury (CE) petitioned that sheriff
(CE) summon John Willis.

29 May. William Robson (DO)
administrator of John Taylor (DO)
petitioned for John Taylor (son of
dec'd) to appear. Said Taylor did not
appear. Sheriff (DO) to repeat summons.

31 May. George Parker (g, Clifts, CV)
exhibited that Thomas Cosden (inn
holder, CV, dec'd) made a devise of his
land between his children, proved by
Michaell Allen, Richard Dawson, &
William Olwant. Richard Ladd (g, CV) to
take depositions from said witnesses.

George Parker for Mary Ireland (CV)
widow of William Ireland (CV) was
granted administration on his estate.
Appraisers: Tobias Miles, Robert
Spickernell. Richard Ladd (CV) to
administer oath.

13:46   John Wattson & his wife Jane (eldest
daughter & administratrix of George
Mackaall (SM)) vs. Robert Graham & his
wife Anne relict & executrix of said
Mackall. Executrix is now dec'd. Said
Wattson exhibited his answer.
13:47   Mentions: bill of (N) Phenix, bill of
James Greene, William Rogers & Co.
13:48   ...
13:49   Kenelm Cheseldyne represented
defendants.

13:50   18 June. Exhibited was will of
Elisabeth Greene (SM).

Sarah Bedworth (AA) widow of Richard
Bedworth (AA) exhibited his will,
constituting her executrix. John Welsh
(g, AA) to prove said will. Said Sarah
was granted administration. Appraisers:
Robert Conant, Richard Deavor. Said
Welsh to administer oath.

Jane Naylor (AA) exhibited will of
Abraham Naylor (AA), constituting her
executrix. Said Jane cannot travel to
Office. Maj. John Welsh to prove said

will. Said Jane was granted
administration. Appraisers: Robert
Conant, Richard Deavor. Said Welsh to
administer oath.

Humphrey Warren (g, CH) exhibited oath
of James Tyer executor of Peter Carr
(CH). Also exhibited was will, proved.
Also exhibited was oath of Robert Henley
& Thomas Clipsham, appraisers. Also
exhibited was inventory.

13:51   Humphrey Warren (CH) exhibited oath of
George Newman administrator, sworn on 21
May 1683. Sureties: William
Hungherford, Eduard Smoothe. Also
exhibited was oath of Thomas Gibson &
Ralph Smith, appraisers sworn same day.

Exhibited was inventory of Thomas Ford
(AA).

Exhibited was will of Darby Donnavan
(SM), proved before Joseph Pyles (g,
SM). Also exhibited was oath of John
Hatton & Samuell Maddocks, appraisers
sworn 4 May 1683.

Henry Ward (CE) exhibited oath of
William Synckler administrator of
William Porter (CE). Also exhibited was
oath of Thomas Hinton & John Cambell,
appraisers. Also exhibited was
inventory.

Henry Ward (CE) exhibited oath of
Richard Roberts administrator of John
Murwant (CE). Also exhibited was oath
of Richard Edmonds & Thomas Skelton,
appraisers.

25 June. Eduard English (high sheriff,
CE) exhibited summons to John Willis
(CE) executor of William Salisbury (CE).

13:52   Exhibited was will of Simon Warford
(KE), proved before Capt. William
Laurence by John Rogers.

Sheriff (SO) exhibited summons to Sarah
Ballard relict of Charles Ballard (SO),
regarding administration of his estate

by Arnold Elzey, unadministered by
Stephen Luffe.

Edward Inglish (g, CE) exhibited verbal
will of Bartholomew Henrickson (CE). 3
sons Matthew, Hendrick, & Bartholomew.
Date: 2 September 1682. Witnesses:
Phillip Burgin, Peter Coole, John West,
John Hagley. Margarett Hagley relict
was granted administration. Appraisers:
Thomas Rumsey, William Ward. Nathaniell
Garrett to administer oath.

13:53 William Hopkins (AA) exhibited will of
Thomas Buckinall (AA), constituting
dec'd's wife Mary executrix. Capt.
Richard Hill to prove said will.
Appraisers: said Hopkins, Nicholas
Greenbery. Said Hill to administer
oath.

Laurence Rowland (CV) who married Grace
relict & administratrix of James
Williams exhibited accounts.

26 June. Henry Hawkins (CH) who married
Elisabeth relict & executrix of Francis
Wyne (CH) exhibited accounts.

Joseph Pyle (g, SM) exhibited oath of
Clement Hely & John Vaudry, appraisers
of Peter Hypkis sworn on 19 June 1683.
Also exhibited was inventory, by
appraisers Clement Heley & John Vadry.

Sheriff (AA) exhibited summons to John
Spencer (AA) administrator of James
Maxwell & administrator of Patrick Hall.
Continuance was granted.

13:54 Sheriff (AA) exhibited summons to John
Bird & his wife Elisabeth relict &
executrix of Henry Lewis regarding suit
by William & Henry Lewis.

Henry Hosier (KE) for Daniell Norris was
granted administration on estate of
Thomas Norris (KE), as next-of-kin.
Appraisers: John Bowle, Charles Tilden.
Said Hosier to administer oath.

Court Session: 1683

Capt. Ninian Beall (CV) exhibited will
of Peter Archer (CV), constituting said
Beall & John Cheltam executors. Said
will is void regarding land legacies,
but good for other legacies. Richard
Marsham (CV) to prove said will.
Appraisers: Thomas Blandford, Richard
Gaunt. Said Marsham to administer oath.

Sheriff (SM) exhibited summons to Gerard
Slye administrator of (N) Chilman.

Sheriff (CV) exhibited summons to Mary
White relict of George Scaroe.

Sheriff (SM) exhibited summons to Thomas
Doxey & Henry Smith, regarding petition
by (N) Skudamore.

Sheriff (DO) exhibited summons to John
Taylor orphan of William Taylor (DO,
dec'd) regarding accounts
13:55   of William Robson administrator of said
dec'd. Payments to: Mr. Stapleford on 9
March 1668 for 900 a., Mr. Stapleford
due when old John Taylor died, Arthur
Wright (subsheriff), Major Taylor,
Thomas Gilbert (subsheriff), John
Haslewood (subsheriff), John Veall
(subsheriff), Stephen Gery (sheriff),
Parson Manroe for christening John
Taylor. Thomas Pattison (DO) endeavored
to contest accounts on behalf of his
son-in-law John Taylor.

Joseph Hopkins (CE) exhibited oath of
Mary Howell administratrix of John
Howell.
13:56   Sureties: Richard Pullen, James Heberne.
Also exhibited was oath of Benjamin
Gundry & Eduard Beck, appraisers sworn
12 May. Date: 19 June 1683. Also
exhibited was inventory.

27 June. Exhibited was inventory of
Patrick Venstone (CH), by appraisers
John Cowar & Alexander Smith.

Capt. Richard Hill (AA) for John Howard
(BA) was granted administration on
estate of Thomas Marshall (BA), as
principle creditor. Appraisers: John

Thomas, John Harding. John Boaring (BA) to administer oath.

Sheriff (CH) exhibited summons to Eduard Maddock (CH) who married Hanna relict & administratrix of Henry Francum (CH), to answer exceptions by Rice Williams (CH) who married a daughter of said Henry Franckum. Exceptions cited.

13:57 Mentions: Zachariah Wade, John England, Benjamin Witchcott, Eduard Ming.

13:58 Signed: Kenelme Cheseldyne for said Williams. Philip Lynes deposed that 8 years ago Dr. Eduard Maddock came to the deponent's house in CH & desired him to draw accounts of said Franckum's estate. Mentions: "Stump's Neck".

13:59 Thomas Gerrard (SM) attorney for Gerrard Slye (g, SM, who is in ENG) administrator of Richard Chilman vs. Robert Carvile et. al. creditors of said Chilman. Continuance was granted.

Letter from Mr. George Parker (Clifts, CV) to Mr. Thomas Grunwin (registrar). Mentions: enclosed inventory of Mr. Thomas Cosden, said Parker is sick, will of Thomas Ford, Thomas Lun (AA). Inventory of said Cosden was appraised by Richard Smith, Sr. & Xpher Banes.

28 June. Exhibited was inventory of Francis Fowkes (CV), by appraisers James Veitch & James Cobb.

13:60 Exhibited was inventory of Robert Andrewes (CV), by appraisers Eduard Blagborne & Francis Higham.

Exhibited was inventory of Derby Donnovan (SM), by appraisers Samuell Maddox & John Hilton.

Exhibited was inventory of Samuell Raspin, by appraisers John Courts & William Ward.

Samuell Abbot (TA) administrator of Joseph Padley (TA) exhibited accounts.

Court Session: 1683

29 June. Charles Cartee (CH)
administrator of Patrick Venstone (CH)
exhibited accounts.

James Mecall (CV) was granted
administration on estate of Peter Browne
(CV), as principle creditor.
Appraisers: George Abbott, William
Taylor. Capt. Richard Ladd to
administer oath.

Col. William Chandler (CH) exhibited
will of Anne Doughty (CH), constituting
Parthenia & Sarah Burdeck executrices.
Robert Doyne (CH) to prove said will.
Appraisers: James Littlepage, Eduard
Mines. Said Doyne to administer oath.

13:61 William Hopkins (AA) guardian of Henry &
William Lewis orphans of Henry Lewis vs.
George Parker attorney for John Bird &
his wife Elisabeth. Said Parker is ill.
Continuance was granted.

Stephen Luffe (SO) exhibited a letter
from Richard Crockett petitioning that
administration on estate of Charles
Ballard to Arnold Elzey be revoked &
given to said Luffe. Said Crockett &
his father-in-law Mr. Richard Whitty
are sureties to said Elzey. Date: 23
June 1683. Witnesses: John Winder,
Thomas Pemberton. Ruling:
administration stands as is.

30 June. Exhibited was inventory of
Alexander Gardner (AA), by appraisers
William Jones & William Treveil.

Exhibited was inventory of Richard
Burton (CV), by appraisers Thomas
Robinson & John Samuell.

13:62 2 July. Cleborne Lomax (CH) exhibited
that Archibald Wahob (CH) administrator
of William Lewis (CH) cannot travel to
Office. Henry Adams (CH) to examine
accounts & administer oath.

Exhibited was will of Edmond Dermott
(SM), proved before Clement Hill by
Thomas Clarke, Dennis Lead, & Timothy

Hess.

3 July. Meverell Hulse (CH) was granted
administration on estate of Thomas
Hatersill (CH), as principle creditor.
Estate consists of debts only. Henry
Adams to administer oath.

Exhibited was inventory of Isaak Gilpin
(KE), by appraisers Thomas Boone &
Richard Lowder.

Exhibited was inventory of Francis
Harmer (CE), by appraisers Richard
Pullen & Thomas Hawker.

Exhibited was inventory of Sarah
Blackiston (CE), by appraisers Richard
Lowder & Daniell Hasse.

Judith Price (TA) widow of Roger Price
was granted administration on his
estate. Appraisers: Alexander
Larramore, John Hunt. James Murphy (TA)
to administer oath.

13:63   4 July. James Philips (BA) for self &
Thomas Heath (BA) was granted
administration on estate of Gervais
Lascells (BA). Appraisers: Robert Low,
Arthur Taylor. Eduard Beedle (g) to
administer oath.

5 July. Exhibited was will of Simon
Warford (KE), proved before William
Laurence (g, KE). John Rousby (TA) for
Hannah Goodhand executrix was granted
administration on his estate.

Martha Arnell (AA) widow of Richard
Arnoll exhibited his will. Maj. John
Welsh (AA) to prove said will.

11 July. Patience Clocker (SM) widow of
Daniell Clocker, who accidentally
drowned, was granted administration on
his estate. Surety: Capt. Thomas
Courteney.

Sheriff (SM) to summon to Madam
Elisabeth Calvert widow & administratrix
of William Calvert, Esq. (Principle

Secretary) to render accounts.

Richard Gardiner administrator of
Richard Craine exhibited accounts.

13:64   20 July. William Blanckensteine (SM)
was granted administration on estate of
Anthony Lamb (SM), as principle
creditor. Appraisers: Eduard Morgan,
Robert Craine. William Hatton to
administer oath.

27 July. Capt. Richard Ladd (CV)
exhibited oath of James Mecall
administrator of Peter Browne (CV).
Sureties: George Abbot, William Taylor.

Capt. Richard Ladd (CV) exhibited oath
of Mary Ireland administratrix of
William Ireland (CV). Sureties: Henry
Kent, John Kent.

Capt. Richard Ladd (CV) exhibited oath
of Mordecai Hunton & George Parker
administrators of Thomas Cosden (CV).
Sureties: Francis Hutchins, William
Parker. George Parker exhibited devises
by Thomas Cosden to:
• land "Den" to son Thomas.
• land "Sadler" to son Alphonso.
• land bought of Mr. Jones to son
  William.
• land "Hopeyard" to daughter
  Margarett.
• land "Adinton" to daughter
  Elisabeth. Witnesses: Michaell
  Allen, Richard Dawson, William
  Olivant.
Affirmed on 5 June 1683.

13:65   Capt. Richard Ladd (CV) exhibited oath
of Robert Reed & Anne Armstrong
administrators of Robert Andrewes (CV).
Sureties: Eduard Armstrong, Eduard
Blagburne.

Said Ladd exhibited oath of James Veech
& James Cobb appraisers of Francis
Fowkes (CV).

28 July. Elisabeth Calvert
administratrix of William Calvert was

granted continuance.

Johanna Barnes (CV) widow of Matthew Barnes (CV) was granted administration on his estate. Appraisers: William Taylor, Thomas How. Capt. Richard Ladd to administer oath.

Exhibited was will of Robert Browne (SM), constituting Thomas Gerrard & John Bayne executors. James Bowling (SM) to prove said will. Appraisers: John Barecroft, Richard Edelen. Said Bowling to administer oath.

13:66 31 July. Judith Goldsmith (SM) widow of John Goldsmith (SM) exhibited his will, constituting her executrix, proved by Edward Turner & Thomas Waring. Said Judith is unable to travel to Office. Appraisers: Edward Turner, Samuell Maddox. Clement Hill (g) to administer oath.

1 August. Richard Morris (CH) administrator of Clement Theobalds (CH) exhibited accounts.

Richard Garforth (CH) administrator of John Price (CH) exhibited accounts.

George Parker (CV) procurator for John Sollars executor of John Shrigley (AA) exhibited accounts, proved before Maj. John Welsh.

Exhibited was inventory of Anthony Lamb (SM).

Exhibited was inventory of Eduard Sike (SM), by appraisers Thomas Keeting & Owen Guyther.

Exhibited was will of William House (CV), proved before Francis Hutchins. Also exhibited was inventory, by appraisers Timothy Yanton & Thomas Eduards.

13:67 Sheriff (BA) exhibited summons to George Wells (g, BA) to render accounts on estate of Samuell Gouldsmith, which was

Court Session: 1683

not served. Said summons was renewed.

2 August. Mary Grey (AA) widow of John
Grey was granted administration on his
estate. Appraisers: Matthew Howard,
William Hopkins. Richard Hill to
administer oath.

George Parker (CV) exhibited that Thomas
Homewood died 3 years ago & his brother
(unnamed, Quaker) would not administer
the estate. James Homewood (eldest son
of dec'd) is of another opinion &
desires administration. Said James was
granted administration. Appraisers:
William Jones, William Penington.
Eduard Dorsey to administer oath.

William Howell (CE) petitioned regarding
the accounts of John Salisbury
administrator of William Salisbury. The
inventory of said estate, which came
into the hands of said John, has a
considerable portion detained by John
Willis (former administrator), which is
now available. When all is available,
an inventory will be produced. Signed:
William Nowell. Date: 14 July 1683.
13:68   Exhibited was inventory, by appraisers
William O'Deary & Ezekiell Jackson.

6 August. Sheriff (CH) exhibited
summons to Eduard Maddock (CH)
administrator of Henry Francum (CH),
regarding suit by Rice Williams.

Col. Diggs (SM) exhibited oath of
Justinian Tennison (SM) executor of John
Tennison (SM), proved by William
Goddard. Also exhibited was oath of
John Cood & Vincent Mansell, appraisers.
Also exhibited was inventory. Sheriff
(SM) to summon said Justinian to render
accounts.

Exhibited was bond of Elisabeth Harris
administratrix of Samuell Harris (SM),
with sureties: Thomas Carvile, John
Hilton.

16 August. Henry Adams (g, CH)
exhibited accounts of Archibald Wahop

Page 27

administrator of William Love.

Margarett Fishwick (SM) widow of Edward
Fishwick was granted administration on
his estate. Appraisers: William
Rosewell, William Shertcliffe. Clement
Hill (g, SM) to administer oath.

13:69 21 August. Henry Adams (CH) exhibited
oath of Meverell Hulse administrator of
Thomas Hateraill (CH). Security: Henry
Hawkins.

28 August. Mary Gray (Magaty River, AA)
widow of John Gray was granted
administration on his estate.
Appraisers: William Hopkins, Matthew
Howard. Capt. Richard Hill (AA) to
administer oath.

Maj. John Welsh (AA) exhibited oath of
Sarah Bedworth executrix of Richard
Bedworth, sworn 30 July 1683. Also
exhibited was oath of Richard Deavor &
Robert Conant, appraisers sworn same
day. Date: 27 August 1683.

Maj. John Welsh (AA) exhibited oath of
Jane Naylor executrix of Abraham Naylor,
sworn 20 August 1683. Appraisers are
very sick.

13:70 John Wattson & Thomas Wahob (SM) both
claim right to administer estate of
Robert Graham. Robert Carvile,
procurator for said Graham, to examine
said Graham's papers & to clear the many
incumbrances. Said Wahob to deliver
said papers. Orphan of said Graham to
remain in the house of said Wahob.

John Wattson (SM) petitioned for
appraisers for estate of James Macaall
(SM): Robert Masson, Peter Watts. Mr.
William Hatton (SM) to administer oath.

Rice Williams who married one of the
daughters of Henry Francum (CH) vs.
Edward Maddock (CH) administrator of
said Francum. Said Maddock is unable to
produce receipts. Ruling: said Maddock
to pay said Williams 1/3rd of residue

for his wife's filial portion. Kenelme
Cheseldyne to be paid attorney's fees.

Thomas Bland (AA) for William Hopkins
(AA) guardian of William & Henry Lewis
orphans of Henry Lewis (AA) vs. John
Bird who married Elisabeth relict of
said Lewis. Not all of the parties were
present. Continuance was granted.

13:71 26 September. Benjamin Williams (AA)
was granted administration on estate of
James Philips (AA), as greatest
creditor. Appraisers: Leonard Wayman,
Walter Phelps. Richard Beard (g, AA) to
administer oath.

Maj. John Welsh (AA) to summon Thomas
Lunn administrator of Thomas Ford (AA) &
to administer oath regarding accounts.

William Meares (CV) was granted
administration on estate of Thomas
Heavernam (AA). Appraisers: Seth Biggs,
Francis Neighbour. Maj. John Welsh
(AA) to administer oath.

Richard Edelen & his wife Elisabeth were
granted administration on estate of
Henry Aspeanwall (CH). Said Elisabeth
is unable to travel to Office.
Appraisers: John Ward, Nathaniell
Barton. William Smith (g, CH) to
administer oath.

John Addisson (SM) vs. administrator of
Robert Hodgeson (CH, lately murdered).
Caveat entered.

13:72 Eduard Pye, Esq. (CH) vs. administrator
of Robert Hodgeson (CH). Caveat
entered.

William Hatton (g, SM) exhibited oath of
John Addisson & Francis Hill, appraisers
of William Berief (SM).

William Hatton (SM) exhibited oath of
Eduard Morgan & Robert Craine,
appraisers of Anthony Lamb (SM).

Exhibited was inventory of George Newman
(CH), by appraisers Ralph Smith & Thomas
Gibson.

28 September. Richard Marsham (CV)
exhibited oath of Capt. Ninian Beall &
John Chittam executors of Peter Archer
(CV), with will proved by John Browne &
Lewis Jones. Also exhibited was oath of
Thomas Gant & Thomas Blandfort,
appraisers. Also exhibited was
inventory.

Clement Hill (SM) exhibited oath of
William Rosewell & William Shercliffe,
appraisers of Edward Fishwick (SM),
sworn 21 September 1683. Also exhibited
was bond of Margarett Fishwick
administratrix, with surety: William
Meekins.

6 October. Capt. Richard Hill (AA)
exhibited will of Thomas Bucknall (AA),
proved by witnesses. Also exhibited was
oath of Mary Bucknall executrix. Also
exhibited was oath of Nich. Greenbery &
William Hopkins, appraisers. Also
exhibited was inventory.

13:73   Grace Fearson (CH) widow of John Fearson
(CH) was granted administration on his
estate. Appraisers: Thomas Gibson,
William Hatche. Humphrey Warren (CH) to
administer oath.

James Turner (CH) was granted
administration on estate of Abraham
Turner (CH), as next-of-kin.
Appraisers: John Gouge, Joseph Cooper.
Humphrey Warren (g, CH) to administer
oath.

13 October. William Smith (g, CH)
exhibited oath of Elisabeth Aspeanwall
administratrix of Henry Aspeanwall (CH).
Also exhibited was oath of John Ward &
Nathaniell Barton, appraisers. Also
exhibited was inventory.

25 October. Eduard Dorsey (AA)
exhibited will of Rowland Nance (BA),
proved. Also exhibited was oath of

Henry Constable (BA), executor. Also
exhibited was inventory, by appraisers
Nich. Greenbery & Richard Gwinn.

11 November. Exhibited was inventory of
Thomas Norris (KE), by appraisers John
Bowls & Charles Tilden. Also exhibited
was bond of administrator. Sureties:
Henry Hosier, John Bowles.

24 November. Elisabeth Gardiner (SM)
widow of John Gardiner (SM) exhibited
his will, constituting her executrix.
Joseph Pile (SM) to prove said will.
Appraisers: William Langworth, Francis
Knott.

13:74   John Godshall (CH) exhibited will of
George Clarke (CH), constituting him
executor. Robert Doyne to prove said
will. Appraisers: Richard Morris,
Richard Garforth. Said Doyne to
administer oath.

Mary Dike (CH) widow of her 1st husband
Thomas Alcocke, who died a year ago,
exhibited his will, constituting Col.
William Chandler & Mr. John Stone
executors. Said will was proved &
executors have renounced executorship on
29 December 1682. John Stone to prove
said will.

John Boaring (BA) exhibited oath of John
Howard administrator of Thomas Marshall
(BA). Sureties: David Jones, Anthony
Demondidier. Also exhibited was oath of
John Thomas & John Arden, appraisers.
Also exhibited was inventory.

Exhibited was inventory of Peter Archer
(CV), by appraisers & Blandfort Tho.
Gant.

13:75   Edward Bedell (BA) exhibited oath of
Arthur Taylor & Robert Low, appraisers
of Gervais Lascell, sworn on 16 July
past. Also exhibited was oath of Thomas
Heath, administrator, sworn on 12 July
past. Sureties: James Mills, John
Parnell. James Philips was the other
administrator; said Heath has whole

administration. Also exhibited was inventory.

James Bowling (g, SM) exhibited oath of Thomas Gerrard one of executors of Robert Browne (SM), sworn on 16 August 1683. Also oath of John Barcroft & Richard Edelin, appraisers, sworn same day.

28 November. Anne Kannedy (SM) widow of William Kannedy was granted administration on his estate. Appraisers: John Evans, Robert Craine. William Hatton (SM) to administer oath.

13:76   Martha Joy (CV) widow of Peter Joy (CV) was granted administration on his estate. Appraisers: David Davies, John Miles. John Darnall (CV) to administer oath.

30 November. Exhibited was inventory of Peter Browne (CV), by appraisers George Abott & William Taylor.

4 December. William Medley (SM) was granted administration on estate of Thomas Medley (SM), as next of kin. Appraisers: Peter Mills, William Shertcliffe. Clement Hill (g, SM) to administer oath.

6 December. William Stevenson (TA) exhibited letter from Vincent Lowe petitioning that said Stephenson be granted administration on estate of Dr. Robert Hilton, formerly granted to Peter Denny. Date: 5 December 1683 at Mattapony Sewall. Said Stephenson was granted administration. James Murphy (TA) to administer oath.

Griffith Jones attorney for David Arbuthnott (merchant) vs. estate of Samuell Tovy (KE). Caveat.

13:77   Jonas Greenwood exhibited petition of Ellin Evitts widow of Nathaniell Evitt for administration on his estate. Date: 1 December 1683 at Chester River. Said Greenwood was granted administration.

Court Session: 1683

Appraisers: MM Charles Tilden, Thomas
Warren. Christopher Goodhand to
administer oath.

Joane West (CE) widow of John West was
granted administration on his estate.
Appraisers: Eduard Play, John Hayburne.
William Peirce to administer oath.

John Hynson was granted administration
on estate of John Jackson (KE).
Appraisers: Matthew Erreckson, John
Butcher. Mr. Lawrence to administer
oath. [Petition was dated 4 November
1683; administration granted on 12
November 1683.]

13:78   Margarett Hagley (CE) widow of
Bartholomew Henrickson (CE) was granted
administration on his estate.
Appraisers: Thomas Rumsey, William Ward.
Nathaniell Garrett to administer oath.

7 December. The widow Stanesby (BA) of
John Stanesby petitioned for new
appraisers. Date: 27 October 1683.

Exhibited was inventory of Eduard
Fishwick (SM), by appraisers William
Rosewell & William Shertcliffe.

8 December. Robert Carvile procurator
for John LeMaire (CH) who married
Margarett (daughter of Archibald Wahob
(CH, dec'd)) & Philip Hoskins who
married Elisabeth (daughter & coheiress
of said Wahob) exhibited that said
Archibald died last Saturday, leaving
Elisabeth (relict & mother-in-law to
said Margarett & Elisabeth),
13:79   & said Elisabeth exhibited a will made
just before his death. Said Archibald
was of insane memory & understanding.
Petition that Col. William Chandler &
Ignatius Causeene examine witnesses.
Said Elisabeth summoned.

Robert Carvile creditor of John Stanesby
(dec'd) petitioned that Mary Stanesby
(widow) had appraisers William Yorke &
Thomas Hedge, & petitioned for new
appraisers. Petition to stay said

request. Ruling: granted. Widow
summoned.

11 December. Abraham Smith (CE) died
last May & his wife has not taken out
administration, intending to defraud
creditors.

13:80 Creditors: Henry Stapells, Philip
Cannedy. Date: 24 October 1683. Widow
summoned.

Maj. James Ringold (KE) petitioned for
administration on estate of Samuell
Tovy, as greatest creditor. Widow is "a
woman to be mistrusted, to embezzle
estate". Date: 1 December 1683. Said
Ringold was granted administration.
Appraisers: Thomas Boone, John Doughty.
Mr. William Frisby to administer oath.
Exhibited was debt of said Tovy (g, inn
holder, KE) to James Ringgold (g, KE).
Date: 4 August 1679.

13:81 Witnesses: William Croshan, Josias
Lanham. Exhibited was second bond.
Date: 22 October 1681. Witnesses:
Josias Lanham, Barbara Lanham.

13:82 **12 December.** Maj. John Welch (AA)
exhibited inventory of Abraham Naylor.
Appraisers were sworn 8 September last.
Date: 11 October 1683.

Eduard Dorsey (AA) exhibited oath of
James Homewood, administrator, sworn 19
November instant.

18 December. John Darnall (CV)
exhibited oath of Martha Joy
administratrix of Peter Joy (CV). Also
exhibited was oath of David Davies &
John Miles, appraisers.

19 December. Absalom Tennison (SM) one
of executors of John Tennison (SM)
exhibited that he is now of age &
petitioned for executorship with his
brother Justinian. Ruling: granted.

John Hance (CV) was granted
administration on estate of Charles
Bathurst (CV), as principle creditor.
Appraisers: William Parker, Francis

Freeman. Capt. Richard Ladd (CV) to administer oath.

13:83 20 December. Luke Gardiner (SM) exhibited nuncupative will of William Woodcocke (SM), bequeathing to said Gardiner. Richard Gardiner (SM) to take depositions. Appraisers: Eduard Cole, Francis Knott. Said Richard to administer oath.

John Morgan (CV) was granted administration on estate of Anne Norman (CV), as next of kin. Appraisers: William Goodman, Eduard Brooke. Francis Collyer (CV) to administer oath.

James Ringgold (KE) exhibited that Samuell Tovy (KE) is dec'd & indebted to said Ringgold. And that Anne Tovey (widow) is likely to waste & embezzle the estate. Mr. Frisby to present LoA to said widow.

13:84 27 December. Robert Carvile (SM) exhibited will of James Bodkin (CH), constituting Clement Hill (SM) & said Carvile joint executors. Joseph Pile to prove said will. Appraisers: William Boareman, James Bowling.

29 December. Anne Tovy (KE) widow of Mr. Samuel Tovy was granted administration on his estate. Appraisers: MM Edward Inglish, William Harris. Charles Tilden to administer oath. Originally, Mr. Henry Hosier was to administer oath, but no longer has said commission. Said Tovy died on 17 October last.

13:85 Mentions: Maj. Ringgold & his son-in-law William Constable.

[CE Co. 14 November last] William Nowell petitioned that Abraham Smith died last May. Mary his widow is now married to John Salisbury & Philip Cannedy is principle creditor.

13:86 LoA were granted. Capt. Joseph Hopkins (one of nearest neighbors) to administer oath.

William Harris (KE) exhibited will of
Eduard Tom (CE), constituting Nathaniell
Toms executor. Said Nathaniell has
renounced administration. Joseph
Hopkins to prove said will. Said Harris
was granted administration. Appraisers:
William Ealmes, Eduard Beck. Said
Hopkins to administer oath.

Exhibited was additional inventory of
Peter Hykes (SM), by appraisers Clement
Haley & John Vaudry.

Matthew Chapman vs. estate of Capt.
Henry Ward. Caveat. Mentions: will in
hands of Governor Markam (in ENG).
Date: 19 December 1683.

13:87   William Digges exhibited will of Eduard
Toms, constituting Nathaniel Toms
executor, who has renounced
administration. Petition that Richard
Pullen or William Harris be granted
administration.

Exhibited was will of Thomas Alcocke
(CH), proved before John Stone (g, CH)
by John Hoskins & William Dike.

1 January. Exhibited was inventory of
John Murvart (CE), by appraisers Thomas
Bolton & Richard Edmonds.

Last October, Henry Hawkins (CH) who
married Elisabeth relict & executrix of
Francis Wyne (CH) who was security with
Michael Ashford (CH) to Thomas Marshall
(millwright, CH) on estate of Samuell
Raspin, exhibited that said Marshall has
fled the Province to VA. James Tyer
(CH) & Mr. Barton (CH) are to take oath.

15 January. Benjamin Evans (CV)
exhibited will of George Collings (CV),
constituting him executor. Richard
Marsham (g, CV) to prove said will.
Said Evans was granted administration.
Appraisers: John Chittam, Capt. Ninean
Beall. Said Marsham to administer oath.

13:88   16 January. William Hatton (SM)
exhibited oath of Robert Masson & Peter

Court Session: 1683

Watts, appraisers of George Mackeall (SM), sworn on 14 December 1683.

Exhibited was inventory of James Bodkin (SM), by appraisers William Boareman & Capt. James Bowling.

Exhibited was inventory of Thomas Medley (SM), by appraisers Peter Miles & William Shertcliffe.

Capt. Richard Hill (AA) petitioned for warrant to examine accounts of William Platt (AA) administrator of Robert Parnafee (AA).

Capt. Richard Hill exhibited oath of Mary Grey widow & administratrix of John Grey (AA).

13:89 Said Mary was summoned.

18 January. Thomas Driskeld (AA) was granted administration on estate of William Fisher (AA), for use of Sarah widow in ENG. Appraisers: Woolfran Hunt, Walter Carr. Capt. Thomas Francis to administer oath.

James Cullen (g, SM) petitioned for Marke Cordea (g, SM) to render accounts on estate of Anthony LeCompte (DO).

Per petition of John LeMaire (CH), Col. William Chandler (CH) & Capt. Ignatius Causeene (CH) to examine witnesses of will of Archibald Wahop

13:90 (CH). Per LeMaire's caveat (f. 78), dec'd was insane.

19 January. Margarett Worrell widow of Robert Worrell (CH) was granted administration on his estate. Appraisers: Joseph Cornall, William Burnam. James Tyer (CH) to administer oath.

Margrett Cole (SM) widow of William Cole (SM) was granted administration on his estate. Appraisers: William Shortley, Peter Mills. Clement Hill (SM) to administer oath.

21 January. Mary Dike (CH) relict of Thomas Alcocke (CH) was granted administration on his estate. Appraisers: John Ward, Eduard Maddock. John Stone (g, CH) to administer oath.

22 January. Jacob Looton (CE) administrator of George Phoenix (SM) exhibited accounts.

Clement Hill (g, SM) exhibited oath of Peter Mills & William Shercliffe, appraisers of Thomas Medley, sworn 11 January 1683.

13:91   Richard Gardiner (SM) exhibited will of William Woodcocke (SM), proved by Henery Coale, Timothy Therall, & Anne Young. Date: 27 December 1683. Also exhibited was oath of Luke Gardiner executor, sworn 9 January 1683. Also exhibited was oath of Eduard Coale & Franc. Knott, appraisers, sworn 8 January 1683.

Exhibited was bond of William Medley (SM) administrator of Thomas Medley (SM). Sureties: Thomas Kerkly, William Husbands.

Humphrey Warren (g, CH) exhibited oath of James Turner, administrator, sworn 8 November 1683. Sureties: Anthony Neall, William Jenkins. Also exhibited oath of John Gooch & Joseph Cooper, appraisers of Arthur Turner, sworn 9 October 1683.

13:92   Humphrey Warren exhibited will of John Fearson. Also exhibited was oath of Grace Fearson, executrix, sworn 9 October 1683. Also exhibited was oath of Thomas Gibson & William Hatch, appraisers.

1 February. Exhibited was inventory of John Fearson (CH), by appraisers Thomas Gibson & William Hatch.

Exhibited was bond of Benjamin Williams (AA) administrator of James Filkes (AA). Sureties: Leonard Waman, Walter Phelps. Also exhibited was inventory, by same as appraisers.

Jane widow of Robert Webb (CV) was granted administration on his estate. Appraisers: John Cobreath, Abraham Clerke. Capt. Samuell Bourne (g, CV) to administer oath.

Nancy Johnson relict of James Gilstrap (CV) was granted administration on his estate. Appraisers: Thomas Hinton, John Hunt. Capt. Samuell Bourne to administer oath.

13:93   George Parker was granted administration on estate of Simon Gibson (carpenter, AA). Appraisers: Thomas Day, Gabriell Parrott. Maj. Nicholas Gassaway to administer oath.

George Parker (g, Clifts, CV) exhibited will of Maj. John Welsh (AA), constituting widow Mary executrix. Col. Thomas Taylor (AA) to prove said will. Said Mary was granted administration. Appraisers: Maj. Nicholas Gassaway, Capt. Henry Hanslap. Said Taylor to administer oath.

4 February. Philip Lyne (CH) vs. estate of William Smithson (DO). Caveat.

14 February. Col. William Burgess (AA) was granted administration on estate of John Barker (Seavearne, AA). Appraisers: Jacob Harness, Eduard Dorsey, Laurence Draper. Capt. Richard Hill to administer oath.

13:94   Richard Pollard (CV) exhibited will of Elisabeth Rope (CV), constituting him executor. Capt. Samuell Bourne (CV) to prove said will. [Estate is only land.]

Isaack Winchester (KE) to prove will of Elisabeth Eareckson (KE), & to administer oath to Mathew Eareckson as executor. Appraisers: Thomas Osbourne, Valentine Suthorne. Said Winchester to administer oath.

James Ellis (AA) exhibited will of Elisabeth Heathcoate (AA), constituting Col. Thomas Taylor & said Ellis executors. Said Taylor has renounced administration. Date: 14 November 1683. Col. William Burgess (AA) to prove said will. Said Ellis was granted administration. Appraisers: Walter Carr, Robert Conant. Said Burgess to administer oath.

Capt. Richard Hill (AA) to prove will of Henry Howard (AA) & to administer oath to Theophilus Hackett as executor. Appraisers: John Benett, Hugh Mercken. Said Hill to administer oath.

13:95 15 February. Richard Royston (TA) was granted administration on estate of George Taylor (AA), on behalf of the orphans. Appraisers: John Power, Richard Phidemon. James Murphy (TA) to administer oath.

James Murphy (TA) to administer oath to appraisers of estate of Robert Hilton (TA), William Stevenson is administrator.

Francis Sheppard vs. estate of Hugh Johnson (TA). Caveat. Mary widow of said Hugh has renounced administration. William Bishop desires administration.

13:96 Date: 27 January 1683. Witnesses: John Holingsworth, William Cowell. Said Bishop & Robert Carvile summoned.

18 February. Exhibited was will of George Collins (CV), proved before Richard Marsham. Also exhibited was oath of Capt. Ninian Beall & John Chittam, appraisers.

25 February. Exhibited was inventory of William Canedy (SM), by appraisers Robert Crane & John Evans.

Summons to Marke Cordea to render accounts on estate of Anthony LeCompte (DO) returned.

Exhibited was inventory of William Heifernam (AA), by appraisers Seth Biggs & Francis Voisin.

Court Session: 1683

13:97   Charles Tilden (KE) exhibited oath of
         Anne Tovy relict & administratrix of Mr.
         Samuell Tovy, sworn 1 January 1683.
         Sureties: Thomas Theaxstone, Michaell
         Miller. Also exhibited was oath of MM
         Eduard Inglish & William Harris,
         appraisers, sworn same day.

         Elisabeth Skipwith (Clifts, CV)
         exhibited will of George Skipwith (CV),
         constituting her executrix. Said
         Elisabeth cannot take oath, for
         conscience sake. Thomas Starling (CV)
         to prove said will.

         27 February. Exhibited was inventory of
         Arthur Turner (CH), by appraisers John
         Gooth & Joseph Cooper.

         James Turner (CH) was granted
         administration on estate of John Bennett
         (CH), as principle creditor.
         Appraisers: Joseph Cooper, William
         Jenkins. Capt. Humphrey Warren (CH) to
         administer oath.

         Daniell Hamond (SM) was granted
         administration on estate of John
         Hartwell (SM), as principle creditor.
         Appraisers: Stephen Gough, Richard
         Burckhead. James Pattison (g) to
         administer oath.

13:98   28 February. John Court executor of
         Robert Henley (CH) was granted
         administration on his estate. James
         Tyer (CH) to prove said will.
         Appraisers: John Fanning (g), Thomas
         Clipsham (g). Said Tyer to administer
         oath.

         Exhibited was bond of Margarett Worall
         (CH) administratrix of Robert Worall
         (CH). Sureties: John Smith, William
         Timothy. Also exhibited was inventory,
         by appraisers Joseph Cornall & William
         Burnam.

         3 March. Joseph Sparnon who married
         Alice relict of Thomas Hinton (CE) was
         granted administration on his estate.
         Appraisers: George Collfeild, William

Curer. William Dare (g) to administer
oath. Said Hinton made a verbal will,
which was set aside. Said will was made
in the presence of Joseph Sparnon,
Howell Lloyd, John Owen, & Robert
Kimball on 16 December 1683. Legatees:
wife Alice. Sworn: 25 January 1683/4.

13:99 Exhibited was inventory of Daniell
Clocker (SM), by appraisers Francis
Catterson & James Cullen.

4 March. Exhibited was inventory of
William Ireland (Clifts, CV), by
appraisers Tobias Miles & Robert
Spickernell.

Capt. Richard Ladd (CV) exhibited oath
of John Hance (CV) administrator of
Charles Bathurst (CV). Sureties: Henry
Kent, Basill Waring. Also exhibited was
inventory, by appraisers William Puker &
Francis Freeman.

Charles Brewer (AA) son & heir of
Elisabeth Brewer (widow, AA) petitioned
for a copy of her will, since he is
going on a voyage to ENG.

5 March. Augustine Herman for his
daughter relict of Henry Ward petitioned
for
13:100 LoA. Matthew Chapman should have
indicated that Capt. Markham has the
will, bequeathing all to his daughter &
making him overseer. When said Ward
fell sick & was asked if he had made a
will, he said: "No." Mentions: son of
said marriage. Date: 10 February 1683/4
at Bohemia Manor. Anna Margaretta
(widow) was granted administration on
his estate. Appraisers: MM Nathaniell
Garratt, Samuell Wheeler. Said Herman
to administer oath.

Maj. Thomas Long (BA) to prove will of
William Cromwell (BA), constituting
Elisabeth Cromwell executrix. Said
Elisabeth was granted administration.
Appraisers: John Thomas, William Ball.
Said Long to administer oath.

William Bishop was granted administration on estate of Samuell Conykear (KE), as principle creditor. Appraisers: Robert Sadler, Thomas Cooper. Christopher Goodhand to administer oath.

13:101   Edward Inglish (CE) was granted administration on estate of Francis Blang (CE), as principle creditor. Appraisers: Gideon Gundry, James Heyborne. Capt. William Peirce (CE) to administer oath.

8 March. George Parker for Ellinor Evendon relict of Thomas Evendon (CV) was granted administration on his estate. She cannot travel as far as SM. Appraisers: John King, Richard Jackson. John Creycroft (CV) to administer oath.

John Waters (AA) was granted administration on estate of Michaell Williams (AA), as principle creditor. Appraisers: James Paschall, Walter Carr. Col. Thomas Taylor (AA) to administer oath.

Marke Cordea (g, SM) was granted continuance on accounts for estate of Anthony LeCompte (DO).

12 March. John Cambell (SM) exhibited will of Dorothy Homan (SM), constituting him executor. Said Cambell was granted administration. Appraisers: Christopher Goodson, Randall Hynson. William Hatton (g) to administer oath.

13:102   William Hatton (g, SM) exhibited bond of Anne Cannedy administratrix of William Cannedy (SM). Sureties: Robert Crane, John Evans.

Henry Clay, Jr. (TA) exhibited will of Henry Clay, Sr., constituting him executor. James Murphy (g, TA) to prove said will. Said Jr. was granted administration. Appraisers: William Leeds, William Gassell. Said Murphy to administer oath.

18 March. Capt. Richard Hill (AA) exhibited will of Stephen Burle (AA), proved. Also exhibited was oath of Blanch Burle executrix. Also exhibited was oath of Theophilus Hackett & Humphrey Boone, appraisers.

Richard Hill exhibited that widow Grey had not accepted administration because of the appraisers. She has since married Patrick Murphie & requests LoA. She was granted administration. Appraisers: John Peasely, William Pennington. Date: 8 March 1683. Capt. Richard Hill to administer oath.

Miles Gibson for Mr. John Boaring petitioned to prove will of Francis Lovelace. Appraisers: Richard Samson, Thomas Durbin. Date: 11 March 1683.

Col. George Wells (BA) to prove will of Robert Jones (BA), constituting William Jones executor. Said William was granted administration. Appraisers: Lawrence Taylor, John Fisher. Said Wells to administer oath.

13:103 19 March. Francis Sheppard exhibited his renunciation of administration on estate of Hugh Johnson (TA). Date: 13 March 1683. William Bishop (TA) was granted administration, as principle creditor. Surety: James Murphy. Appraisers: John Offley, Richard Gould. William Hemsley (TA) to administer oath.

Juletta Carr (AA) exhibited will of Thomas Daborne (AA), constituting her executrix. Col. Thomas Taylor to prove said will. Said Carr was granted administration. Appraisers: Richard Gott, Robert Lockwood. Said Taylor to administer oath.

Court Session: 1684

25 MarchCol. William Burges (AA) exhibited oath of Walter Carr & Robert Conant, appraisers of Elisabeth Heathcoate (AA). Also exhibited was her will.

Exhibited was inventory of William
Woodcocke (SM), by appraisers Eduard
Coule & Francis Knott.

Exhibited was inventory of George
Macaall (SM), unadministered by Robert
Graham (SM, dec'd).

Clement Hill exhibited oath of Peter
Mills & William Shertcliffe, appraisers
of William Coale (SM). Also exhibited
was bond, with sureties: William Medley,
John Nevit.

13:104 Capt. Richard Hill (AA) exhibited will
of Henry Howard (AA), proved. Also
exhibited was oath of Theophilus Hackett
executor.

William Robson (DO) administrator of
John Taylor (DO) was granted discharge.

Exhibited was bond of Ellinor Evitts
(KE) administratrix of Nathaniell
Evitts. Sureties: Thomas Theatstone,
Morgan Jones.

Ebenezar Blackiston (CE) exhibited will
of Francis Harmer (CE, died 2 years
ago), constituting him executor. Said
will was proved in 1681, but he never
took oath as executor. LoA issued.

Anthony Holland & Benjamin Capell
exhibited will of Thomas Person (AA),
constituting them executors. Col.
Thomas Taylor to prove said will. Said
Holland & Capell were granted
administration. Appraisers: Richard
Gott, John Waters. Said Taylor to
administer oath.

26 March. Capt. Richard Ladd (CV)
exhibited oath of Johanna Barnes
administratrix of Matthew Barnes (CV).
Sureties: John Manning, George Abbot.
Also exhibited was inventory, by
appraisers William Taylor & Thomas Howe.

James Ellis (AA) petitioned for sheriff
(AA) to summon John Heathcoat & Joseph
Heathcoat & Samuell Roberts (all of AA)

to render accounts on estate of
Nathaniell Heathcoate (AA).

13:105   29 March. Henry Coursey, Jr. (TA)
exhibited petitions for:
- LoA on estate of Dr. Eustace (TA).
- LoA to Mrs. Elisabeth Coursey
  relict of William Coursey & said
  Coursey's son who is with his cousin
  Henry.
Maj. Peter Sayer to take bond of
Elisabeth Coursey & William Coursey
administrators of Maj. William Coursey.
Appraisers: Thristram Thomas, William
Hemsley. Said Sayer to administer oath.

Said Sayer to administer oath to
Elisabeth Eustace widow & administratrix
of Dr. Eustace. Appraisers: Richard
Jones, Robert Smith. Said Sayer to
administer oath.

John Gallwith (CV) was granted
administration on estate of Thomas
Jackson (CV), who died with neither wife
nor children nor kindred in this
Province, as principle creditor.
Appraisers: John Grover, Joseph
Williams. Roger Brookes (g, CV) to
administer oath.

2 April. Exhibited was inventory of
Ambrose Sanderson (CV), by appraisers
Thomas Tasker & Robert Smith.

William Richards (merchant, CV) was
granted administration on estate of John
Hamond, as principle creditor. Surety:
Col. Henry Jowles. Appraisers: Simon
Stacy, Joseph Goosey. John Darnall,
Esq. to administer oath.

John Wattson (SM) was granted
administration on estate of Robert
Graham
13:106   (SM). Mentions: Thomas Wahob.

4 April. Richard Boughton for Elisabeth
Hambleton (CH) widow of John Hambleton
(CH) was granted administration on his
estate. Appraisers: John Stone, William
Smith. Robert Doyne (g, CH) to

Court Session: 1684

administer oath.

Richard Boughton (g, CH) petitioned for
sheriff (CH) to summon Elisabeth
Hambleton (CH) widow of John Hambleton,
Parthenia Burditt (CH), & Sarah Burditt
(CH) to show cause why administration on
estate of Samuell Eaton should not be
granted to said Boughton in right of his
wife Verlinda as next of kin.

John LeMaire vs. estate of Archibald
Wahop. Col. William Chandler (g, CH) &
Ignatius Causen (g, CH) exhibited
depositions for Elisabeth relict of
Archibald Wahop (CH) & John Lemaire
(chirurgeon, CH). Date: 5 February
1683.
• Cleborne Lomax (g, CH), age 40,
deposed on 1 December 1683 that
Archibald Wahop requested the
deponent to write his will.
13:107 ...
• Danill Murphy (CH), age 31, deposed
on 1 December 1683.
• Peter Fernandis (p, CH), age 36,
deposed on 1 December 1683.
• John Boyce (p, CH), age 40, deposed
on 1 December 1683.
13:108 ...
• Thomas Jenkins (p, CH), age 44,
deposed on 1 December 1683.

Ruling: to make will void, several
defects could concur:
1. disability of testator.
2. unlawfulness in legacies.
3. incapacity of executor.
4. compulsion of testator by fear.
5. circumvention by fraud or flattery.
6. induction by any unlawful manner.
7. testator had not "Animum testandi".

John LeMaire vs. estate of Archibald
Waughob. Testator was over-persuaded by
his wife & threatened by same. Ruling:
allegation without due proof.
13:109 Col. William Chandler to prove said
will. Elisabeth (widow), who is not
able to travel as far as Office, by
reason of great age, was granted
administration on said estate.

Page 47

Appraisers: John Godshall, John Clerke.
Said Chandler to administer oath.

Dennis Hurley (SM) one of executors of
Derby Donnovan (SM) exhibited accounts.

Thomas Marshall (millwright, CH)
administrator of Samuell Raspin
exhibited accounts, proved before
William Barton (g) & James Tyre (g).

13:110 7 April. Exhibited was inventory of
William Coale (SM), by appraisers Peter
Mills & William Shertcliffe.

Lt. Col. Thomas Taylor (AA) exhibited
will of Maj. John Welsh (AA), proved.

Maj. Thomas Long (BA) was granted
administration on estate of Ambrose
Gellut (BA), as principle creditor.
Appraisers: Francis Watkins, Richard
Enoch. Charles Gorsuch to administer
oath.

8 April. Miles Gibson (g) for Elisabeth
Harris (BA) widow of William Croshow was
granted administration on his estate.
Appraisers: John Yeo, Peter Ellis.
Eduard Bedell (g, BA) to administer
oath.

9 April. William Richardson & Benjamin
Laurence renounced executorship of
estate of Thomas Hooker (AA). Mentions:
Thomas Hooker (son of dec'd) as
executor, other children.

Capt. Richard Hill (AA) exhibited oath
of Mary Murphy (AA) widow &
administratrix of John Grey.
13:111 Sureties: John Peasely, William
Pennington.

Capt. Richard Hill (AA) exhibited will
of Stephen Burle (AA), proved. Also
exhibited was oath of Blanch Burle
executrix.

10 April. Michaell Tawney (CV)
exhibited that John Gallwith (CV)
obtained LoA on estate of Thomas Jackson

(CV) on 29 March last. Said Tawney
petitioned for John Herbert as next of
kin to dec'd. Petition of William
Hubert (orphan). Mentions: petitioner's
father William Herbert (CV) who d.
about 5 years ago intestate leaving petitioner
& 1 daughter Mary who married Thomas
Jackson (CV). Said Jackson, for his
wife, administered estate of said
Herbert. Said Jackson died 13 March
last. His wife, said petitioner's
sister, also died. Petitioner was very
sick. Court should appoint a guardian
for petitioner.

13:112 Signed: William Hubert. Ruling: said
Herbert is of age to choose his
guardian. LoA to said Gallwith revoked.

James Tyre (g, CH) exhibited will of
Robert Henley, proved by Eduard Lee,
Richard Ghent, Cleborne Lomax, &
Margaret Maystie on 8 March 1683. Also
exhibited was oath of John Court
executor, sworn same day. Also
exhibited oath of John Fanning & Thomas
Clipsham, appraisers sworn 31 March
1684.

James Murphey (TA) exhibited oath of
Alexander Laremore & John Hunt,
appraisers of Roger Price, sworn 26
October 1683.

13:113 Also exhibited bond of Judith widow &
administratrix. Also exhibited was
inventory.

21 April. Robert Kembell (CE) who
married Abigaill only daughter of
Rowland Williams (CE, dec'd) was granted
administration on his estate.
Appraisers: William Price, John
Reycroft. Col. George Talbot (CE) to
administer oath.

Abraham Comb (SM) who married relict &
administratrix of Eduard Fishwick (SM)
exhibited accounts.

Nathaniell Garrett (g, CE) exhibited
oath of Katherine Linsey administratrix
of Robert Morrison (CE). Sureties:
William Drake, John Hagley. Also

exhibited oath of John Cox & Andrew
Peterson, appraisers.

Capt. Humphry Warren (CH) exhibited
oath of James Turner (CH) administrator
of John Bennett. Sureties: John Gooch,
Thomas Humphrey. Also exhibited oath of
Joseph Cooper & William Jenckins,
appraisers.

Letter from Lord Baltimore: Henry
Darnall, Esq. & William Diggs, Esq.
appointed keepers of great seal. Date:
27 January 1682.

13:114 Mr. K. Chesildine attorney for George
Hodgson (SM) petitioned for recovery of
remainder of judgements in CH County
Court vs. Thomas Marshall administrator
of Mr. Samuell Raspin. Said Marshall
has wasted estate & is a fugitive. Bond
to be delivered to petitioner. Signed:
C. Baltemore. Date: 5 April 1684.
Received of Eustachius Turin (reg.).
Signed: Thomas Burford. Date: 24 April
1684.

Jonathon Goosey (CV) appointed guardian
to 2 orphans of Thomas Kemp (CV, dec'd).
13:115 Richard Steevens ordered to deliver
goods to said Goosey. Signed: Eust.
Turin.

Andrew Abinghton for Sarah Downes (TA)
widow of James Downes was granted
administration on his estate.
Appraisers: Richard Swetnam, Andrew
Abington. George Robotham (g, TA) to
administer oath.

22 April. James Crawford for Sarah
Dorington (CV) widow of Francis
Dorington was granted administration on
his estate. Appraisers: John Cobreadth,
Marke Clare.

Thomas Bland attorney for Providence
Renolds (AA) relict & executrix of
Robert Davidge (AA) was granted
discharge.

Court Session: 1684

Capt. Richard Hill (AA) to summon John
Howard administrator of Thomas Marshall
to take oath on his accounts.

Anastasia Thompson (widow) was granted
administration on estate of Michael
Thompson (SM). Appraisers: Cuthbert
Scott, Abraham Coombs. Clement Hill (g,
SM) to administer oath.

13:116 William Herbert (orphan, CV) petitioned
for Michaell Tawney (CV) as guardian &
to administer estate of his kinsman
Thomas Jackson (CV). Ruling: granted.
Thomas Brookes to administer oath.

William Hopkins (AA) guardian of William
& Henry Lewis vs. John Bird & his wife
Elisabeth relict & executrix of Henry
Lewis. Hearing set.

William Blankensteine (merchant, SM) vs.
estate of William Cocke (SM). Caveat.
Sheriff (DO) to summon Simon Awdery
("wid" of dec'd).

23 April. Exhibited was inventory of
John Jackson (KE), by appraisers Matthew
Eareckson & John Butcher.

24 April. Eduard Ladamore (CE)
exhibited will of Thomas Shelton (CE),
constituting him executor. Capt.
William Peirce (g, CE) to prove said
will. Appraisers: Henry Eldersley,
Nicholas Allum. Said Peirce to
administer oath.

Thomas Furby who married Hannah (TA)
relict & executrix of Thomas Baxter (KE)
exhibited accounts. "They could not
take the oath for conscience sake."

13:117 Nathaniell Garrett (g, CE) exhibited
oath of Margarett Hagley (CE)
administratrix of her 1st husband
Bartholomew Henrickson (CE). Also
exhibited oath of William Ward & Thomas
Rumsey, appraisers. Also exhibited
inventory.

Court Session: 1684

Capt. Thomas Francis (AA) to prove will
of Richard Arnall (AA). Appraisers:
Woolfan Hunt, Nicholas Nicholson. Said
Francis to administer oath. [Note:
"Quaker" written in margin.]

Lt. Col. Thomas Taylor (AA) to prove
will of Thomas Hooker (AA). Appraisers:
Richard Lockwood, John Wattkins. Said
Taylor to administer oath. [Note:
"Quaker" written in margin.]

Anthony Neale (CH) one of executors of
Capt. James Neale petitioned for Capt.
Humphrey Warren (g, CH) to prove said
will. Anne & Anthony Neale executors
were granted administration.
Appraisers: John Fanning, John Coates.
Said Warren to administer oath.

Sarah Jones (AA) widow of William Jones
exhibited his will. Capt. Richard Hill
(AA) to prove said will. Said Sarah was
granted administration. Appraisers:
James Oroke, William Peninton. Said
Hill to administer oath.

13:118 25 April. Richard Bowen (CV) exhibited
will of Robert Standley (CV),
constituting him executor. Richard
Marsham (CV) to prove said will. Said
Bowen was granted administration.
Appraisers: John Chittam, William Selby.

George Robotham (g, TA) to prove will of
Eduard Moseley (TA). Appraisers: John
Lane, Richard Dudley. Said Robotham to
administer oath. [Note: "Quaker"
written in margin.]

William Combes (g, TA) to prove will of
Leonard Jinnings (TA). Appraisers:
Arthur Norwood, William Moore. Said
Combes to administer oath. [Note:
"Quaker" written in margin.]

Col. Henry Coursey (TA) exhibited will
of George Carall (TA, who d. 9-10 years
ago), constituting said Coursey
executor. Col. Philemon Lloyd (TA) to
prove said will.

Court Session: 1684

Col. Philemon Lloyd (TA) to prove will
of Robert Noble (TA). Cornelia Noble
was constituted executrix. [Note:
"Quaker" written in margin.]

Sheriff (CE) to summon Joana West relict
of John West (CE) to accept or
relinquish administration on said
estate.

Francis Catterton (inn holder, SMC) vs.
estate of William Cocks (SMC). Caveat.

13:119 29 April. Exhibited was inventory of
Henry Howard (AA).

Exhibited was inventory of Stephen Burle
(AA).

Exhibited was inventory of Dorothy Homan
(SM), by appraisers Randall Hinson &
Christopher Goodson.

James Mecall (CV) administrator of Peter
Browne (CV) exhibited accounts.

Capt. Thomas Francis (AA) exhibited
oath of Thomas Drifeld administrator of
William Fisher (AA), sworn 23 February
1683. Also exhibited oath of Wolfran
Hunt & Walter Carr, appraisers sworn
same day. Also exhibited inventory.

Exhibited bond of Elisabeth Hamilton
(CH) administratrix of John Hamilton.
Sureties: Richard Boughton, Thomas
Robinson. Also exhibited inventory, by
appraisers John Stone & William Smith.

13:120 Robert Carvile vs. estate of (N)
Stanesby. Administratrix is widow
Stanesby. Caveat subducted. Date: 11
April 1684.

Exhibited was inventory of George Clarke
(CH), by appraisers Richard Morrice &
Richard Garforth. Will was not proved,
as not being endorsed, & was returned to
Mr. Robert Doyne.

2 May. Amy Peters (SM) widow of Thomas
Bramstone (SM) was granted

Court Session: 1684

administration on his estate.
Appraisers: Clement Heley, John Hilton.
Joseph Piles (g, SM) to administer oath.

Thomas Bowdle (TA) exhibited will of
Timothy Goodridge (TA), constituting
Phebe Loftis executrix, now wife of said
Bowdle. Eduard Man (g, TA) to prove
said will. Said Phebe was granted
administration. Appraisers: Samuell
Hatton, Thomas Delahay. Said Man to
administer oath.

Rachell Baily (TA) widow of Richard
Bayly was granted administration on his
estate. Appraisers: John Stanley,
William Wintersell. Eduard Man (g) to
administer oath.

13:121 James Greene (SM) was granted
administration on estate of Elisabeth
Greene. Appraisers: John Cood, Benjamin
Mansell. Clement Hill (g, SM) to
administer oath.

6 May. Katherine Townehill (AA) widow
of Edmond Townehill (AA) exhibited his
will, constituting her executrix. Col.
William Burges (AA) to prove said will.
Appraisers: Eduard Carter, Richard
Tidings. Said Burges to administer
oath.

Richard Ghott & Benjamin Capill
appointed appraisers of Thomas Daborne
(AA). Col. Thomas Taylor to administer
oath.

Richard Ghott & Walter Carr appointed
appraisers of Thomas Persons (AA). Lt.
Col. Thomas Taylor to administer oath.
Executors are: Anthony Holland, Benjamin
Capell.

8 May. Isaak Winchester (g, KE)
exhibited oath of Thomas Osborne &
Valentine Southarne, appraisers of
Elisabeth Eareckson. Date: 26 April
1684. Also exhibited will of said
Eareckson, proved.

Page 54

Court Session: 1684

Capt. Samuell Bourne (CV) exhibited
oath of Leucy Johnson administratrix of
her 1st husband James Gilstrop.
Sureties: Jeremia Johnson, James
Cranford. Also exhibited oath of Thomas
Hinton & John Hunt, appraisers. Also
exhibited inventory.

13:122 Capt. Samuell Bourne (CV) exhibited
oath of Jane Webb widow & administratrix
of Robert Webb. Sureties: Thomas
Hinton, John Hunt. Also exhibited oath
of John Cobreath & Abraham Clarke,
appraisers. Also exhibited inventory.

Said Bourne exhibited oath of Richard
Pollard (CV) executor of Elisabeth Roap
(CV), with will.

10 May. Clement Hill (SM) exhibited
oath of Anastasia Thompson
administratrix of Michaell Thompson.
Sureties: Henry Spinke, William Meekins.
Also exhibited oath of Cuthbert Scott &
Abraham Coombes, appraisers sworn 8 May.
Also exhibited inventory.

17 May. Augustine Herman (CE) exhibited
oath of Nathaniell Garrett & Samuell
Wheeler, appraisers of Henry Ward, sworn
14 April. Also exhibited inventory.
Also exhibited oath of Anna Margaretta
Ward administratrix. Sureties: Ephraim
Herman, Nathaniell Garrett.

13:123 Richard Roberts (CE) administrator of
John Morment (CE) exhibited accounts.

Capt. Richard Hill (AA) exhibited oath
of Capt. William Burgess (AA)
administrator of John Barker (AA).
Surety: William Michell.

Exhibited was inventory of John Grey
(AA), by appraisers John Peasely &
William Penington.

2 June. Miles Gibson (g, BA) exhibited
oath of Mary Stanesby administratrix of
John Stansby (BA). Sureties: Benjamin
Gundry, John Hall. Also exhibited was
oath of James Collyer & John Tilliard,

Court Session: 1684

appraisers. Also exhibited was
inventory.

James Pattisson (g, Crosse Mannor, SM)
exhibited oath of Daniell Hammond
administrator of John Hartwell (SM).
Sureties: Thomas Nottingham, John Fosse.
Also exhibited oath of Stephen Gough &
Richard Burkhead, appraisers.

6 June. Capt. Richard Hill (AA)
exhibited oath of Elisabeth Plott
executrix of Robert Parnafee (AA).

Exhibited was oath of James Greene (SM)
administrator of Elisabeth Greene (SM).
Sureties: Neh. Blakiston, John Tennison.

Exhibited was will of Stephen Murty.
William Hatton to prove.
13:124 Clement Hill executor was granted
administration on said estate.
Appraisers: Cuthbert Scott, Abraham
Coombes. Said Hatton to administer
oath.

John Balden (AA) exhibited will of his
father John Balden (AA), constituting
him executor. Capt. Richard Hill to
prove said will. Said executor was
granted administration. Appraisers:
Henry Ridgely, Jacob Harniss. Said Hill
to administer oath.

10 June. William Hatton (g, SM)
exhibited oath of Cuthbert Scott &
Abraham Coombes, appraisers of Stephen
Murty (SM). Also exhibited was will,
proved.

Exhibited was will of William Jones
(AA), proved before Capt. Richard Hill.

John Boaring (g, BA) exhibited oath of
Miles Gibson (BA) executor of Francis
Lovelace. Also exhibited was oath of
Thomas Durbine & Richard Samson,
appraisers. Also exhibited was
inventory.

12 June. Capt. Richard Hill (AA)
exhibited oath of John Howard (AA)

Court Session: 1684

administrator of Thomas Marshall (AA),
on his accounts.

13:125 William Harris who married Elisabeth
widow of William Croshaw petitioned that
new LoA be granted in both names.

13 June. Charles Pine (BA) was granted
administration on estate of James Denton
(BA). Miles Gibson (g) to administer
oath.

Miles Gibson exhibited summons to Thomas
Heath administrator of Gervais Lascalles
(BA) to render accounts.

Mich. Judd (BA) petitioned sheriff (BA)
to summon William Burden & Israell
Skelton executors of Thomas Cooke (BA)
to render accounts.

Mich. Judd (BA) was granted
administration on estate of William
Evens, who died at his house, having an
inconsiderable estate. Miles Gibson (g,
BA) to swear appraisers.

14 June. Exhibited was bond of Alice
Sparnon widow of Thomas Hynson (CE).
Sureties: Joseph Spernon, George
Oldfeild, William Currer.

21 June. Exhibited was inventory of
Robert Henley (CH), by appraisers John
Fanning & Thomas Clipsham.

13:126 Anthony Underwood (SM) procurator for
James Ellis (BA) executor of Elisabeth
Heathcoate (AA) vs. Robert Carvile (g,
SM) for John Heathcoate administrator of
Nathaniell Heathcoate. Libel exhibited.
Mentions: said Elisabeth is relict of
said Nathaniell; said Nathaniell died
December 1681 leaving widow Elisabeth;
under pretense, said John "is a very
near relation" to said Nathaniell; said
Elisabeth made will constituting Col.
Thomas Taylor & plaintiff James Ellis
executors; said Taylor has renounced
administration;
13:127 said John has departed the Province.
Said Ellis was granted administration

Page 57

Court Session: 1684

dbn on estate of Nathaniell Heathcoate.
Col. Thomas Taylor (AA) to administer
oath. Sheriff (AA) exhibited the
summons to John Heathcoate.

Letter to Office: Date: 26 April 1684.
Edmond Beetonson (AA) who married Lydia
widow of Thomas Watkins (AA) exhibited
accounts on 31 July 1680.

13:128 James Phillips (BA) vs. William Harris
& his wife Elisabeth administratrix of
William Croshaw. Caveat. Date: 6 June
1684.

23 June. John Biggs (CV) exhibited will
of Oliver Stockley (CV). George Lingham
(g, CV) to prove said will. Said Biggs
was granted administration. Appraisers:
Matthew Beale, John Davies. Said
Lingham to administer oath.

Mary Jessup (CV) widow of Thomas Jessup
(CV) exhibited his will,
13:129 constituting her executrix. George
Lingham (g, CV) to prove said will.
Said Mary was granted administration.
Appraisers: John Biggs, John Leech.
Said Lingham to administer oath.

Sarah Tucker (AA) widow of Thomas Tucker
(AA) exhibited his will, constituting
her executrix. Capt. Richard Hill (AA)
to prove said will. Said Sarah was
granted administration.

Exhibited was will of William Davies
(CV), proved before Henry Darnall, Esq.
Thomas Gant executor was granted
administration. Appraisers: John
Chittam, John Bowlin. Richard Marsham
(CV) to administer oath.

James Cullen (g, SMC) vs. Marke Cordea
administrator of Anthony LeCompte (DO).
Petition to render accounts.

Anthony Underwood (g, SM) procurator for
Richard Boughton & his wife Verlinda vs.
Elisabeth Hamilton (CH) relict of John
Hamilton (CH) & vs. Sarah & Parthenia
Barditt executrices of Ann Doughty (CH).

Libel exhibited.

13:130 Mentions: Verlinda wife of Richard Boughton is sole sister of Samuell Eaton (CH, dec'd). Said Eaton made a will in April 1681, constituting his mother Ann Doughty executrix. Said Doughty took possession of said Eaton's estate & leased to John Hamilton (CH). Said Doughty died without proving said Eaton's will. Said John Hamilton died January 1683. Petition for administration.

13:131 24 June. Said Elisabeth Hamilton & Sarah Burditt summoned. Said Parthenia Burditt is not to be found. Date: 22 April 1684.

Exhibited was will of Archibald Waughob (CH), proved before Col. William Chandler. Also exhibited was inventory, by appraisers John Godsahll & John Clarke.

Capt. Humphrey Warren (CH) exhibited warrant to swear Anne Neale & Anthony Neale executors of Capt. James Neale (CH). Warrant is unserved. Mrs. Anne Neale refuses executorship; he requests her 1/3rds. Date: 19 June 1684. Ruling: will is valid.

13:132 Sheriff (CH) to summon said Anne Neale to appear at Nottley Hall before Col. William Digges.

Exhibited was inventory of Thomas Daborne (AA), by appraisers Richard Ghott & Benjamin Capell.

Exhibited was inventory of Thomas Parsons (AA), by appraisers Walter Carr & Richard Ghott.

Maj. Thomas Long (BA) exhibited oath of Elisabeth Cromwell executrix of William Cromwell (BA). Also exhibited was oath of John Thomas & William Baall, appraisers. Also exhibited was inventory.

25 June. CV County Court on 16 June 1684. Present: John Darnall, Esq.,

Court Session: 1684

Capt. Samuell Bourne, Mr. John Griggs,
Capt. Richard Ladd, Mr. Thomas Brooke,
Mr. George Lingam, Mr. John CreyCroft,
Mr. Francis Hutchins. Regarding:
estate of Thomas Kemp (CV).

13:133 Symon Stacey was appointed administrator
& guardian of orphans. Signed:
Christopher Kellet. Thomas Brooke (g,
CV) to administer oath.

James Tyer (CH) executor of Peter Carr
was granted continuance.

Thomas Bland (AA) exhibited will of
William Yieldhall (AA), constituting
Katherine Yieldhall (widow) executrix.
Said Katherine is unable to travel to
Office. Said Katherine was granted
administration. Appraisers: Adam
Shipley, Henry Peirpoint. Eduard Dorsey
(g, AA) to administer oath.

26 June. Capt. William Peirce (high
sheriff, CE) exhibited summons to
Margarett Hagley relict of Bartholomew
Henrickson (CE, dec'd).

13:134 Said Hagley was granted administration
on his estate. Appraisers: Nicholas
Alum, Henry Eldersly. Nathaniell Garett
to administer oath.

Sheriff (CE) exhibited summons to Joane
West (CE) relict of John West. She
could not come without "great damage to
my life & having none but small children
& none else to leave them with." She
cannot take oath for conscience sake.
Said Joane was granted administration.

Capt. William Peirce (CE) exhibited
oath of Eduard Ladamore executor of
Thomas Shelton, sworn 24 May 1684. Also
exhibited was oath to Henry Eldersly &
Nicholas Alum, appraisers. Also
exhibited was inventory.

George Warner (g, CE) exhibited will of
Robert Sanders (CE), proved. Also
exhibited was oath of Eduard Play &
Joseph Langley, appraisers.

Court Session: 1684

13:135 27 June. Maj. Peter Sawyer (TA) exhibited that Capt. Jonathon Sybrey (TA) accidentally drowned. Said Sawyer was granted administration on his estate. Appraisers: Richard Mirax, Nicholas Broadway. Capt. William Hemsley (TA) to administer oath.

Lt. Col. Thomas Taylor (TA) exhibited will of Francis Holland (AA), proved, constituting Margarett (widow) executrix. Said Margarett cannot swear for conscience sake. Appraisers: William Meares, Robert Conant. Col. Taylor to administer oath.

Exhibited was inventory of Robert Richardson (SO), by appraisers John Osborne & William Walton.

John Shankes (SM) exhibited petition for guardianship of orphans of William Watts (St. Clement's Hundred, SM). Date: 3 October 1682.
13:136 Gerrard Slye was executor. Children are to be raised in Church of ENG. John Shankes (grandfather of orphans, Protestant) was appointed guardian. Mentions: Justinian Gerrard, Vincent Mansfeild, Colline Mackensie, Emma wife of said Watts, Emma Rosewell.
13:137 Sureties: Nehemiah Blakiston (St. Clement's Hundred), Eduard Russell. Orphans: Charles Watts, William Watts, Eduard Watts. Date: 9 June 1684. Signed: MM William Hatton, Clement Hill, Joseph Piles, James Bowling, Thomas Mudd, John Dent. Per: John Blomfeild (clerk).
13:138 Said Shankes & family "visited with sore & tedious sickness". Children & Negro woman were abused "by stripes & burning with hot iron in ye private parts" by John Oliver (overseer to Gerrard Slye (g)). Said Oliver was committed to custody of sheriff.

13:139 Anthony Underwood attorney for Marke Cordea (g, SM) appeared to answer summons to render accounts on estate of Anthony LeCompte (DO).

Page 61

Court Session: 1684

Eduard Day (SO) who married Elisabeth relict & executrix of Thomas Walker (SO) was summoned to render accounts. Said Elisabeth is also dec'd.

Col. George Wells (BA) was summoned to render accounts on estate of Samuell Goldsmith.

13:140 28 June. Thomas Starling (g, CV) exhibited oath of Sarah Dorington (CV) widow & administratrix of Francis Dorington (CV). Sureties: Marke Clare, Thomas Crowder. Also exhibited was oath of Marke Clare & John Cobreadth, appraisers. Also exhibited was inventory.

Thomas Starling (g, CV) exhibited will of George Skipwith (CV), proved. ["Quaker" is written in the margin.]

Exhibited was inventory of Thomas Hinton (CE), by appraisers George Oldfeild & William Currer.

George Robotham (g, TA) exhibited oath of Sarah Downes administratrix of James Downes (TA). Sureties: John Pemberton, William Kendall. Also exhibited was oath of Andrew Abington & Richard Swetnam, appraisers. Also exhibited was inventory.

William Harris exhibited inventory of Eduard Toms (KE), by **13:141** Eduard Beck & William Elmes. Signed: Mr. Eust. Turin.

Ellioner Hamond widow of Daniell Hammond (SM) administrator of John Hartwell (SM) was granted administration on said Hartwell's estate. Appraisers: Stephen Gouh, John Taunt. Clement Hill (SM) to administer oath.

Nicholas Sylvester (SM) was granted administration on estate of Henry Phillips (SM), having no relations in Province, as principle creditor. Appraisers: John Broome, Peter Mills. Clement Hill (SM) to administer oath.

Court Session: 1684

30 June. Exhibited was will of Thomas
Daborne (AA), proved before Lt. Col.
Thomas Taylor (AA).

Exhibited was will of Thomas Persons
(AA), proved before Lt. Col. Thomas
Taylor (AA).

Joseph Pile (g, SM) exhibited oath of
Amy Peters administratrix of Thomas
Bramstone. Sureties: Clement Haley,
John Hilton. Also exhibited was oath of
said Haley & said Hilton, appraisers.
Also exhibited was inventory.

13:142 John CreyCroft (g, CV) exhibited oath of
John King & Richard Jackson, appraisers
of Thomas Evenden (SM). Also exhibited
was bond of Ellinor Evenden
administratrix. Sureties: Thomas
Finley, John Gigges. Also exhibited was
inventory.

Exhibited was bond of William Bishop
(TA) administrator of Samuell Conybear
(TA). Sureties: John Louday, Griffith
Jones. Also exhibited was inventory, by
appraisers Robert Sadler & Thomas
Cooper.

Col. William Burgess (AA) exhibited
oath of Katherine Townehill (AA)
executrix of Edmond Townehill (AA).
Also exhibited was oath of Eduard Carter
& Richard Tiding, appraisers. Also
exhibited was inventory.

Exhibited was bond of Richard Royston
(TA) administrator of George Taylor
(TA). Surety: Griffith Jones, Also
exhibited was inventory, by appraisers
John Power & Richard Phidemond.

Exhibited was inventory of John Barker
(AA), by appraisers Laurence Draper &
Jacob Harniss.

Letter: date: 15 September 1682, SM.
Anthony Holland (SM) administrator of
13:143 Christopher Gardiner (SM) exhibited
accounts. Distribution: 3 orphans.
Signed: East. Turin. Mentions:

Commissioners of AA.

Sheriff (TA) to summon John Bird & his wife Elisabeth (AA) executrix of Henry Lewis (AA).

Exhibited was will of Eduard Toms (CE), proved before Joseph Hopkins (g, CE), with renunciation of Nathaniell Toms (executor, brother). Said Nathaniell recommended Richard Pullen & William Harris. Date: 18 December 1683. Witnesses: Francis Midellton, Jane Jones.

13:144 William Harris (g, KE) was granted administration on his estate. Sureties: Benjamin Gandry, George Higgimbotom. Appraisers: Eduard Beck, William Elmes. Joseph Hopkins (g, CE) to administer oath.

Exhibited was oath of Symon Stacy & Jonathon Goosey, appraisers of John Hammond (CV), sworn by John Darnall, Esq. Also exhibited was inventory.

Capt. Joseph Hopkins (CE) exhibited return of LoA to Philip Cannedy & Mary Salisbury administrators of Abraham Smith. They refused, saying they never requested them. Said Mary Salisbury & William Cannedy sued for LoA. (cf. f. 85.) Said Mary Salisbury & Philip Cannedy summoned.

Exhibited was oath of Elisabeth Coursey & her son William Coursey as joint administrators of Maj. William Coursey, sworn by Maj. Peter Sayer (TA). Also exhibited was oath of Thrustram Thomas & William Hemsley, appraisers.

Exhibited was oath of Elisabeth Eustace administratrix of Dr. James Eustace (TA), sworn by Maj. Peter Sayer. Sureties: Henry Coursey, Jr., John Serjeant. Also exhibited was oath of Richard Jones & Robert Smith, appraisers.

13:145 Exhibited was will of Robert Noble (TA), proved before Col. Philemon Lloyd (TA).

Court Session: 1684

Exhibited was inventory of Samuell Tovy
(KE), by appraisers Eduard Inglish &
William Harris.

7 July. Exhibited was inventory of John
Bennett (CH), by appraisers Joseph
Cooper & William Jenkins.

15 July. Rebecca Daley (SM) widow of
Bryant Daley exhibited his will,
constituting her executrix. Said
Rebecca was granted administration.
Appraisers: James Yeare, Owen Guyther.

Miles Gibson (g, BA) exhibited oath of
William Harris & his wife Elisabeth
Harris administrators of William Croshow
(BA). Sureties: John Yeo, Eduard
Reeves. Also exhibited was inventory,
which contains items belonging to
orphans of (N) Hollis. Orphan (male) of
said Hollis is of age to choose a
guardian. Their estate is much
embezzled by
13:146 so many step-fathers & an "uncareful"
mother. Said mother summoned.
Inventory for Croshow to be redone,
which is little or none. Said orphan
(male) to be apprised of his & his
sisters condition.

Charles Jones (CE) administrator of
Charles Howell (CE) exhibited accounts.
Discharge was granted.

23 July. Anne Devine (now Anne
DelaVallee, SM) relict of Daniell Devine
(SM) exhibited his will, constituting
her executrix, proved before Col. Henry
Darnall, Esq. Said Anne was granted
administration. Appraisers: Thomas
Doxey, Eduard Chester. James Pattisson
(g, Crosse Mannor) to administer oath.

25 July. Per William Blankensteine
(SM), sheriff (SM) to re-summon Audery
Cocks widow of William Cocks (SM).

26 July. Said Audery Cocks appeared;
however, business called Col. William
Digges away. Ruling: nothing done.

13:147 28 July. Exhibited was oath of Thomas
Linsey & his wife Katherine
administratrix of Robert Morris (CE) on
their accounts, sworn by Capt. William
Peirce.

John Rousby (g, TA) exhibited petition
to Court, dated 21 June 1684. Mrs.
Cornelia Vaughan widow of Mr. Charles
Vaughan, who drowned with Capt. Sybery,
was granted administration on said
Charles' estate. Appraisers: Isaak
Winchester, Lewis Blangey. Mr.
Christopher Goodhand (KI) to administer
oath.

Stephen Luffe petitioned for Arnold
Elzey administrator of Mr. Charles
Ballard to render accounts. Date: 24
July 1684.

29 July. Exhibited was inventory of
Thomas Bramson (SM), by appraisers
Clement Heley & John Hilton.

13:148 12 August. Elisabeth Mobberly (St.
George's Hundred, SM) widow of John
Mobberly (St. George's Hundred, SM)
exhibited his will, constituting her
executrix. William Hatton (g, SM) to
prove said will. Said Elisabeth was
granted administration. Appraisers:
John Addisson, Peter Watts. Said Hatton
to administer oath.

Robert Ardis (SM) was granted
administration on estate of Abraham
Reede (CV), as principle creditor.
Appraisers: Capt. Thomas Courtney,
Joseph Edloe. Maj. Nicholas Sewall to
administer oath.

Exhibited was will of James Littlepage
(CH), proved before John Stone (g, CH).
Also exhibited was oath of Col. William
Chandler, Robert Chandler, Anne Fowke,
Gerrard Fowke, Mary Fowke, & Elisabeth
Fowke executors. Also exhibited was
oath of John Hanson & Eduard Maddock,
appraisers.

Court Session: 1684

Exhibited was oath of Nicholas Sylvester administrator of Henry Philips (SM), sworn by Clement Hill (SM). Sureties: Abraham Coombs, John Bailey. Also exhibited was oath of John Browne & Peter Mills, appraisers, sworn 14 July 1684.

13:149 Exhibited was oath of Ellinor Hammond administratrix of Daniell Hamond (SMO, sworn by Clement Hill (g, SM). Sureties: Eduard Feild, Ignatius Warren. Also exhibited was oath of Stephen Gough & John Taunt, appraisers, sworn 30 July 1684.

Dennis Hurley exhibited additional accounts on estate of Derby Donnovan (SM), proved before Clement Hill (SM).

Miles Gibson (g, BA) exhibited directions to appraisers of William Croshow. Also exhibited was that William Hollis (age 19, orphan of William Hollis) chose said Gibson as his guardian. Date: 11 August 1684. Elisabeth Harris (mother of said orphan) appeared
13:150 & said orphan was given his share. Accounting: inventory of William Hollis was exhibited in 1680. In January 1681/2, Elisabeth Russell, now Elisabeth Harris, relict of said Hollis exhibited accounts & disbursement. Said Russell, now a widow, married William Croshow (lately dec'd) & then married William Harris. Exhibited was inventory of William Croshow &
13:151 Elisabeth Harris exhibited accounts on estate of her 1st husband William Hollis, retaining her widow's 1/3rds. Estate to be divided amongst children: son paid to tutor/guardian, 2 others (under age).

18 August. Miles Gibson (g, BA) to administer oath to William Harris & his wife Elisabeth administrators of William Croshow. Sureties: John Yeo, Eduard Reeves. Also exhibited was inventory of said Croshow.

Miles Gibson (g, BA) exhibited oath of Charles Pine administrator of James Denton (BA). Sureties: Robert Bendger, Thomas Richardson. Also exhibited oath of Robert Love & Mich. Judd, appraisers. Also exhibited inventory.

13:152 Richard Marsham (g, CV) exhibited oath of Richard Bowen, Sr. executor of Robt. Standley (CV). Also exhibited will, proved.

Anthony Neale (g, CH) executor of Capt. James Neale exhibited that his mother Mrs. Anne Neale (widow) cannot be persuaded to take oath as executrix, alleging invalidity of will. Capt. Humphrey Warren (CH) to administer oath to said Anthony & said Anne. Refusal of said Anne is no longer a barrier to administration of said estate.

19 August. Miles Gibson (g, BA) to prove will of Christopher Topley (BA), constituting Jane Topley executrix.

13:153 20 August. Nicholas Skidmore & his wife Anne vs. Henry Smith & Thomas Doxey. Robert Lardger (SM) summoned.

Sheriff (SM) to summon Sarah Priest (SM) widow of Charles Priest to show cause why she does not administer his estate.

22 August. Richard Swetnam (TA) was granted administration on estate of John Climer (TA), who drowned accidentally, as principle creditor. Appraisers: Capt. William Hemsley, William Kendall. George Robotham (g, TA) to administer oath.

25 August. Summons to Robert Lardge (SM) returned.

Summons to Sarah Priest (SM) returned.

William Burne (BA) one of executors of Thomas Cooke (BA) exhibited accounts.

Miles Gibson (g, BA) to administer oath to Elisabeth Harris (BA) relict of

William Croshaw (BA) & her husband
William Harris as administrators of said
Crowshaw.

13:154 27 August. Court at SM. Robert Carvile
procurator for Nicholas Skidmore & his
wife Anne (CH) relict of Joseph Brough
(SM) vs. Kenelme Cheseldine attorney
for Henry Smith & Thomas Doxey. Libel
exhibited. Said Brough's estate
administered by George Marshall (SM,
dec'd). Said Anne came to the Province
to inhabit & found the estate of both
said Brough and said Marshall gone &
wasted. Said Smith & Doxey were
sureties on the administration. Answer
exhibited. Examination: Robert Large
(p, SM) summoned.
13:155 Ruling: continuance.

John Wattson (SM) vs. Robert Graham.
Re: estate of George Macaal. Objections
cited. Mentions payments to: Dominick
Bodkin, Samuell Hall, Thomas Spinke
attorney for (N) Bagnall (merchant,
Bristoll), Robert Williams (merchant,
Falmouth), Gerrard Slye attorney for (N)
Cocke (London).
13:156 Thomas Waughop (St. George's Hundred,
SM) was granted administration on estate
of Robert Graham (SM), on behalf of
orphan. Appraisers: John Addisson,
Robert Masson. William Hatton (g, SM)
to administer oath. Said Graham
appeared in Court on 5 April 1683 & died
soon thereafter. Said Wattson married
one of daughters of said Macaal.
13:157 John Addisson & Robert Masson, neighbors
to aforesaid parties, to hear arguments.

Audery Cocks widow of William Cocks (SM)
was granted continuance. Mentions
caveats by: William Blankensteine,
Francis Catterton (TA).

13:158 Robert Carvile & Kenelme Cheseldine
attorneys for James Cullen (g, SM) vs.
Anthony Underwood attorney for Marke
Cordea (g, SM). Petition for accounts
on estate of Anthony LeCompte (DO).
Said Cordea who married Hester relict &
executrix. Said Hester not cited.

Court Session: 1684

Ruling: Cordea to exhibit accounts.

Nicholas Skidmore & his wife Anne (CH) vs. Capt. Henry Smith (SM) & Thomas Doxey (SM). Sheriff (SM) exhibited summons to Robert Large (SM) to testify.

Sheriff (SM) exhibited summons to Sarah Priest.

George Parker procurator for Margarett Smith (AA) widow of Nathan Smith (AA) exhibited his will, constituting her executrix.
13:159 Col. Thomas Taylor (AA) to prove said will. Said Margarett was granted administration. Appraisers: Maj. Nicholas Gassaway, Maj. Thomas Francize. Said Taylor to administer oath.

Robert Carvile (g, SM) & Clement Hill (g, SM) executors of James Bodkin (CH) exhibited accounts. Continuance was granted.

Exhibited was inventory of Stephen Murty (SM), by appraisers Cuthbert Scott & Abraham Combe.

Maj. Nicholas Sewall (CV) exhibited oath of Robert Ardis (SM) administrator of Abraham Reede (CV). Sureties: William Aisquith, Eduard Horne. Also exhibited was oath of Capt. Thomas Courtney & Joseph Edloe, appraisers.

Eduard Dorsey (g, AA) exhibited will of William Yieldhall, proved by Henry Peirpoint, Nicholas Shepard, & James Williams on 26 July 1684. Also exhibited was oath of Jane Yieldhall executrix, sworn same day. Also exhibited was oath of Henry Peirpoint & Adam Shipley, appraisers, sworn same day.
13:160 Date: 28 July 1684.

Exhibited was will of John Ashcombe (CV), proved before Col. Henry Darnall.

Court Session: 1684

13 September. Exhibited was inventory
of Bryant Daley (SM), by appraisers
James Yore & Owen Guyther.

Exhibited was inventory of Daniell
Devine (SM), by appraisers Thomas Doxey
& Eduard Chester.

23 September. Richard Marsham (g, CV)
exhibited oath of Mr. Thomas Ghant
executor of William Davies (CV), sworn 1
July 1684. Also exhibited was oath of
John Chittam & John Smith, appraisers,
sworn same day.

13:161   Also exhibited was inventory.

Exhibited was inventory of Robert
Standlye (CV), by appraisers John
Chittam & William Selby.

Also exhibited was inventory of Thomas
Kemp (CV), by appraisers John Rumsey &
Jonathon Goosey.

Sheriff (SM) exhibited summons to Marke
Cordea & his wife Hester executrix of
Anthony LeCompte (DO).

Col. Thomas Taylor (AA) exhibited oath
of Margarett Smith (AA) widow &
executrix of Nathan Smith. Also
exhibited was inventory, by appraisers
Maj. Nicholas Gassaway & Maj. Thomas
Francis.

Exhibited was inventory of Henry Philips
(SM), by appraisers Peter Mills & John
Browne.

26 September. Eduard Inglish (CE)
administrator of Francis Blang (CE) was
granted continuance.

29 September. John Stone (CV) & his
wife Mary relict of John Feild (CV) were
granted administration on his estate.
Appraisers: John Broome, Henry Trueman.
John CreyCroft to administer oath.

13:162   30 September. Jacob Seath (TA)
exhibited will of John Hartley (TA),
constituting him executor. William

Byshop (g, TA) to prove said will. Said
Seath was granted administration.
Appraisers: Alexander Cuningham, William
Coursey. Said Byshop to administer
oath.

Christopher Goodhand & his wife Hanna
(KE) exhibited will of Sarah Harris
(KE), constituting them executors.
Philip Connor (KE) to prove said will.
Said Christopher & Hanna were granted
administration. Appraisers: Isaak
Winchester, Anthony Workman. Said
Connor to administer oath.

Henry Hosier (KE) exhibited will of
William Fawson (KE), constituting him
executor with Richard Clowder. Charles
Tilden (g, KE) to prove said will. Said
Hosier & Clowder were granted
administration. Appraisers: William
Harris, Michael Miller. Said Tilden to
administer oath.

Anne widow of Anthony Norwood (TA) was
granted administration on his estate.
Appraisers: Joseph James, Richard Moore.
William Comb (TA) to administer oath.

James Mecall (CV) was granted discharge
on estate of Peter Browne.

13:163-166 <does not exist>

13:167   Mary Welsh (AA) executrix of Maj. John
          Welsh (AA) was granted continuance.

          2 October. Joseph Cornell (CH)
          exhibited will of John Pope (CH),
          constituting him executor. Capt.
          Humphrey Warren (CH) to prove said will.
          Said Cornell was granted administration.
          Appraisers: John Fanning, John Beand.
          Said Warren to administer oath.

          Susanna Clothier (TA) widow of Lewis
          Clothier (TA) was granted administration
          on his estate. James Murphy (TA) to
          administer oath.

          Thomas Dakins (SM) who married relict of
          Daniell Hammond (SM) was granted

continuance.

Richard Chandler (CH) who married
Elisabeth relict & administratrix of
John Hamilton (CH) exhibited accounts.

Miles Gibson (g, BA) exhibited that he
refused to give security for estate of
orphan of William Hollis (BA), he being
the guardian.

13:168 Anne Neale (CH) widow & one of executors
of Capt. James Neale (CH) petitioned
that Anthony Neale, petitioner's son &
joint executor, has taken away most of
chattel as well as her jewelry, plate, &
church plate, depriving petitioner of
support & maintenance. Petitioner is in
old age. Said Anne had objected to
will. Kenelme Chiseldyne had urged her
to be joint executor & indicated the
consequences of not doing so.
13:169 Ruling: case dismissed.

Matthew Eareckson (KE) was granted
administration on estate of Hans
Rosomonson (KE), who died leaving no
kindred in Province, as principle
creditor. Appraisers: John Coppidge,
Joseph Sudler. Capt. William Laurence
(KE) to administer oath.

6 October. Eduard James (KE) who
married Catherine relict of Thomas
Browne (KE) was granted administration
on his estate. Appraisers: Matthew
Eareckson, William Temple. Isaak
Winchester (g, KE) to administer oath.

Elisabeth Jones (SO) widow of Andrew
Jones (SO), who accidentally drowned,
was granted administration on his
estate. Appraisers: Thomas Pemberton,
Stephen Luffe. William Brereton (SO) to
administer oath.

Eduard Swetnam (KE) administrator of
Eduard Rogers (KE) exhibited accounts.

Exhibited was will of William Vaughan
(KE), appointing Maj. James Ringgold
(KE) as guardian of his 2 children.

Philip Connor to prove said will. Said Ringgold was granted administration. Appraisers: Walter Kerby, Francis Barnes. Said Connor to administer oath.

13:170 Mary Evens (KE) widow of Thomas Evens was granted administration on his estate. Appraisers: Anthony Workman, Walter Kerby. James Ringgold (g, KE) to administer oath.

(N) Quillaine widow of Daniell Quillaine (SO) was granted administration on his estate. Appraisers: Col. William Colebourne, Capt. John Osborne. Col. William Stevens (SO) to administer oath.

Col. William Stevens (SO) exhibited will of William Innis (SO), constituting Thomas Pointer & Samuell Hopkins executors. Said Steevens to prove said will. Said Pointer & Hopkins were granted administration. Appraisers: Matthew Scarborough, Charles Rackliffe. Said Steevens to administer oath.

7 October. LoA to Richard Swetnam (TA) administrator of John Climer (TA) revoked. Anne widow of said Climer was granted administration. Appraisers: William Finny, Thrustram Thomas. Col. Philemon Lloyd (TA) to administer oath.

13:171 George Immins who married Hester relict of Charles Stewart (KE) was granted administration on his estate. Appraisers: Thomas Osborne, Francis Barnes. Philip Connor (g, KE) to administer oath.

Anne Neale renounced executorship with her son Anthony Neale on estate of her husband Capt. James Neale. Date: 26 August 1684. Witnesses: Hum. Warren, John Faning. (cf. f. 168.)

Robert Carvile (g, SM) & Griffith Jones (g, TA) attorneys for said Mrs. Elisabeth Coursey vs. Kenelme Cheseldyne (g, SM) for William Coursey. Elisabeth Coursey petitioned for LoA on estate of her husband Maj. William

Court Session: 1684

Coursey. Mentions: her son-in-law
William Coursey.
13:172 Appraisers: Capt. William Hemsley,
Thrustram Thomas. Date: 28 September
1684. Question: should the joint
administration of said Elisabeth & said
William be recalled? Ruling: defendant.
Said William then renounced
administration. Said Elisabeth was
granted sole administration. Appraisers
as aforesaid. Maj. Peter Sayer (TA) to
administer oath. Considerable estate of
orphan of (N) Beedle is intermixed with
said Coursey's estate.

13:172½ 8 October. Philip Lynes (SM) was
granted administration on estate of
William Smithson (DO), as principle
creditor. Security: William Rosewell
(SM). Appraisers: Dr. John Brookes,
Thomas Pattisson. Capt. Henry Tripp
(DO) to administer oath.

9 October. Eduard Man (g, TA) exhibited
oath of Mrs. Rachell Baily
administratrix of her husband Richard
Bayly (also Richard Baily), sworn 19 May
1684. Sureties: James Murphy, Henry
Newman. Also exhibited was inventory.

George Lingham (CV) exhibited oath of
John Leach & John Bigger, appraisers of
Thomas Jessup, sworn 27 July 1684. Also
exhibited was inventory.

13:173 George Lingham (CV) exhibited oath of
Matthew Beale & John Davies, appraisers
of Oliver Stockley. Also exhibited was
inventory.

William Combes (TA) exhibited will of
Leonard Jinnings, proved. One of the
appraisers drowned; inventory was
exhibited by William Sharpe appraiser.
New appraisal ordered.

Exhibited was a list of goods of estate
of William Watts (SM) by John Shankes
(SM) grandfather & guardian to orphans.

Col. Thomas Taylor (AA) exhibited oath
of John Far (AA) administrator of Jacob

Page 75

Walker, sworn 16 December 1678.
Sureties: William Alcocke, John Kindall.

13:174   Exhibited was will of George Carall
(TA), proved before Col. Philemon Lloyd
(TA).

Exhibited was will of John Mobberly
(SM), proved before William Hatton (SM).

William Hatton (g, SM) exhibited oath of
Thomas Waughop administrator of Robert
Graham (SM). Sureties: Francis Hill,
Robert Masson.

Thomas Lurky administrator of Robert
Morris (CE) exhibited accounts.

Exhibited was bond of Joane West (CE)
administratrix of John West (CE).
Sureties: Philip Helger, William Jones.

Col. George Wells (BA) exhibited oath
of William Jones (BA) executor of Robert
Jones. Also exhibited was oath of
Laurence Taylor & John Fisher,
appraisers. Also exhibited was
inventory.

Philip Lynes (SM) vs. estate of Thomas
Alanson (CH). Caveat entered.

Exhibited was will of Robert Sanders
(CE), proved before George Warner (g,
CE). Also exhibited was inventory.

13:175   Capt. Richard Hill (AA) exhibited oath
of Sarah Jones executrix of William
Jones (AA).

Exhibited was inventory of Elisabeth
Eareckson (KE).

Richard Hill (g, AA) exhibited oath of
John Baldwin executor of John Baldwin
(AA). Also exhibited was inventory.

Capt. Richard Hill (AA) exhibited oath
of Sarah Tucker executrix of Thomas
Tucker (AA). Also exhibited was
inventory.

13:176 John Addisson (g, SM) & Robert Masson (g, SM) exhibited examination of accounts of John Wattson administrator of George Macaall (SM) & of Thomas Waughop administrator of Robert Graham (SM). Mentions: Mr. Robert Williams, Mrs. Jane Macaall, Dominick Bodkin, Samuell Hall, Dr. John Wyne, Marmaduke Semme, Stephen Murty, James Beamont, Joshua Guybert, John Baker, Richard Moy, John Wattson, Thomas Spinke for (N) Bagnall, (N) Cox (of London), Capt. (N) Rickey for said Company Merchants, (N) Baker on (N) Welch, Mr. Rogers, Robert Cole, (N) Stanley, Bryant Thompson, George Dundoet, (N) Rickey & (N) Thompson, (N) Graham.

13:177 Date: 17 September 1684. Ruling: said Wattson & Waughop to contact Mr. Robert Williams & Co. Mentions: Robert Graham married Anne relict & executrix of George Macaall, John Watson married Jane eldest daughter of said George, said Robert died leaving only a son by said Anne. Letter to:

13:178 MM Robert Williams, Bryan Rogers, (N) Grille, Bryan Thompson & Co. (merchants, Falmouth).

Marke Cordea (g, SM), summoned to render accounts on estate of Anthony LeCompte (DO), did not appear. Ruling: attachment against him, per request of James Cullen who married Catherine (daughter of said LeCompte). Mentions: Hester wife of said Cordea.

13:179 Attachment by Joshua Doyne (sheriff). Anthony Underwood procurator for Marke Cordea & his wife Hester exhibited accounts. Ruling: disallowed.

Audery Cocks (SM) widow of William Cocks (SM) renounced administration on his estate. William Blankensteine (SM) was granted administration, as principle creditor. Security: Marmaduck Seeme. Appraisers: John Wattson, Marmaduck Seeme. William Hatton (SM) to administer oath.

Thomas Brooke (CV) exhibited bond of Symon Stacy administrator of Thomas

Kemp. Sureties: James Rumsey, Jonathon Goosey. Date: 19 August 1684. Also exhibited was oath of James Rumsey & Jonathon Goosey, appraisers sworn 4 July 1684.

15 October. Dennis Hurlow (SM) administrator of Darby Donnovan (SM) was granted discharge.

13:180   Susanna widow of Thomas Clipsham (CH) was granted administration on his estate. Appraisers: John Beaumont, John Worrall. Capt. Humphrey Warren (CH) to administer oath.

Capt. Humphrey Warren (CH) to summon John Fanning (CH) administrator of John Cooper (CH).

22 October. Henry Exon (inn holder, SM) petitioned for Thomas Wahop & Robert Masson to appraise additional chattel of John Garnish (SM). William Hatton (SM) to administer oath.

24 October. Martha Baker (CH) widow of Thomas Baker (CH) exhibited his will. Ignatius Cawseene (g, CH) to prove said will. Appraisers: John Fanning, Joseph Cornell. Said Cawseene to administer oath.

1 November. Col. George Talbot (CE) was granted administration on estate of John Faghey (CE), as principle creditor. Appraisers: George Oldfeild, Cornett Philemurphy. William Dare (g, CE) to administer oath.

6 November. Thomas Simpson (SM) was granted administration on estate of John Hartwell, unadministered by Daniell Hamond (lately dec'd), as principle creditor. Appraisers: John Taunt, William Rosewell. Joseph Pile (g, SM) to administer oath.

10 November. LoA to Maj. James Ringgold (KE) administrator of Charles Vaughan revoked. Said Ringgold was guardian to children of said Vaughan, &

all children are lately dec'd.
Elisabeth Vaughan widow was granted
administration. Appraisers: Walter
Kerby, Alexander Walters. Philip Connor
to administer oath.

13:181 Thomas Seward (KE) was granted
administration on estate of John Clarke
(KE), as principle creditor.
Appraisers: John Hynson, William Harris.
James Ringgold (g, KE) to administer
oath.

Exhibited was will of William Fawson
(KE), proved.

Exhibited was inventory of Capt. James
Neale, by appraisers John Fanning & John
Courts.

Thomas Anderson (TA) exhibited will of
George Allumby (TA), constituting his
daughter Dorothy (infant, under age)
executrix. Eduard Man (g, TA) to prove
said will. Said Anderson was granted
administration & guardianship.
Appraisers: William Combes, Richard
Gurlin. Said Man to administer oath.

14 November. Mary Bowlin (CV) widow of
John Bowlin (CV) exhibited his will,
constituting said Mary now Mary Evens
executrix. Maj. Thomas Trueman (CV) to
prove said will. Said Evens was granted
administration. Appraisers: Thomas
Ghant, Thomas Blandford. Said Trueman
to administer oath.

Robert Carvile (g, SM) procurator for
Mr. Leonard Greene vs. estate of James
Bourne. Caveat entered.

13:182 15 November. William Rosewell (inn
holder, SM) vs. estate of Dr. James
Bourne. Caveat entered.

19 November. Capt. Henry Smith (SO)
exhibited that Thomas Pemberton (SO),
appraiser of Andrew Jones (SO), is
runaway. New appraiser: Daniell Hast.

Robert Thompson (SM) & Robert Morehouse (SM) exhibited nuncupative will of Dr. James Bourne (SM), bequeathing all to said Thompson & Morehouse. William Hatton to prove said will. Said Thompson & Morehouse were granted administration. Appraisers: Marmaduck Semms, William Blankensteine. Said Hatton to administer oath.

26 November. Mary Husbands relict of William Bowen (SM) was granted administration on his estate. Appraisers: John Wade, John Cambell. William Hatton to administer oath.

13:183   Thomas Gerrard (g, SM) was granted administration on estate of Daniell Johnson (SM), as principle creditor. Appraisers: John Barecroft, Richard Edelen. William Boareman, Jr. to administer oath.

28 November. Nathaniell & Samuell Ashcome 2 sons & joint executors of John Ashcome (CV) exhibited will, proved before Col. Henry Darnall. Said Nathaniell & Samuell were granted administration. Appraisers (CV): John Cooper, Gustavus White. Capt. Samuell Bourne (CV) to administer oath. Appraisers (distant parts): James Ketch, Richard Gardiner. John Darnall, Esq. to administer oath. Appraisers (DO): Gustavus White, Joseph Stannaway. Henry Hooper (g, DO) to administer oath.

Exhibited will of Thomas Baker (CH), proved before Ignatius Causeene (g, CV).

George Robotham (TA) exhibited oath of Richard Swetnam administrator of John Climer (TA). Sureties: George Robins, James Sedwick. Also exhibited was oath of Capt. William Hemsley & William Kendall, appraisers.

13:184   William Hatton exhibited oath of John Wattson & Marmaduck Semms, appraisers of William Cocks (SM).

Court Session: 1684

Exhibited inventory of Thomas Alcocke
(CH), by appraisers John Ward & Eduard
Maddock.

Nathaniell Garrett (CE) exhibited oath
of John Hagley & his wife Margarett
administers of Bartholomew Hendrickson
(CE), sworn 29 September 1684.
Sureties: Philip Holleger, John Cock.
Also exhibited oath of Richard Allum &
Henry Eldersley, appraisers, sworn same
day.

Richard Willhouse (DO) was granted
administration on estate of Richard
Dawson (DO), on behalf of the children.
Appraisers: James Peterkin, Bartholomew
Ennalls. John Brooke (DO) to administer
oath.

Bartholomew Ennalls (DO) exhibited will
of Ednor Conner (DO), constituting him
executor on behalf of Thomas Conner
(orphan), proved by John Searles &
Humphry Mould. John Brookes to
administer oath to Frances Mould (other
witness). Said Ennalls was granted
administration. Appraisers: Capt.
Anthony Dawson, Richard Willhouse. Said
Brookes to administer oath.

13:185   Judith Newfinger widow of William
Newfinger (SM) was granted
administration on his estate.
Appraisers: John Vaudry, Phillip
Briscoe. Joshua Piles (g, SM) to
administer oath.

Elisabeth Neves widow of Robert Neves
(KE) was granted administration on his
estate. Appraisers: Richard Lowder,
William Deane. Eduard Inglish (CE) to
administer oath.

Mary Twiney widow of John Twiney (KE)
exhibited his will, constituting her
executrix. Charles Tilden to prove said
will. Said Mary was granted
administration. Appraisers: Thomas
Warren, John Chandler. Said Tilden to
administer oath.

Elisabeth Baker widow of Hugh Baker (SM) was granted administration on his estate. Appraisers: Gilbert Turberville, Thomas Spinke. James Pattison (g, SM) to administer oath.

John Sickes (SM) exhibited verbal will of Robert Hudson (SM), constituting him executor. William Hatton (g, SM) to prove said will. Said Sickes was granted administration. Appraisers: John Mitchell, John Wynne. Said Hatton to administer oath.

13:186 Exhibited will of John Wheeler (AA), constituting his son John Wheeler (orphan, under age) executor & Richard Beard & John Belt overseers. Said Beard & Belt have renounced overseership. Date: 22 November 1684. Witness: Thomas Taillor. Henry Hanslap was granted administration, on behalf of orphan. Appraisers: Maren Duvall, Walter Phelps. Col. William Burges to administer oath.

Col. Thomas Taillor (AA) to take bond of John Stevenson (AA).

13:187 Edward English was administrator of Francis Blang (CE). Richard Edmonds (CE) was granted new administration on said estate. Appraisers: James Heybourne, Gideon Gundry. Eduard English (CE) to administer oath.

1 December. William Dossey (DO) was granted administration on estate of his brother John Dossey (DO). Appraisers: Daniell Clark, Benjamin Priestly. Maj. Thomas Taylor (DO) to administer oath.

2 December. Elisabeth Coursey (TA) vs. William Coursey, Jr. administrator of George Carrall. Caveat entered.

Francis Jenckins (high sheriff, SO) exhibited summons to Arnold Elzey to render accounts of estate of Charles Ballard.

Robert Thompson (CH) administrator of William Wright (CH) exhibited accounts.

Court Session: 1684

3 December. Exhibited inventory of
William Wright (CH), by appraisers
Thomas Cranson & John Wood.

Letter to: Mr. James Ringgold
administrator of Mr. William Vaughan &
guardian of his 2 children.
13:188 Said children are both dec'd & said
Ringgold ordered to restore said estate
to Elisabeth Vaughan (widow).

4 December. Exhibited will of James
Hall (TA), constituting Sarah Hall &
William Combes executors. Said Combes
renounced executorship.
13:189 Date: 1 December 1684. Witnesses: Edw.
Man, Thomas Vaughan, Fran. Catterson,
John Woodward. James Murphy (g, TA) to
prove said will. Said Sarah was granted
administration. Appraisers: Hugh
Sherwood, John Power. Said Murphy to
administer oath.

Maj. Thomas Trueman (CV) exhibited oath
of Mary Evans executrix of John Bowlin
(CV), sworn 24 November 1684. Also
exhibited oath of Thomas Gaunt & Thomas
Blamford, appraisers, sworn same day.

James Phillips was granted
administration on estate of Richard Sims
(BA), as principle creditor.
Appraisers: Nicholas Hampstead, Edward
Waters. Miles Gibson to administer
oath.

13:190 Exhibited will of John Bowlin (CV),
proved before Col. Henry Darnall by
Maj. Thomas Truman, Richard Marsham, &
William Truman.

8 December. Hans Hanson (KE) was
granted administration on estate of
Stephen Cuthbert (KE), as principle
creditor. Appraisers: Charles Hynson,
William Harris. John Hynson (g, KE) to
administer oath.

Charles Hutchins (DO) on behalf of
Thomas Cocker (DO) exhibited will of
William Bennett (TA), constituting his
sisters Mary Bennett & Margarett Bennett

Court Session: 1684

(both in ENG) executrices. Edward
Pindar (g, DO) to prove said will. Said
Cocker was granted administration.
Appraisers: Charles Hutchins, Thomas
Hicks. Said Pindar to administer oath.

George Cocks who married Mary Wright
sister to William Wright (SM) was
granted administration on his estate.
Appraisers: Peter Kerwarden, John
Redmond. William Hatton (g, SM) to
administer oath.

Thomas Evans (SM) & John Taunt (SM)
summoned to render accounts on estate of
George Bayton (SM). Also John Taunt was
summoned

13:191 to render accounts on estate of Henry
Neale (SM). Summons to Robert Drury to
testify regarding estate of George
Bayton. Also petition for LoA to Susan
Clarke (CV) widow of John Clarke (CV).
Said Susan was granted administration on
her husband's estate.

9 December. Kenelm Chiseldyn (g, SM)
for Col. George Wells appeared,
regarding accounts of George Goldsmith.
Said Chiseldyne was also summoned to
answer libel. Robert Carvile & Anthony
Underwood summoned.

Sheriff (SM) to summon Audery Cocks,
James Cullen, & Elisabeth Baker to
appear before James Pattison to render
accounts on estate of William Cocks, at
request of William Blankenston.

Sheriff (SM) to summon Thomas Evans (SM)
& John Taunt (SM) to render accounts on
estate of George Bayton (SM). Summons
to Robert Drury to testify regarding
said estate. Summons to John Taunt to
render accounts on estate of Henry
Neale.

13:192 Sheriff (SO) to summon Arnold Elzey (SO)
to render accounts on estate of (N)
Ballard.

10 December. Sarah Priest (SM) widow of
Charles Priest (SM) was granted

Page 84

administration on his estate.
Appraisers: John Doxey, Charles Smith.
James Pattison (g, SM) to administer
oath.

11 December. Mary Tanshall (CH) widow
of Edward Tanshall (CH) relinquished
administration. Phillip Lynes was
nominated. Date: 18 November 1684.
Said Lynes was granted administration.
Appraisers: William Burnham, John Smith.
James Tyer (CH) to administer oath.

13:193 12 December. Exhibited inventory of
Thomas Baker (CH), by appraisers John
Fanning & Joseph Cornell.

John Fanning administrator of Robert
Cooper (CH) exhibited accounts, proved
before Humphrey Warren.

Humphrey Warren (CH) exhibited oath of
Susanna Clipsham administratrix of
Thomas Clipsham, sworn 25 October 1684.
Sureties: John Fanning, John Worland.
Also exhibited oath of John Bayne & John
Worland, appraisers, sworn same day.

Humphrey Warren (CH) exhibited oath of
Joseph Cornell administrator of John
Pope, sworn 12 October 1684. Also
exhibited oath of John Bayne & John
Fanning, appraisers, sworn 18 October
1684. Also exhibited will, proved by
Laurence Young, James Halliman, William
Warder, & Edward Boteler.

13:194 William & Elisabeth Harris
administrators of William Croshaw (BA)
exhibited accounts, proved before Miles
Gibson (BA).

Thomas Heath administrator of Gervais
Lassells (BA) exhibited accounts, proved
before Miles Gibson.

James Pattison exhibited oath of Thomas
Doxey & Edward Chester, appraisers of
Daniell Divine, sworn 26 August.

Phillip Conner (KE) exhibited oath of
Elisabeth Vaughan widow & administratrix

of William Vaughan, sworn 22 November
1684. Sureties: Thomas Smith, Michaell
Miller. Also exhibited oath of Walter
Kerby & Alexander Walter, appraisers,
sworn 20 November.

Exhibited inventory of Nathaniell Evett
(KE), by appraisers Charles Tilden &
Thomas Warren.

Exhibited inventory of John Poper (CH),
by appraisers John Bayne & John Fanning.

Thomas Smith (KE) who married Ellinor
relict of Nathaniell Evett (KE)
exhibited accounts.

13:195 William Hatton (SM) exhibited will of
James Bourn (SM), proved by Randolph
Hinson & John Pote on 27 November 1684.
Other witness Barbara Hinson did not
appear due to sickness. Also exhibited
oath of Richard Thompson & Robert
Morehouse executors of Dr. James Bourne
(SM), sworn 29 November 1684. Sureties:
Marmaduke Seems, Abraham Rhodes.

William Hatton (SM) exhibited oath of
Mary Husbands administratrix of William
Bowen, sworn 28 November 1684.
Sureties: John Wade, John Cambell. Also
exhibited oath of John Wade & John
Cambell, appraisers, sworn same day.

17 December. Thomas George was granted
administration on estate of his brother
Benjamin George (SM). Appraisers:
Phillip Jones, Peter Carwarden. William
Hatton (SM) to administer oath.

13:196 19 December. Hanna Hungerford widow of
John Hungerford (DO) was granted
administration on his estate.
Appraisers: William Robinson, Richard
Meekins. William Traverse (g, DO) to
administer oath.

Margarett Stubberfield widow of John
Stubberfield (AA) was granted
administration on his estate.
Appraisers: Nicholas Greenberry, George
Eager. Henry Constable (g, AA) to

Court Session: 1684

administer oath.

Col. William Burges exhibited will of
Nicholas Painter (AA), constituting said
him executor. Col. Thomas Taillor (AA)
to prove said will. Said Burges was
granted administration. Appraisers:
Henry Hanslap, Maren Duvall. Said
Taillor to administer oath.

Joseph Pile (g, SM) exhibited will of
Bartholomew Piggott (SM), constituting
him executor. William Hatton (SM) to
prove said will. Said Pile was granted
administration. Appraisers: Dr.
Patrick Innis, Thomas Clarke. William
Boarman, Jr. to administer oath.

24 December. Adam Head (SM) was granted
administration on estate of Samuell
Burges (SM). Appraisers: Joshua
Guibert, Cuthbert Scott. Clement Hill
(SM) to administer oath.

13:197 Katherine Wheeler (CH) widow of James
Wheeler (CH) exhibited his will,
constituting her executrix. William
Chandler (CH) to prove said will. Said
Katherine was granted administration.
Appraisers: John Godsall, John Clarke.
Said Chandler to administer oath.

10 January 1684/5. Kenelm Cheseldyn (g,
SM) was granted administration on estate
of Jonathon Squire (SM). Appraisers:
John Shankes, John Tenneson. Clement
Hill (g, SM) to administer oath.

22 January. Thomas Mattenly (SM) was
granted administration on estate of
Robert Curtis (SM). Appraisers: Luke
Gardiner, Francis Knott. Clement Hill
(g) to administer oath.

27 January. James Cullen was appointed
Register of the Court & Clerk of the
Office.

Margarett Combes (SM) widow of Abraham
Combes (SM) exhibited his will,
constituting her executrix. Clement
Hill (g) to prove said will. Said

Court Session: 1684

Margarett was granted administration.
Appraisers: William Roswell, Stephen
Gough. Said Hill to administer oath.

Court Session: 1684/5

13:197.A*[1]. 20 February. Mr. William Boarman,
Jr. (SM) exhibited oath of Joseph Pile
executor of Bartholomew Piggott (SM),
sworn 2 February 1684. Also exhibited
oath of Patrick Innes & Thomas Clarke,
appraisers, sworn same day.

Mr. Thomas Brook (CV) exhibited oath of
John Dossett & Jonathon Goosey,
executors of Thomas Allwell, sworn 6
February. Also exhibited oath of
Richard Clarke & John Hunt, appraisers,
sworn same day. Also exhibited
inventory.

Court Session: 1685

29 April. Exhibited inventory of
Bartholomew Piggott (SM).

Mr. Clement Hill exhibited oath of John
Taunt & Richard Birkett, appraisers of
Augustine Warren (SM).

13:197.B* 29 April 1685. Mr. Clement Hill
exhibited oath of John <torn> & Richard
Birkett, appraisers of George Henderson
(SM), sworn 26 February 1684. Also
exhibited inventory.

Exhibited inventory of Augustine Warren
(SM). Mr. Clement Hill exhibited oath
of John Hoskins & Henry Powlter,
appraisers of John Shanks (SM), sworn 2

---

[1]   6 unnumbered folios appear between folios
197 & 198. For the purposes of
identification, they are cited as
197.A<...>197.F. The asterisk (*) is
indicated to call the reader's attention to
the fact that the order on the microfilm is
different from the order in the liber; the
order presented is the order in the liber.

March 1684.

Mr. Thomas Sterling (CV) exhibited oath
of Marke Clare & John Russell,
appraisers of Henry Robinson, sworn 23
February 1684.

Exhibited inventory of John Shanks (SM).

Exhibited inventory of Henry Robinson
(CV).

Mr. John Craycroft (CV) exhibited oath
of John Hunt & William Whittington,
appraisers of Anthony Kingsland (CV),
sworn 2 March 1684. Also exhibited
inventory.

13:197.C* Exhibited bond of John Hillen & Ralph
Foster, administrators of Samuel Maddox.
Securities: Thomas Carvile, John Vandry,
Thomas Stonestreet.

Mr. William Hatton (SM) exhibited oath
of Henry Laurence & Walter Woolverstone,
appraisers of James Pagrave (SM). Also
exhibited inventory. Also exhibited
bond of Margaret Pagrave administratrix.
Securities: Henry Lawrence, Walter
Woolverstone.

Mr. William Hatton exhibited oath of
Daniel Smith & John Mitchell, appraisers
of John Wynn (SM). Also exhibited
inventory.

Mr. Clement Hill exhibited oath of
Henry Spink & Richard Walker, appraisers
of Peter Mills (SM), sworn 17 March
1684. Also exhibited oath of Mary Mills
executrix.

13:197.D* Francis Hutchens (g, CV) exhibited
oath of Elisabeth Daniell administratrix
of John Daniell (CV). Securities (CV):
Edward Hurlock, Joseph Baker. Also
exhibited oath of William Turner & James
Dossey, appraisers. Also exhibited
inventory.

Mr. Clement Hill exhibited oath of John
Smith & John Hilton, appraisers of John

Gee (SM), sworn 9 March 1684. Also exhibited bond of Edward Smoote administrator. Securities: John Hilton, Thomas Reves. Also exhibited inventory.

Mr. Hill exhibited oath of Edward Turner & Thomas Reeves, appraisers of Samuel Maddox (SM). Also exhibited inventory.

13:197.E* Clement Hill exhibited oath of Henry Spinke & Richard Walker, appraisers of Joseph Harding (SM), sworn 17 March 1684. Also exhibited was bond of William Shirtcliffe administrator of said Harding. Sureties: Francis Knott, Peter Howard.

Exhibited was inventory of Peter Mills (SM).

Mr. Henry Constable (g, AA) exhibited oath of Johannah Randall administratrix of Christopher Randall (g, AA), sworn on 24 March. Sureties: John Corens, John Medcalfe. Also exhibited was oath of Francis Mead & Mathew Howard, appraisers. Also exhibited was inventory.

Mr. Clement Hill exhibited oath of Joshua Guibert & Adam Head, appraisers of William Thomas (SM), sworn 26 March 1685.

Court Session: 1685

13:197.F* 30 April. George Lingan (CV) exhibited oath of John Sunderland & Mark Clar, appraisers of William Hitchcock (CV), sworn 28 March 1685. Also exhibited inventory.

Mr. Samuel Bourne exhibited oath of Thomas Parsloe (CV) administrator of John Cooper (CV). Sureties: John Hambleton, Henry Mackdowell. Also exhibited oath of John Skippers & Jeremiah Sympson, appraisers. Also exhibited inventory.

13:198 27 January. Susanna Clarke exhibited will of George Acheson (CV),

constituting her executrix. Thomas
Brooke (g, CV) to prove said will. Said
Clarke was granted administration.
Appraisers: Arthur Ludford, Thomas
Davis. Said Brooke to administer oath.

John Dossett & Jonathon Goosey (CV)
exhibited will of Thomas Allwell (CV),
constituting them executors. Thomas
Brooke (CV) to prove said will. Said
Dossett & Goosey were granted
administration. Appraisers: Richard
Clarke, John Hunt. Said Brooke to
administer oath.

Exhibited will of Nicholas Painter (AA),
proved before Col. Thomas Tailler.

28 January. Exhibited inventory of
Simon Gibson (AA), by appraisers
Gabriell Parrott & Thomas Day.

Col. Thomas Tailler (AA) exhibited oath
of Col. William Burges executor of
Nicholas Painter, sworn 29 December
1684. Also exhibited oath of Henry
Hanslap & Maren Duvall, appraisers,
sworn same day.

13:199 John Creycroft (g, CV) exhibited oath of
John Brome & Henry Truman, appraisers of
John Fields (CV). Also exhibited bond
of John Stone administrator. Sureties:
John Cooper, Richard Broughton.

Lavina Kingsland (CV) widow of Anthony
Kingsland (CV) exhibited his will,
constituting her executrix. John
Creycroft (g, CV) to prove said will.
Said Lavina was granted administration.
Appraisers: William Whittington, John
Hunt. Said Creycroft to administer
oath.

Abraham Thornbury (AA) exhibited will of
Matthew Axon (AA), constituting him
overseer. John Sollers (g, AA) to prove
said will. Said Thornbury was granted
administration. Appraisers: William
Sewick, Charles Bowen. Said Sollers to
administer oath.

Court Session: 1685

Abraham Thornbury (AA) was granted
administration dbn on estate of Richard
Bedworth (AA). Appraisers: William
Sewick, Charles Bowen. John Sollers
(AA) to administer oath.

Elisabeth Daniell (CV) widow of John
Daniell (CV) was granted administration
on his estate. Appraisers: William
Turner, James Dosey. Francis Hutchens
(g, CV) to administer oath.

13:200 Thomas Cocker exhibited his renunciation
of administration of estate of William
Bennett (TA), on behalf of Mary Bennett
& Margarett Bennett, sisters of dec'd,
recommending Mr. William Dolbery.
Date: 20 January 1684. Witnesses:
William Hill, James Pearell. Said
Dobery was granted administration, on
behalf of the sisters. Appraisers:
Thomas Martin, Thomas Atthow. Edward
Pindar (DO) to administer oath.

29 January. Elisabeth Frazier widow of
Dennis Hurly (SM) was granted
administration on his estate.
Appraisers: Thomas Clarke, Clement Hely.
Joseph Pile (g, SM) to administer oath.

John Hance administrator of Charles
Bathurst (CV) exhibited accounts, proved
before Col. William Digges.
Continuance was granted.

Dr. Patrick Innes vs. estate of William
Thomas (Clement's Bay). Caveat entered.

13:201 30 January. Exhibited will of John
Darnall (CV), constituting Col. Henry
Darnall & Col. Philemon Lloyd
executors. Capt. William Hemsley (g,
TA) to prove said will. Susanna Darnall
(widow) was granted administration.
Said Hemsley to administer oath.

Robert Cole (SM) was granted
administration on estate of Daniell
Haley (SM), as principle creditor.
Appraisers: Edward Cole, Nathaniell
Jenkinson. Clement Hill to administer
oath.

Page 92

2 February. Clement Hill (SM) exhibited
oath of William Roswell & Stephen Gough,
appraisers of Abraham Coombes (SM),
sworn 30 January 1684. Also exhibited
oath of Margarett Coomb (relict)
executrix, sworn same day. Also
exhibited will of said Abraham, proved
by Henry Paine, Thomas Swailes, & Peter
Mills.

5 February. William Brereton (SO)
exhibited oath of Daniell Hast & Stephen
Luffe, appraisers of Andrew Jones (SO).
Also exhibited bond of Elisabeth Jones
administratrix. Sureties: John Winder,
Stephen Luffe. Also exhibited
inventory.

13:202 Clement Hill (g, SM) exhibited oath of
MM Cuthbert Scott & Joshua Guybert,
appraisers of Samuell Burges (SM), sworn
20 January. Date: 24 January 1684.
Also exhibited bond of Adam Head
administrator. Sureties: James French,
John Dash.

9 February. Mr. Cullen exhibited
inventory & bond about the
administration of Susan Clarke. Julian
Ledgett widow of Thomas Ledgett (CV) was
granted administration on his estate.
Maj. Thomas Truman (CV) to administer
oath.

10 February. John Bed son of Margarett
Stagg was granted administration on her
estate. Col. Darnall to administer
oath.

12 February. John Warren (SM) was
granted administration on estate of
George Henderson (SM), as principle
creditor. Appraisers: John Tant,
Richard Burkett. Clement Hill (SM) to
administer oath.

13:203 Ignatius Warren brother to Augustine
Warren (SM) was granted administration
on his estate. Appraisers: John Tant,
Richard Burkett. Clement Hill to
administer oath.

Col. Darnall exhibited oath of
Nathaniell Sprigg & John Nuthall,
appraisers of John Clarke (CV), sworn 31
January 1684/5. Also exhibited
inventory.

Clement Hill (g, SM) exhibited oath of
Luke Gardiner & Francis Knott,
appraisers of Robert Curtis (SM), sworn
2 February 1684. Also oath of Edward
Cole & Nathaniell Jenkinson, appraisers
of Daniell Hely (SM), sworn same day.
Date: 6 February 1684.

13 February. Abigall Shanke widow of
John Shanke exhibited his will,
constituting her executrix.
13:204 Clement Hill (g, SM) to prove said will.
Said Abigall was granted administration.

Joseph Edloe (CV) exhibited will of
Edward Mollens (CV), constituting him
executor. Maj. Nicholas Sewall to
prove said will. Said Edloe was granted
administration. Said Sewall to
administer oath.

Sarah Renolds (CV) exhibited will of
Henry Robinson (CV), constituting her
executrix. Thomas Starling (CV) to
prove said will. Said Renolds was
granted administration. Appraisers:
Marke Clare, John Russell. Said
Starling to administer oath.

Col. William Digges exhibited will of
Rice Williams (CH), constituting him
executor. Clement Hill (g, SM) to prove
said will. Said Digges was granted
administration.

John Sikes executor of Robert Hudson
(SM) petitioned for new appraisers:
Robert Mason, John Mitchell. John Wynne
(appraiser) is dec'd. William Hatton to
administer oath.

13:205 14 February. William Bishop (g, TA)
exhibited oath of Jacob Seth executor of
John Hartley (TA), sworn 19 December
1684. Also exhibited oath of Alexander
Cunningham, & William Coursey, Jr.,

Court Session: 1685

appraisers, sworn same day. Also
exhibited will of said Hartley, proved
by John Hollinworth, John Hamer, &
Thomas Wyatt. Also exhibited inventory.

Joseph Edloe (CV) executor of Dr.
Edward Mollens (CV) took oath, &
exhibited codicil, proved by Thomas
Sloper, John Ellis, & Henry Giffard.

Exhibited inventory of William Bowen
(SM), by appraisers John Waid & John
Cambell.

18 February. John Heard (SM) exhibited
will of Anthony Laughlin (SM),
constituting him & Richard Gardiner
executors. Clement Hill (g) to prove
said will. Said Heard & Gardiner were
granted administration. Appraisers:
John Brown, Stephen Gough. Said Hill to
administer oath.

13:206 21 February. Anthony Underwood attorney
for Johanna Goldsmith vs. Col. George
Wells. Libel exhibited. Plaintiff is
executrix & relict with said Wells of
Maj. Samuell Goldsmith. Said Wells is
son-in-law to said Johanna.
13:207 Petition for her portion.

Ralph Bartley (CV) was granted
administration on estate of Francis
Everett (CV), as principle creditor.
Appraisers: John Wood, John Godshall.
Robert Doyne (g) to administer oath.

Joseph Bowle (CE) brother to James Bowle
(CE) was granted administration on his
estate. Appraisers: Nathaniell Dare,
Richard Whitton. William Dare (g, CE)
to administer oath.

13:208 Martha Wamsley widow of Thomas Wamsley
(CE) was granted administration on his
estate. Appraisers: George Oldfield,
John Hyland. William Dare to administer
oath.

23 February. Rachell Bailly
administratrix of Richard Bailly (TA)
exhibited inventory of his estate & she

Court Session: 1685

died before she could render accounts.
John Bailly (son of said Richard) was
granted administration on estate of said
Richard. Appraisers: Thomas Robins,
Robert Bryan. Edward Man (g) to
administer oath.

William Coombes (TA) for Anne Norwood
widow of Arthur Norwood (TA) exhibited
inventory. Before the return of said
inventory, said Anne died. Appraisers:
Joseph James, Richard Moore.

13:209 John Eson (son of said Anne) was granted
administration on estate of said Arthur.

John Smith (SM) exhibited will of
Samuell Maddox (SM), bequeathing all to
his 4 children, & constituting Capt.
Justinian Gerrard, John Hilton, Ralph
Foster, & said Smith overseers. Clement
Hill (g, SM) to prove said will.
Appraisers: Edward Turner, Thomas
Reeves. Said Hill to administer oath.

Edward Smoote who married widow of John
Gee (SM) was granted administration on
his estate. Appraisers: John Smith,
John Hilton. Clement Hill to administer
oath.

Nicholas Hackett (TA) vs. estate of
Thomas Watkins (TA). Caveat exhibited.

13:210 29 February. Thomas Mitchell (CH) was
granted administration on estate of
Edward Abbott (CH), as principle
creditor. Appraisers: Michaell
Mynoakes, John Boswell. John Stone (g,
CH) to administer oath.

Thomas Waghop administrator of Robert
Graham was granted continuance.

25 February. Johanna Randall widow of
Christopher Randall (AA) was granted
administration on his estate.
Appraisers: Francis Mead, Matthew
Howard. Henry Constable (g, AA) to
administer oath.

Exhibited bond of Elisabeth Coursey
administratrix of Maj. William Coursey.

Court Session: 1685

Sureties: John Edmondson, John Hawkins.

Maj. Nicholas Sewall exhibited oath of
Thomas Courtney & John Wyseman,
appraisers of Dr. Edward Mollens (CV),
sworn 23 February 1684. Also exhibited
inventory.

13:211 Henry Constable (g, AA) exhibited oath
of Margarett Stubberfield administratrix
of John Stubberfield, sworn 15 February
1684. Sureties: Roger Newman, Henry
Chappell. Also exhibited oath of
Nicholas Greenbury & George Eager, sworn
8 January 1684/5. Also exhibited
inventory.

William Boarman, Jr. exhibited oath of
Joseph Pile executor of Bartholomew
Piggott (SM), sworn 2 February 1684.
Also exhibited oath of Patrick Innis &
Thomas Clarke, appraisers, sworn same
day.

13:212 Exhibited will of William Bennett,
proved before Edward Pindar. Also
exhibited bond of William Dolebery
administrator. Sureties: Henry Hooper,
Thomas Smithson.

26 February. William Meakin (SM)
exhibited will of Robert Beard (SM),
constituting him executor. Clement Hill
(g) to prove said will. Said Meakin was
granted administration. Appraisers:
Robert Foard, Adam Head. Said Hill to
administer oath.

27 February. Exhibited inventory of
Hans Rosmanson, by appraisers John
Coppedge & Joseph Sadler.

Elisabeth Ricaud (KE) widow of Benjamin
Ricaud exhibited his will, constituting
her executrix. John Hynson to prove
said will. Said Elisabeth was granted
administration. Appraisers: Henry
Hosier, Charles Tilden. Said
Christopher Goodhand [sic] to administer
oath.

Court Session: 1685

William Hatton (g, SM) exhibited oath of
Peter Carwarden & John Redmond,
appraisers of William Wright, sworn 11
December 1684. Also exhibited bond of
George Cox administrator. Sureties:
Peter Carwarden, John Redman.

Said Hatton exhibited oath of the
abovementioned, appraisers of Benjamin
George, sworn 18 December 1684. Also
exhibited bond of Thomas George
administrator. Sureties: Peter
Carwarden, Phillip Jones.

13:213 William Hatton (SM) exhibited oath of
Robert Masson & John Mitchell,
appraisers of Robert Hudson (SM), sworn
23 February 1684. Also exhibited verbal
will of said Hudson.

Exhibited will of Bartholomew Piggott
(SM), proved before William Hatton (g).

Mary Smith widow of Lewis Blangy (KE)
exhibited his will, constituting her
executrix. Christopher Goodhand (g, KE)
to prove said will. Said Smith was
granted administration. Appraisers:
Edward Sweatnam, Thomas Smith. Said
Goodhand to administer oath.

Exhibited will of John Darnall, proved
before William Hemsley (g).

Exhibited inventory of Stephen Cuthbert
(KE), by appraisers Charles Hinson &
William Harris.

Exhibited inventory of John Dassey (DO),
by appraisers Daniell Clarke & Benjamin
Priestly.

Exhibited will of George Allumby, proved
before Edward Man (g, TA).

13:214 Exhibited will of George Billingsly
(VA), by Capt. John Cobreath (CV),
proved in VA.

Robert Kent (TA) exhibited will of
Matthew Reed (TA), constituting him
executor. Col. Henry Coursey to prove

Page 98

said will. Said Kent was granted
administration. Appraisers: Nathaniell
Tucker, Richard Jones, Sr. Said Coursey
to administer oath.

Margarett Peterson (TA) widow of Mathyes
Peterson exhibited his will,
constituting her executrix. Col. Henry
Coursey to prove said will. Said
Margarett was granted administration.
Appraisers: John Chafe, John Chaires.
Said Coursey to administer oath.

William & Richard Powell (TA) exhibited
will of John Wilkinson (TA),
constituting them executors. Col.
Henry Coursey to prove said will. Said
William & Richard were granted
administration. Appraisers: John Chafe,
John Chaires. Said Coursey to
administer oath.

Susan Evans (TA) widow of Robert Evans
(TA) exhibited his will, constituting
her executrix. Edward Man (g, TA) to
prove said will. Said Susan was granted
administration. Appraisers: Thomas
Robbins, William Bexley. Said Man to
administer oath.

13:215 Mary Hitchcock (CV) widow of William
Hitchcock exhibited his will,
constituting her executrix. George
Lingan (g, CV) to prove said will. Said
Mary was granted administration.
Appraisers: John Sunderland, Marke
Clare. Said Lingan to administer oath.

Robert Smith (TA) was granted
administration on estate of Samuell
Graves (TA), as principle creditor.
Appraisers: John Chafe, John Chaires.
Col. Henry Coursey to administer oath.

Robert Smith (TA) was granted
administration on estate of Henry Gill
(TA), as principle creditor.
Appraisers: John Chafe, John Chaires.
Col. Henry Coursey to administer oath.

Ursula Gold widow of Robert Gold (TA)
was granted administration on his

estate. Appraisers: Thomas Ford, James
Smith. Col. Henry Coursey to
administer oath.

Rachell Denny widow of Phillip Denny
(TA) was granted administration on his
estate. Appraisers: Thomas Brough,
Henry Green. Col. Henry Coursey to
administer oath.

13:216 Exhibited will of Dr. Edward Mollens
(CV), proved before Col. Henry Darnall
by Nehemiah Blakiston & Richard Keen.

Clement Hill (g, SM) exhibited oath of
John Browne & Stephen Gough, appraisers
of Anthony Loghlin (SM), sworn 23
February 1684. Also exhibited oath of
John Heard executor, sworn same day.
Mr. Richard Gardiner refused to take
oath. Also exhibited will, proved
before said Hill by William Farding,
John Bright, & Thomas Sigsworth.

Ebenezar Blakiston was granted
administration on estate of John White
(CE), as principle creditor.
Appraisers: George Sturton, Edward
Skidmore. Capt. Joseph Hopkins to
administer oath.

28 February. Sarah Cox (TA) widow of
Thomas Cox (TA) exhibited his will,
constituting her executrix. Edward Man
(g, TA) to prove said will. Said Sarah
was granted administration. Appraisers:
Richard Holland, William Wintersell.
Said Man to administer oath.

Exhibited will of Thomas Taylor (TA), to
be proved by George Robotham (g, TA).

13:217 Jane Fanning (CH) widow of John Fanning
(CH) exhibited his will, constituting
her executrix. Henry Adams (g, CH) to
prove said will. Said Jane was granted
administration. Appraisers: John
Courts, Thomas Gibson. Said Adams to
administer oath.

Exhibited will of Bryan O'Maly (TA), to
be proved by James Murphy (TA).

Court Session: 1685

2 March. Exhibited will of Thomas Price (TA), to be proved by Edward Man.

Exhibited will of Henry Wilcocks (TA), to be proved by George Robotham (g, TA).

George Thompson attorney for Thomas Evans & his wife Sarah exhibited scroll regarding estate of George Bayton (SM). Date: 21 January 1684/5. Mentions: said Sarah was employed by Stephen Murty, Robert Letherland, Charles Carpenter,
13:218 Robert Drury, Governor Notley, John Tant, William Meakin. Deposition of Robert Drury (SM), age 50. Mentions: Thomas Evans,
13:219 John Taunt.

Summons to John Taunt (SM) administrator of Henry Neale (SM) to render accounts.

Robert Parke (KE) son of Robert Parke (KE) exhibited his will, constituting him executor. William Frisby (g, KE) to prove said will. Said son was granted administration. Appraisers: Thomas Thaxton, William Deane. Said Frisby to administer oath.

Elisabeth Warren (KE) widow of Thomas Warren exhibited his will, constituting her executrix. Charles Tilden (g) to prove said will. Said Elisabeth was granted administration. Appraisers: Michaell Miller, John Chandler. Said Tilden to administer oath.

13:220 3 March. Shary Wansey exhibited will of Joseph Sone (TA), constituting him executor. George Robotham (g, TA) to prove said will. Said Wansey was granted administration. Appraisers: Samuell Clarke, Thomas Flow. Said Robotham to administer oath.

Exhibited inventory of Hugh Baker (SM), by appraisers Gilbert Turberville & Thomas Spinke.

4 March. Thomas Evans (SM) appeared, per summons.

Page 101

Phillip Lynes was granted administration
on estate of Seth Sergeant (SM).

Phillip Lynes (CH) administrator of
Edward Tanshall (CH) was granted
continuance.

Hester Stuart administratrix of her
husband petitioned for new LoA. (cf. f.
171.)

13:221 6 March. Randall Hinson executor of
Zachary Wade exhibited accounts.

7 March. Col. William Burges exhibited
accounts of estate of Robert Franklin
(AA). Continuance was granted.

Arnold Elzey vs. estate Charles Ballard.
Deferred.

William Coursey, Jr. exhibited will of
George Carrall (TA). Said Coursey was
granted administration, as greatest
legatee. Appraisers: Andrew Price,
Richard Mirax. Capt. William Hemsley
(TA) to administer oath.

Joseph Freeman (SO) & his wife Mary &
Ruth Stevens widow of Edward Stevens
(SO) vs. Florence Tucker executrix of
said Stevens. Caveat entered.
Mentions: wife, children.

Edward Sweatnam (KE) administrator of
Edward Roger exhibited additional
accounts.

13:222 10 March. Anne Wynne (SM) widow of John
Wynne exhibited his will, constituting
her executrix. Said Anne was granted
administration. Appraisers: Daniell
Smith, John Mitchell. William Hatton
(g) to administer oath.

Kenelm Chiseldyn petitioned that John
Tenneson & James Green be appraisers of
estate of Jonathon Squires (SM).
Clement Hill (g) to administer oath.

11 March. John Bevan (BA) was granted
administration on estate of Maurice Lane

(BA). Appraisers: Charles Pyne, John Bird. Maj. Thomas Long to administer oath.

Mary Mills (SM) widow of Peter Mills exhibited his will, constituting her executrix. Clement Hill (g, SM) to prove said will. Said Mary was granted administration. Appraisers: Henry Spinke, Richard Walker. Said Hill to administer oath.

William Shertcliffe (SM) was granted administration on estate of Joseph Harding (SM), as principle creditor. Appraisers: Henry Spinke, Richard Walker. Clement Hill (g, SM) to administer oath.

13:223 12 March. Richard Haseldyne who married Abigall sister of Francis Brooke (TA) was granted administration on his estate. Col. Philemon Lloyd to administer oath.

13 March. Margarett Pagrave (SM) widow of James Pagrave (SM) was granted administration on his estate. Appraisers: Henry Lawrence, Walter Woolverstone. William Hatton to administer oath.

16 March. Thomas Long (SM) & his wife Lucie (daughter of Samuell Dobson (SM)) vs. estate of said Dobson. Caveat entered.

19 March. Capt. Samuell Bourne (CV) to prove will of Christopher Rousby (CV).

Col. William Stevens exhibited oath of Lidia Quillaine administratrix of Daniell Quillaine, sworn 28 October 1684. Also exhibited oath of Col. William Coulbourne & Capt. John Osborne, appraisers, sworn same day.

Exhibited will of William Innis (SO), proved before Col. William Stevens.

Exhibited bond of Lidia Quillaine administratrix of Daniell Quillaine

Court Session: 1685

(SO). Sureties: Henry Williams, Rowland
Bevans.

13:224 Col. William Stevens exhibited will of
William Innes (SO), proved 12 November
1684. Also exhibited oath of Matt.
Scarbrough & Charles Ratcliffe,
appraisers, sworn same day. Also
exhibited inventory, by appraisers
Mathew Scarbrough & Charles Racliffe.

Maj. Thomas Taylor exhibited oath of
Daniell Clarke & Benjamin Priestly,
appraisers of John Dossey (DO), sworn 3
January 1684.

Exhibited inventory of Samuell Burges
(SM), by appraisers Cuthbert Scott &
Joshua Guybert.

Exhibited inventory of William Wright
(SM), by appraisers Peter Carwarden &
John Rodman.

Exhibited inventory of Benjamin George
(SM), by appraisers Phillip Jones &
Peter Carwarden.

Exhibited inventory of Abraham Coomb
(SM), by appraisers William Roswell &
Stephen Gough.

13:225 23 March. Exhibited will of William
Thomas (SM), constituting widow
Elisabeth executrix. She is since
dec'd. John Bayley (Clement's Bay,
neighbor) was granted administration,
for benefit of orphans. Mentions: Dr.
Patrick Innis (creditor). Date: 21
March 1684. Appraisers: Joshua Guybert,
Adam Head. Clement Hill (g) to
administer oath.

24 March. Ellinor Morris widow of John
Morris (TA) was granted administration
on his estate. Appraisers: Richard
Royston, Thomas Vaughan. James Murphy
to administer oath.

13:226 Anthony Rumball (merchant) was granted
administration on estate of Symon Parker
(TA), as principle creditor.

Court Session: 1685

Appraisers: John Davies, Anthony Mayle.
James Murphy to administer oath.

Richard Sweatnam (TA) was granted
administration on estate of William
Turke (TA), as principle creditor.
Appraisers: Griffin Jones, Anthony
Rumball. James Murphy (g, TA) to
administer oath.

Court Session: 1685

25 March. Thomas Stone (CH) exhibited
will of Giles Tomkins (CH), constituting
his son Giles Tomkins (under age)
executor. Overseers are dec'd. James
Tyer (CH) to prove said will. Said
Stone was granted administration, for
the executor. Appraisers: Anthony
Neale, John Courts. Said Tyer to
administer oath.

William Hemsley, Jr. petitioned for
Richard Jones, Jr. & Isaac Winchester to
appraise estate of Charles Vaughan (KE).
Lewis Blangy (one of former appraisers)
is dec'd. Christopher Goodhand (g, KE)
to administer oath.

William Hemsley, Jr. petitioned for
Richard Sweatnam (g, TA) & Andrew
Abington (g, TA) to appraise estate of
Robert Noble. George Robotham to
administer oath.

13:227 Capt. John Coode was granted
administration on estate of James Green
(SM), as principle creditor.
Appraisers: Richard Cloud, John Smith.
Col. William Digges to administer oath.

26 March. Sarah Powell (CV) widow of
George Powell exhibited his will,
constituting her executrix. Maj.
Thomas Truman to prove said will. Said
Sarah was granted administration. Said
Truman to administer oath.

27 March. George Parker procurator for
John Edwards (AA) petitioned for sheriff
(AA) to summon Richard Beard & Peter
Barnard executors of Daniell Taylor (AA)

Court Session: 1685

to render accounts.

Elinor James widow of Richard James (AA)
exhibited his will, constituting her
executrix. John Soller (g, AA) to prove
said will. Said Elinor was granted
administration. Appraisers: William
Sewick, Charles Powell. Said Sollers to
administer oath.

Nicholas Buttram (CV) exhibited will of
John Rede (CV), constituting him
executor. George Lingan (g, CV) to
prove said will. Said Nicholas was
granted administration. Appraisers:
Symon Wooten, Joseph Higgens. Said
Lingan to administer oath.

13:228   Pheby Little widow of John Little (CV)
was granted administration on his
estate. Appraisers: William Howes,
Newman Barber. Francis Hutchins to
administer oath.

Col. Henry Jowles was granted
administration on estate of John Mantle
(CV), as principle creditor.
Appraisers: William Parker, James
Cranford. Maj. Thomas Truman to
administer oath.

31 March. Jane Maggison widow of John
Maggison (KE) exhibited his will,
constituting her executrix. Phillip
Conner (KE) to prove said will. Said
Jane was granted administration.
Appraisers: Lewes Meredath, Henry
Carter. Said Conner to administer oath.

Exhibited will of Morgan Williams (KE),
constituting widow Amy executrix.
Christopher Goodhand to prove said will.
Said Amy was granted administration.
Appraisers: Thomas Osborne, Alexander
Waters. Said Goodhand to administer
oath.

Capt. John Coode petitioned for sheriff
(SM) to summon Justinian Tennison
administrator of John Tennison to render
accounts.

Court Session: 1685

2 April. John Mustian was granted
administration on estate of Mr. Robert
Jones, who died at Mr. Bankes, as
greatest creditor. Capt. Richard Ladd
refused administration. Appraisers:
Francis Freeman, Bazil Warring. Francis
Hutchins to administer oath.

13:229   4 April. Thomas Seaward (TA) & Nicholas
Clouds (TA) exhibited will of William
Bishop (TA), constituting them
executors. George Robotham (TA) to
prove said will. Said Seaward & Clouds
were granted administration.
Appraisers: Robert Smith, Robert Jones,
Sr. Said Robotham to administer oath.

Exhibited will of Albert Johnson (TA),
constituting Thomas Foord & John Offley
executors. Said Offley is dec'd & said
Foord (p, Chester River, TA) has
renounced administration to Alice widow,
now wife of Henry Green (TA). Date: 2
March 1684/5. Witnesses: Thomas Beckle,
Alice Ford. George Robotham (g, TA) to
prove said will. Said Henry Green was
granted administration in right of his
wife. Appraisers: Robert Smith, Richard
Jones, Sr. Said Robotham to administer
oath.

Exhibited will of John Best (TA),
constituting Charles Hollingsworth
executor. George Robotham to prove said
will. Said Hollingsworth was granted
administration. Appraisers: Robert
Smith, Richard Jones, Sr. Said Robotham
to administer oath.

8 April. Thomas Parslow was granted
administration on estate of John Cooper
(CV), as principle creditor.
Appraisers: John Skipper, Jeremiah
Simpson. Capt. Samuell Bourn to
administer oath.

13:230   Kenelm Chiseldyn (g, SM) exhibited that
James Green (one of appraisers of
Jonathon Squires (SM)) is dec'd. New
appraisers: Thomas Mosely, John
Tenneson. Clement Hill to administer
oath.

Page 107

13 April. Barbara Cullis (CH) widow of Charles Cullis exhibited his will, constituting her executrix. Henry Adams (g, CH) to prove said will. Said Barbara was granted administration. Appraisers: John Wood, John Godshall. Said Adams to administer oath.

Phillip Lynes was granted administration on estate of Hugh Mungarah (CH), as principle creditor. Appraisers: Francis Chalmley, John Wood. John Stone (CH) to administer oath.

Henry Coffin was granted administration on estate of George Buckston (TA), as principle creditor. Col. Philemon Lloyd to administer oath.

Leonard Green (SM) was granted administration on estate of John Hawkins (SM). Appraisers: Marmaduke Sims, Abraham Rhodes. William Hatton to administer oath.

17 April. Samuell Wheeler (CE) was granted administration on estate of Alexander Nash (KE), as guardian to Richard Nash & Thomasin Nash (under age, children of Richard Nash (brother of dec'd, dec'd)). Said Wheeler married the widow of said Richard Nash. Appraisers: Miles Miller, Thomas Joce. Phillip Conner to administer oath.

13:231 Exhibited will of Marke Blomfield (SM). John Blomfield (brother) was granted administration. Sureties: Elias Beech, John Evans. Appraisers: Henry Smith, John Evans.

23 April. Alice Watts (SM) widow of William Watts exhibited his will, constituting her executrix. Said Alice was granted administration. Appraisers: Robert Mason, John Evans. William Hatton (g) to administer oath.

Alice Boteler widow of Charles Boteler (CV) was granted administration on his estate. Appraisers: Henry Truman, Christopher Bayne. John Griggs to

Court Session: 1685

administer oath.

24 April. Daniell Phillips (CV) was
granted administration on estate of
Richard Hewson (CV). Appraisers: James
Veetch, William Suttle. John Griggs to
administer oath.

27 April. Elisabeth Boyden widow of
William Boyden (CH) was granted
administration on his estate.
Appraisers: Francis Adams, John Buoges.
John Stone to administer oath.

28 April. Hannah Browne widow of Robert
Brown (SM) was granted administration on
his estate. Appraisers: William
Boarman, Jr., Samuell Cook. Joseph
Piles to administer oath.

13:232 Isabella Abbott (CV) widow of George
Abbott exhibited his will, constituting
her executrix. Francis Hutchins to
prove said will. Said Isabella was
granted administration. Appraisers:
Samuell Holdsworth, John Manning. Said
Hutchins to administer oath.

Christian Sterling (CV) widow of Thomas
Sterling exhibited his will,
constituting her executrix. George
Lingan (g, CV) to prove said will. Said
Christian was granted administration.
Appraisers: Francis Mauldin, Francis
Freeman. Said Lingan to administer
oath.

Mary Chandler widow of William Chandler
exhibited his will, constituting her
executrix. Col. Digges to prove said
will.

William Lyle (CV) exhibited will of
Phillip Jones (CV), constituting him &
Samuell Griffith executors. George
Lingan to prove said will. Said Lyle &
Griffith were granted administration.
Appraisers: John Moffett, Gawin
Hambleton. Said Lingan to administer
oath.

Jane King widow of John King (CV) was granted administration on his estate. Appraisers: George Hardish, Richard Jackson. John Creycroft to administer oath.

13:233   29 April. Ralph Fishbourne (TA) exhibited will of Alexander Nash (KE), constituting Thomas Taylor & said Fishbourne executors. Phillip Conner to prove said will. Said Fishbourne was granted administration; said Taylor is dec'd. Appraisers: Isaac Winchester, Christopher Goodhand. Said Conner to administer oath.

Exhibited will of Thomas Furbey (TA). Col. Philemon Lloyd (TA) to prove said will.

2 May. Thomas Seaward (TA) & Nicholas Clouds (TA) exhibited will of Thomas Lewis (TA), constituting them executors. Col. Henry Coursey to prove said will. Said Seaward & Clouds were granted administration. Appraisers: Richard Jones, Sr., Robert Smith. Said Coursey to administer oath.

Barbara Chapman (CH) exhibited will of William Hensey (CH), constituting William Chapman (under age, son of said Barbara) executor. Henry Adams to prove said will. Said Barbara was granted administration, on behalf of her son. Appraisers: Thomas Hussey, Cleborne Lomax. Said Adams to administer oath.

Barbara Chapman widow of Richard Chapman (CH) was granted administration on his estate. Appraisers: Thomas Hussey, Cleborne Lomax. Henry Adams to administer oath.

Thomas Bayley was granted administration on estate of Thomas Bingham (TA), as principle creditor. Appraisers: John Johnson, John Tillison. Col. Henry Coursey to administer oath.

13:234   Thomas Seaward (TA) & Nicholas Clouds (TA) executors of William Bishop were

granted administration on estate of
William Wood (TA), as principle
creditors. Appraisers: Richard Jones,
Robert Smith. Col. Henry Coursey to
administer oath.

4 May. Phillip Lynes was granted
administration on estate of Seth
Sergeant (SM), as principle creditor.
Appraisers: Thomas Grunwin, James
Mackewen. Garrett Vansweringen to
administer oath.

Henry Tayler who married a daughter of
Thomas Wynne (SM) was granted
administration on his estate.
Appraisers: Thomas Price, Abraham
Rhoades. James Pattison to administer
oath.

Estate of John Waterton (g;, BA).
Witnesses to will live remote from SMC.
Miles Gibson (g, BA) to prove said will.

13:235   12 May. Mary Ward (CH) widow of William
Ward (CH) exhibited his will,
constituting her executrix. Ignatius
Causeen (g) to prove said will. Said
Mary was granted administration.
Appraisers: John Courts, Sr., John
Poosey. Said Causeen to administer
oath.

16 May. Robert Burman (TA) was granted
administration on estate of James Cooke
(TA). Appraisers: Symon Stevens, Henry
Costin. Col. Philemon Lloyd to
administer oath.

26 May. Rhoda Earle (TA) widow of James
Earle exhibited his will, constituting
her executrix. George Robotham (g) to
prove said will. Said Rhoda was granted
administration. Appraisers: Robert
Bryan, John Earle. Said Robotham to
administer oath.

27 May. William Harris (KE) exhibited
will of Thomas Boon (KE), constituting
him executor. John Hynson to prove said
will. Said Harris was granted
administration. Appraisers: Charles

Tylden, Michaell Miller. Said Hynson to administer oath.

Vertue Reader (SM) widow of Symon Reader exhibited his will, constituting her executrix. Clement Hill (g) to prove said will. Said Vertue was granted administration. Appraisers: John Paler, John Bullock. Said Hill to administer oath.

13:236 Mary Bridgin widow of Robert Bridgin (SM) was granted administration on his estate. Appraisers: John Paler, John Bullock. Clement Hill (g) to administer oath.

Anthony Chilcutt (DO) who married widow (now dec'd) of James Harper (DO) was granted administration on his estate. Appraisers: Anthony Taylor, Benjamin Priestly. Maj. Thomas Taylor to administer oath.

18 May. Ralph Fishbourne one of executors of Alexander Nash (KE) petitioned for LoA. He is a Quaker & not willing to take oath. Former administration to Samuell Wheeler is void.

Exhibited will of Thomas Rumsey (CE), constituting Matthias Mattson & Nicholas Allum executors. Nathaniell Garrett (CE) to prove said will. Said Mattson & Allum were granted administration. Appraisers: Henry Eldersly, Andrew Peterson. Said Garrett to administer oath.

Richard Way (CH) was granted administration on estate of Elisabeth Gent (CH). Appraisers: John Wright, John Falkner. Robert Doyne (g) to administer oath.

13:237 Thomas Dillon (SM) exhibited will of Peirce Wall (SM), constituting him executor. Clement Hill (g) to prove said will. Said Dillon was granted administration. Appraisers: Edward Cole, William Shearly. Said Hill to

administer oath.

James Phillips (BA) was granted
administration on estate of William
White (gunsmith, BA). Appraisers:
Israell Skelton, Michaell Judd. Miles
Gibson to administer oath.

30 May. Martha Morris (CV) exhibited
will of John Gill (CV), constituting her
executrix. Francis Hutchins (g) to
prove said will. Said Martha was
granted administration. Appraisers:
William Williams, Joseph Baker. Said
Hutchins to administer oath.

John Larkin (AA) exhibited will of
George Holland (AA), constituting him
executor. Maj. James Ringold (KE) to
prove said will.

Exhibited will of Thomas Lewis (TA),
constituting William Bishop (TA), now
dec'd) executor. George Robotham to
prove said will. Thomas Seaward &
Nicholas Clouds executors of said Bishop
were granted administration.
Appraisers: Richard Jones, Sr., Robert
Smith. Said Robotham to administer
oath.

13:238 Martin Muggenbury exhibited will of
Isaac Daniell (CE), constituting him
executor. Nathaniell Garrett to prove
said will. Said Muggenbury was granted
administration. Appraisers: John
Wheeler, Lodowick Martin. Said Garrett
to administer oath.

John Harding who married Elisabeth widow
& executrix of Morgan Peniviy (?) (CE)
exhibited his will. George Warner to
prove said will. Said John was granted
administration in right of his wife.
Appraisers: John Briscoe, Samuell
Weatherly. Said Warner to administer
oath.

Isaack Calke & his mother Anne were
granted administration on estate of
Oliver Calke (CE). Appraisers: Lawrence
Christian, Lodowick Martin. Nathaniell

Court Session: 1685

Garrett to administer oath.

Thomas Bayle (TA) was granted administration on estate of Thomas Bingham (TA), as principle creditor. Appraisers: John Hinson, John Tillison. George Robotham to administer oath.

Nicholas Clouds & Thomas Seaward were granted administration on estate of William Wood (TA), as principle creditors. Appraisers: Richard Jones, Robert Smith. George Robotham to administer oath. Mary Veetch widow of James Veetch (CV) was granted administration on his estate. Appraisers: John Turner, William Hutchins. John Griggs (g) to administer oath.

13:239 Katherine Davenport widow of Humphry Davenport (TA) relinquished administration on his estate to Robert Smith (TA). Date: 10 May 1685. Witnesses: Richard Burcut, Richard Triggs.

Exhibited will of William Palmer (CH), constituting his mother Anne Atkins executrix. Said Atkins was granted administration. Appraisers: Edward Ming, Richard Harrison. Robert Doyne (g) to administer oath.

Exhibited will of Richard Pinner (CH), constituting Mary Pinner executrix. Appraisers: Edward Ming, Richard Harrison. Robert Doyne (g) to administer oath.

Exhibited will of Hendrick Mattson (alias Hendrick Freeman, CE), constituting his son Mathias Mattson (alias Mathias Freeman) executor. Said Mathias was granted administration. Appraisers: Nicholas Allum, Henry Eldersly. Nathaniell Garrett (g) to administer oath.

Miles Gibson on behalf of Jane Taply exhibited will of Christopher Taply (BA). Maj. Edward Inglish to prove

Page 114

said will, since witnesses live in CE.

Elisabeth Swinborne (CH) widow of
Nicholas Swinborne exhibited her
renunciation, naming Edward Rookwood
(CH) administrator. Date: 19 May 1685.
Witnesses: John Hoskins, Thomas Hussey.

Exhibited will of Benjamine Lawrence
(AA). Col. Thomas Taillor to prove
said will.

1 June. Exhibited will of Samuell
Maddocks (SM), proved by Robert Fletcher
& Edward Smoote. John Hilton & Ralph
Foster, 2 of the overseers, were granted
administration. The other 2 overseers
are unwilling & incapable of giving
security. Capt. Joshua Doyne to
administer oath.

13:240 Exhibited will of Nicholas Swinborne
(CH), constituting his wife Elisabeth
executrix, who renounced administration
to Edward Rookwood (CH). Said Rookwood
was granted administration. Appraisers:
Cleborne Lomax, Mathew Dike (?). Robert
Doyne to administer oath.

Susanna Cooper widow of John Cooper (TA)
was granted administration on his
estate. Appraisers: John Newman, Ralph
Dawson. Col. Vincent Lowe to
administer oath.

Renewal of appraisers of Maj. William
Coursey: Thomas Smithson, James Murphy.
Mr. Edward Mann to administer oath.

John Gough was granted administration on
estate of William Arfitt (CH), as
principle creditor. Robert Doyne (CH)
to administer oath.

Phillip Hoskins was granted
administration on estate of Richard
Garworth (CH), as principle creditor.
Appraisers: Francis Harrison, John
Davis. Mr. Robert Doyne to administer
oath.

Court Session: 1685

Sarah widow of John Gwinn (CH) was
granted administration on his estate.
Appraisers: Henry Hardy, William
Burneham.

Exhibited will of Henry Hickson (CH),
constituting Richard True executor. Mr.
Robert Doyne to prove said will &
administer oath.

2 June. Honor Furnis widow of William
Furnis (SO) was granted administration
on his estate. Appraisers: John King,
Andrew Whittington. Capt. David Browne
to administer oath.

Margaret Nuthall widow of James Nuthall
(CV) & John Nuthall guardian to orphan
(infant) were granted administration on
his estate. Appraisers: Robert Dove,
Richard Charleton. Thomas Brooke to
administer oath.

10 June. Exhibited inventory of William
Thomas, by appraisers Joshua Gwibert &
Adam Goad.

Ann Craft widow of Robert Craft (SM) was
granted administration on his estate.
Appraisers: John Cecill, John Riley.
Clement Hill to administer oath.

13:241 23 June. Margarett Nuthall & James
Nuthall, Jr. executors of James Nuthall
vs. John Nuthall. Sheriff (CV) to
summon said John.

2 July. Exhibited inventory of Charles
Cullis (CH), by appraisers Thomas
Grunwin, John Wood, & John Godshall.

Exhibited will of Philemon Lloyd (TA).
Col. Vincent Lowe to prove said will.
Henrietta Maria Lloyd was granted
administration. Bondsman: James Cullen.
Appraisers: Maj. Peter Sayer, George
Robotham, Thomas Smithson, John Davis.

10 July. Mr. Robert Carvile was
granted administration on estate of
James Bodkin (SM). Appraisers: Garrett
Vansweringen, Thomas Grunwin.

Court Session: 1685

Sheriff (CE) to summon Samuell Wheeler
administrator of Alexander Nash to
answer complaint of Ralph Fishbourne
executor of said Nash.

13 July. Sarah widow of George Powell
(CV) exhibited his will, constituting
her executrix, & was granted
administration on 26 March last. Said
Sarah is now married to John Crook.
Said John & Sarah were granted
administration. Appraisers: Richard
Gardiner, Thomas Hall. Maj. Thomas
Trueman to administer oath.

Exhibited will of John Munns (CH),
constituting his widow Winifred Muns
executrix, who has since married (N)
Speake. Appraisers: Thomas Middleton,
P. Hoskins. Mr. Robert Doyne to
administer oath.

13:242   14 July. Exhibited will of Thomas Love
(AA), constituting his widow Diana Love
executrix. Said Diana was granted
administration. Appraisers: Walter
Carr, Mathew Hughes. Col. Thomas
Taillor to administer oath.

Johanna widow of Robert Clarkeson (AA)
was granted administration on his
estate. Appraisers: Nicholas Gassaway,
Fardinando Batty. Col. Thomas Taillor
to administer oath.

Elisabeth widow of Theodorus Young (AA)
was granted administration on his
estate. Col. Thomas Taillor to
administer oath.

Exhibited inventory of James Veitch
(CV).

17 July. Exhibited will of James Rumsey
(CV). Mr. Thomas Brooke to prove said
will. Richard Jenkins & his wife Ann
were granted administration.
Appraisers: John Dawsett, Michael Bayly.
Said Brooke to administer oath.

Exhibited will of Jonathon Pearce (CV),
constituting James Moore executor. Said

Moore was granted administration.
Appraisers: James Ellwis, Michael Ball.
Mr. Thomas Brooke to administer oath.

Exhibited will of John White (SO),
constituting widow Sarah White
executrix. Said Sarah was granted
administration. Appraisers (SO):
Richard Lewis, Richard Warren. Col.
William Colebourne to administer oath.

John Makitt (alias John Makitrick) was
granted administration on estate of
Henry Cole (CO). Appraisers: Josias
Seaward, John Walton. Mr. Edmond
Howard to administer oath.

Sheriff (SO) to summon Florence Tucker
executrix of Edward Stevens (SO) to
prove his will. Also summons to John
Heath, Thomas Williams, & William
Morrice witnesses to said will.

Sheriff (SO) to summon Joseph Freeman &
his wife Mary & Ruth Stevens widow of
Edward Stevens (SO) to contest will of
said Edward.

13:243   18 July. Robert Clarke & his wife Sarah
(daughter of Abraham Combes (dec'd)) vs.
John Reswick & his wife Margaret
executrix & widow of said Combes.
Summons to said Reswick.

Phillip Willan (SM) was granted
administration on estate of Thomas Wynne
(SM). Appraisers: Abraham Rhodes,
Thomas Price. Garrett Vansweringen (g)
to administer oath.

20 July. Joseph Edlo guardian to
William Window son of Thomas Window (CV)
was granted administration on estate of
said Thomas. Appraisers: William Kerby,
John Wiseman. Maj. Nicholas Sewall to
administer oath.

27 July. Exhibited will of Joseph
Dawkins (CV). Mr. John Griggs to prove
said will. Margarett Dawkins widow was
granted administration. Appraisers:
Francis Hiham, Christopher Beanes. Said

Court Session: 1685

Griggs to administer oath.

28 July. Sheriff (TA) to summon Ralph Fishbourne to show cause why administration granted to Samuell Wheeler administrator of Alexander Nash is not good.

Sheriff (SM) to summon John Tannt to render accounts on estate of Henry Neale (SM).

30 July. Robert Carvile procurator for Francis Hamersly (g, VA) exhibited will of Nathan Barton (CH), constituting widow Martha executrix.

13:244 Not long after death of said Nathan, said Martha fell sick & gave care of her children Nathan, Thomas, & Martha to said Francis Hammersley. Said Martha also made nuncupative will, constituting said Francis executor. She died at beginning of March last. Petition for Mr. Ignatius Causeene (CH) to prove both wills. Said Hamersly was granted administration on both estates, as greatest creditor. Appraisers: Maj. John Wheeler, Robert Middleton. Mentions: bill of John Munne, bill of Richard Gibson. Said Hamersly was called to VA. Mr. Robert Doyne (sheriff, CH) to prove said wills.

Exhibited will of Thomas Goddard (TA), constituting widow Ann Goddard executrix. Said Ann was granted administration. Appraisers: Richard Roystone, Thomas Vaughan. James Murphy (g) to administer oath.

5 August. Exhibited will of Phillip Jones (CV), constituting Samuell Griffith & William Lile executors. Said Griffith has renounced administration George Lingan to prove said will.

13:245 Lawrence Draper was granted administration on estate of Walter Smith (AA), as greatest creditor. Appraisers: Thomas Freeborne, Andrew Norwood. Capt. Edward Dorsey to administer oath.

Court Session: 1685

William Marshall was granted
administration on estate of William
Jenkins (CV), as greatest creditor.
Appraisers: Robert Wood, John Muffett.
George Lingan (g) to administer oath.

George Lingan (g) to take oath of Robert
Mines & his wife Margarett
administratrix of Patrick Due, regarding
additional accounts.

6 August. Exhibited will of Thomas
Darcy (alias Thomas Matchett, CV),
constituting widow Frances executrix.
Col. Henry Joweles to prove said will.

John Tannt exhibited accounts on estate
belonging to children of Henry Neale.
Said children are dec'd since the
division of estate of said Neale. The
sum of right belongs to Lord Proprietor.

Kenelm Cheseldyne attorney for Arnold
Elzey administrator of Charles Ballard
ordered to render accounts.

Exhibited will of Thomas Banks, proved
before Col. Henry Darnall. Ann Banks
executrix was granted administration.
Appraisers: Col. Henry Jowls, (N).
John Griggs (g) to administer oath.

Summons to John Reswick & his wife.

Summons to James Bigger regarding estate
of (N) Nuttwell.

13:246   Samuell Wheeler (CE) exhibited will of
Alexander Nash.

Alice Watts (SM) exhibited will of
William Watts.

7 August. Susan Edwards widow of Symon
Edwards (CV) was granted administration
on his estate. Appraisers: Christopher
Banes, William Chittle. John Griggs (g)
to administer oath.

13 August. Exhibited will of Edward
Howard (CV), constituting widow Mary
executrix.

Court Session: 1685

22 August. John Bowles was granted
administration on estate of John
Ferckleton (KE). Appraisers: John
Dobbs, John Butcher. Phillip Connor to
administer oath.

Appraisers of estate of Mr. John
Darnall to be sworn by Col. Henry
Darnall.

Exhibited will of Emanuel Jenkenson
(TA). Mr. Edward Mann to prove said
will.

Exhibited will of Henry Parratt (TA).
George Robotham (g) to prove said will.

Exhibited will of George Sealy (DO),
constituting widow Mary executrix. John
Alford (g) to prove said will.

31 August. Exhibited will of Robert
Chapman (KE). Appraisers: William
Deane, George Browne. Edward Inglish
(g) to administer oath.

Sheriff (KE) to summon Thomas Joce & his
wife Ann administratrix of Samuel Tovy
to render accounts, at request of Maj.
James Ringold.

Exhibited will of Thomas Binks (CV),
constituting widow Elisabeth, Thomas
Cleverly, & John Gary executors. Mr.
John Griggs to prove said will. Said
Cleverly & Gary are since dec'd.
Nathaniel Dare who married said
Elisabeth was granted administration.
Appraisers: John Hance, James Cranford.
Basill Warren (g) to administer oath.

13:247   4 September. Kenelm Cheseldyne attorney
for Arnold Elzey (SO) administrator of
Charles Ballard exhibited that said
Elzey cannot render accounts until
Stephen Luffe & his wife Sarah render
their accounts. Said Stephen & Sarah
summoned. Said Elzey summoned.

Exhibited will of James Rumsey (CV).
Exhibited also inventory. Mr. Thomas
Brooke (CV) exhibited oath of Richard &

Court Session: 1685

Ann Jenkins executors of James Rumsey, sworn 19 August 1685. Also exhibited oath of Michael Bayley & John Dawsett, appraisers, sworn same day.

Maj. Thomas Trueman (CV) exhibited oath of John Crooke & his wife Sarah executors of George Powell (CV), sworn 19 July 1685. Also exhibited oath of Capt. Richard Gardiner & Thomas Hall, appraisers, sworn same day.

13:248 Exhibited renunciation of Samuel Griffith one of executors of Phillip Jones (CV). Date: 4 June 1685. Witnesses: George Lingan, William Hutchison.

Mr. John Griggs exhibited oath of Daniel Phillips administrator of Richard Hewson. Also exhibited oath of John Veitch & William Suttle, appraisers.

Said Griggs exhibited oath of Alice Boteler administratrix of Charles Boteler (CV). Also exhibited oath of Henry Trueman & Christopher Baynes, appraisers.

Mr. William Hatton exhibited oath of Leonard Greene administrator of John Hawknett, sworn 19 April 1685. Also exhibited oath of Marmaduke Semm & Abraham Rhodes, appraisers, sworn same day.

Said Hatton exhibited oath of Robert Mason & John Evans, appraisers of William Watts, sworn 8 May 1685.

13:249 Griffith Jones procurator for Rebeccah Bingham relict of Thomas Bingham exhibited her renunciation, recommending Thomas Bayly, creditor. Date: 31 January 1684. Witnesses: Solomon Wright, Daniell Norman, Robert Norris.

Griffith Jones procurator for Frances Wood relict of William Wood exhibited her renunciation,
13:250 recommending William Bishop, creditor. Date: 29 January 1684. Witnesses: James

Court Session: 1685

Greenwood, Walter Jones.

Margarett Bigger executrix of James
Nuthall was granted administration on
his estate. James Nuthall, the other
executor, is under age, as are the other
children. Col. Henry Jowles to
administer oath.

John Reswick & his wife did not appear.
Summons renewed.

9 September. Col. Jowles to swear
appraisers of estate of James Nuthall,
on behalf of James Bigger & his wife.

12 September. John Harper & his wife
Grace relict of William Collins (CV)
were granted administration on his
estate. Appraisers: Richard Bourke,
John Browne. Richard Marsham to
administer oath.

13:251 14 September. Eleanor Loggin widow of
John Loggin (CV) was granted
administration on his estate.
Appraisers: John Scott, James Macall.
John Griggs to administer oath.

16 September. Exhibited will of Thomas
Doxey (SM), constituting Ann Doxey,
Thomas Haddock, & Thomas Lee executors.
Said executors were granted
administration. Appraisers: Charles
Edgerton, Richard Attwood. James
Pattison to administer oath.

18 September. Sheriff (SM) to summon
James Hall & his wife Hannah
administratrix of Robert Browne to
render an inventory. Timothy Richardson
& Peter Card exhibited objections.

28 September. John Edwards was granted
administration on estate of James
Mitchell (AA), as principle creditor.
Appraisers: Walter Phelps, Benjamin
Williams. Edward Burgess to administer
oath.

29 September. Mabell Offly widow of
John Offly (TA) was granted

administration on his estate.
Appraisers: Robert Smith, William
Sparkes. Mr. Henry Coursey to
administer oath.

Sybella Broadrib was granted
administration on estate of Samuell
Randall (TA), as principle creditor.
Appraisers: John Hayman, William Sparke.
Mr. Henry Coursey to administer oath.

Exhibited will of Edward Stevens (SO),
proved.

(N) Wheeler vs. Mr. Robert Carvile for
(N) Fishbourne.

Robert Clarke vs. Mr. Anthony Underwood
for (N) Reswick & his wife.

Susanna Keene summoned to render
accounts on estate of John Hunt (CV), at
request of John Godscross.

13:252   John Tannt was granted administration on
estate of Henry Neale, Jr. (SM) on
behalf of Lawrence Tetershall & James
Tannt, they being next of kin.

2 October. Exhibited will of Joseph
Woolfe (CH), constituting Mary Wolfe
executrix, who is since dec'd. Mr.
Robert Doyne to prove said will. Rice
Wayman was granted administration, as
principle creditor. Appraisers: John
Wheeler, John Clarke. Said Doyne to
administer oath.

William Stevens (Pocomoke, SO) exhibited
receipt from Edward Day who married
executrix of Capt. Thomas Walker & is
therefore bound to Thomas Walker &
Susanna Walker, children of said Walker.
Date: 17 September 1685. Witnesses: Sa.
Cooper, Stephen Luffe, Edm. Beauchamp.

Exhibited will of Robert Robbins (CH),
constituting widow Margarett executrix,
who has since married Francis Harrison.
Mr. Robert Doyne to prove said will.

Court Session: 1685

Thomas Stonehouse who married Mary widow
of Thomas Steed (CH) was granted
administration on his estate. Mr.
Robert Doyne to administer oath.

13:253 Elisabeth Guest widow of George Guest
(CH) was granted administration on his
estate. Mr. Robert Doyne to administer
oath.

John Magruther was granted
administration on estate of James
Magruther (CV). Appraisers: Ninian
Beal, Thomas Allice. Francis Collyer to
administer oath.

Thomas Wilson who married widow of James
Carr (CV) was granted administration on
his estate. Appraisers: William Jones,
John Chettham. Francis Collyer to
administer oath.

Susanna Benfey widow of Paul Benfy (CV)
was granted administration on his
estate. Appraisers: William Lyles, John
Wipps. Mr. George Lingan to administer
oath.

3 October. Elisabeth Boullay relict &
executrix of James Boullay (CV)
renounced administration on his estate.
Date: 26 September 1685. Witnesses:
George Parker, William Holland.
13:254 Michaell Miller (KE) was granted
administration on said estate.
Appraisers: Maj. Joseph Weeks, William
Harris.

Anney Jones widow of Hugh Jones (KE) was
granted administration on his estate.
Appraisers: Thomas Osborne, Alexander
Waters. Phillip Connor to administer
oath.

5 October. John Larkin was granted
administration on estate of George
Holland (AA). Appraisers: Henry
Hanslapp, Otho Holland. Col. Thomas
Taillor to administer oath.

Samuel Bourne was granted administration
on estate of Dorothy King (CV).

Court Session: 1685

Appraisers: Nathaniell Ascomb, Thomas Parthlo. John Griggs to administer oath.

Capt. Richard Hill (AA) to examine accounts of William Trevele who married widow of William Luffman.

6 October. Richard Sweatnam (TA) was granted administration on estate of Edward Hardgrave (TA). Appraisers: James Benson, James Derumple. George Robins to administer oath.

Richard Sweatnam was granted administration on estate of John Stevens (TA), as principle creditor. Appraisers: Thomas Brough, Robert Smith. George Robotham to administer oath.

Allice Parsons relict of Francis Parsons (TA) renounced administration, recommending William Young (TA).
13:255 Date: 12 January 1685. Witnesses: Thomas Vaughan, John Stephens, James Clarke, Simon Harris. William Young (TA) was granted administration. Henry Coursey, Jr. to administer oath.

Rebecca widow of Joseph Serjeant (DO) was granted administration on his estate. Appraisers: John Edwards, Richard Mallice. John Brooke (g) to administer oath.

John Purnell & Israell Skelton to appraise estate of John Evans. Miles Gibson to administer oath.

Miles Gibson to administer oath to John Bevin administrator of Morris Lane.

Mr. Heyden who married widow of Mr. Henry Ward
13:256 was granted administration on his estate. Date: 22 September 1685 Elk River.

9 October. Edward Day was granted administration dbn on estate of Capt. Thomas Walker (SO). Appraisers: William Brereton, Stephen Luffe. Col. William

Court Session: 1685

Stevens to administer oath.

10 October. Exhibited will of David
Johnson (TA), constituting widow
Bridgett executrix. Said Bridgett was
granted administration. Appraisers:
Peter Sydes, Symon Stevens. Henry
Coursey, Jr. to administer oath.

Abraham Blagg was granted administration
on estate of Hugh Abell (DO), as
principle creditor. Appraisers:
Benjamin Preistly, Phineas Blackwood.
Maj. Thomas Tailler to administer oath.

Exhibited will of William Hemsley (TA),
constituting widow Judith executrix.
Henry Coursey, Jr. to administer oath.

13:257   13 October. James Tyer (CH) was granted
administration on estate of Nathaniel
Veirin. Mentions: sloop at (N)
Underwood. Appraisers: Joseph Cornell,
Anthony Neale. Mr. Robert Doyne to
administer oath.

14 October. George Warner & James Wrath
to appraise estate of John Darnall, Esq.
in CE. Gideon Gundry to administer
oath.

15 October. Garratt Vansweringen &
Thomas Grunwin to appraise estate of
James Bodkin (SM).

26 October. Exhibited will of Abraham
Birkhead (AA), constituting Ann Birkhead
executrix. Col. Thomas Tailler to
administer oath.

27 October. William Dawkin (CV) was
granted administration on estates of
Thomas Cleverly & his wife Ann.
Appraisers: Isaac Baker, Thomas Purnell.
John Griggs to administer oath.

28 October. William Lawthorp (KE) was
granted administration on estates of
Hugh Jones & his wife Ann (KE).
Appraisers: Anthony Workman, Allen
Smith. Christopher Goodhand to
administer oath.

Exhibited will of Patrick Sullivant (KE), constituting widow Frances executrix. Appraisers: Henry Hosier, Hance Hanson. Charles Tilden to administer oath.

13:258 7 November. Exhibited will of Michael Cusick (AA), constituting Francis Stockett executor. Col. Thomas Tailler to prove said will. Said Stockett was granted administration. Appraisers: Woolfran Hunt, Capt. Richard Hill. Said Tailler to administer oath.

10 November. (N) Dobson widow of Samuel Dobson (p, SM) was granted administration on his estate. Appraisers: Samuel Cooksey, Robert Toate. Mr. Thomas Mudd to administer oath.

20 November. Benjamin Bond (AA) was granted administration on estate of William Bateman (AA). Appraisers: John Cross, John Rutter. Capt. Richard Hill to administer oath.

Petition of James Bisco (SM) for search for inventory of his father's estate.

23 November. Thomas Mudd (SM) was granted administration on estate of Edward Turner (SM). Appraisers: Robert Greene, Thomas Simpson. William Boarman (g) to administer oath.

John Llewellin (g, SMC) was granted administration on estate of John Day (SM). Appraisers: James Cullen, Thomas Grunwin.

25 November. Exhibited will of Thomas Harris (CH), constituting widow Mary executrix. Mr. Robert Doyne to administer oath.

William West (CH) was granted administration on estate of Robert Castleton (CH). Mr. Robert Doyne to administer oath.

Court Session: 1685

26 November. Richard Iles (CH) was granted administration on estate of John Probat (CH). Mr. William Barton (CH) to administer oath.

Petition of John Lynham (AA) for search for accounts of (N) Heathcoate in 1682.

Robert Cole (SM) administrator of (N) Healey exhibited accounts.

13:259 James Godsgrace was granted administration on estate of Alice Goldson (CV). Appraisers: James Dorsey, William Turner. Thomas Tasker (g) to administer oath.

Petition of Henry Leake (CV) for copy of inventory of Dr. Mollens.

George Greene (KE) was granted administration on estate of Henry Naish (KE). Appraisers: John Mills, John Bowler. Cornelius Comegys to administer oath.

Robert Smith was granted administration on estate of Samuel Grave. Henry Coursey, Jr. to administer oath.

Robert Smith was granted administration on estate of Henry Gill. Henry Coursey, Jr. to administer oath.

Exhibited will of Mathias Peters (TA), constituting widow Margarett Peters executrix. Mr. Henry Coursey, Jr. to administer oath.

Ursula Gould was granted administration on estate of Richard Gould. Henry Coursey, Jr. to administer oath.

Robert Smith was granted administration on estate of Humphry Davenport (TA). Mr Henry Coursey, Jr. to administer oath. See widow's renunciation.

Edward Tomlines who married widow of Nathaniel Reed (TA) was granted administration on his estate. Henry Coursey, Jr. to administer oath.

27 November. Exhibited will of William
Jones (TA). James Murphy to prove said
will. Fees to be charged to Ralph
Fishbourne (TA).

Exhibited inventory of Thomas Window
(TA), by appraisers John Wiseman &
William Kerby.

Exhibited will of Edmond Webb (TA),
constituting his sons Edmond & William
Webb executors. Said sons were granted
administration. Appraisers: John
Newman, John Power. James Murphy to
administer oath.

13:260 Charles Gost (TA) was granted
administration on estate of Robert
Wischeart (TA), as principle creditor.
Appraisers: Jasper Hall, Thomas Smith.
James Murphy (g) to administer oath.

Exhibited inventory of Thomas Furby, &
will of said Furby proved before Col.
Lloyd.

George Greene (KE) was granted
administration on estate of Henry Naish
(KE). Appraisers: John Mills, John
Bowles. Cornelius Comegys to administer
oath.

Exhibited inventory of John Munne (CH),
by appraisers Robert Middleton & Phillip
Hoskins.

30 November. Exhibited inventory of
Thomas Doxey, by appraisers Charles
Edgerton & Richard Atwood.

Exhibited will of Trustrum Thomas (TA),
constituting his widow Ann Thomas
executrix. George Robotham (g) to prove
said will.

1 December. Exhibited will of Francis
Catterton (TA), constituting his widow
Catherine Catterton executrix. Mr.
Edward Mann to prove said will.
Appraisers: Thomas Robbins, William
Wintershall.

Mr. Robert Carvile exhibited note to
Mr. William Taylard that he was going
across the Bay. John Reswick
13:261 to answer libel of Robert Clarke & to
give security to perform will of (N)
Combs.

2 December. Exhibited will of George
Carroll (TA). William Coursey (TA) was
granted administration on his estate, as
greatest legatee. Mr. Henry Coursey,
Jr. to administer oath.

Exhibited inventory of Thomas Goddard,
by appraisers Richard Roystone & Thomas
Vaughan. James Murphy (g, TA) exhibited
will of Thomas Goddard, proved by John
Whittington & Samuel Crayker. Edward
Hardgrave, the other witness, is since
dec'd.

Exhibited inventory of Michael Cusick,
by appraisers Richard Hill & Woolfran
Hunt. Exhibited will of said Cusick,
proved before Col. Thomas Taillor by
Humphry Jones, Elisabeth Proctor, &
Richard Kilbourne. Executor is Francis
Stockett.

Jacob Seth executor of John Hartly
exhibited accounts, proved before Col.
Henry Darnall on 11 November last.

Maj. Nicholas Sewall exhibited oath of
Joseph Edlo administrator of Thomas
Winans. Also exhibited oath of John
Wiseman & William Kerby, appraisers.

Edward Dorsey exhibited oath of Laurence
Draper administrator of Walter Smith.
13:262 Also exhibited inventory, by appraisers
William Foreman & Thomas Freborne.

John Griggs (CV) exhibited oath of
Elioner Loggins administratrix of John
Loggins. Also exhibited oath of John
Scott & James Macall, appraisers.

Said Griggs exhibited oath of Margarett
Dawkins executrix of Joseph Dawkins.

Court Session: 1685

Said Griggs exhibited oath of Susann
Edwards administratrix of Symon Edwards.
Also exhibited oath of Christopher Bands
& William Chittle, appraisers.

Said Griggs exhibited oath of Nathaniel
Dare & his wife Elisabeth executrix of
Thomas Binks. Also exhibited will,
proved by Robert Talbott, William
Herron, & John Davis.

Thomas Haddock (SM) petitioned for copy
of will of Thomas Doxey.

Mr. Phillip Lynes administrator of
William Smithson was granted
continuance.

Mr. Phillip Lynes was granted
administration on estate of George
Hodgson (CH), as principle creditor.
Appraisers: Henry Hardy, Michael
Ashford. James Tyer (CH) to administer
oath.

13:263 Phillip Lynes administrator of Edward
Tanshall (CH) was granted continuance.

Phillip Lynes administrator of Hugh
Mongomery was granted continuance.

Sheriff (SM) to summon Richard Thompson
& Robert Morehouse executors of James
Bourne to render accounts, per request
of Cuthbert Scott (g).

Richard Cloud (SM) was granted
administration on estate of John Butler
(SM). Appraisers: Justinian Gerrard,
Thomas Jourdain. Col. William Diggs to
administer oath.

Henry Darnall, Esq. & Clement Hill, Esq.
appointed Judges for Probate.
13:264 Date: 20 August 1685. William Taylard
appointed Register.

Summons to Richard Thompson (SM) &
Robert Morehouse (SM) executors of Dr.
James Bourne to render accounts, per
request of Mr. Cuthbert Scott (SM).

Court Session: 1685

Richard Cloud (SM) was granted
administration on estate of John Butler
(SM). Appraisers: Justinian Gerrard,
Thomas Jourdaine. Col. William Diggs
to administer oath.

4 December. Cornelius Comegys (KE) was
granted administration on estate of
Isabella Broadrib (KE). Appraisers:
Edward Fry, Thomas Piner. Charles
Tilden to administer oath.

Michael Miller (g, KE) for Robert Herne
was granted administration on estate of
John Lawrence (mariner, later commander
of ship Endeavor, London) on behalf of
widow Abigall. There are no children.
Appraisers: Michael Miller, Hance
Hansen. Charles Tilden to administer
oath.

13:265 8 December. Jane King was granted
administration on estate of Edward
Fletcher (CV), as principle creditor.
Appraisers: John Tawmen, Thomas Tinsily.
George Lingan (CV) to administer oath.

9 December. Mr. James Cullen note to
Mr. Taylard exhibited:
• will of his father, constituting his
  mother & himself as executors. Will
  was dated 6 November last.
  Appraisers: Capt. Thomas Courtney,
  Thomas Grunwin.
• James Pattison (g) as guardian of
  Katherine Ward daughter of Edward
  Ward (SM, dec'd) was granted
  administration on his estate.
  Appraisers: Gilbert Turberfeild,
  Thomas Spinke. Garrett Vansweringen
  (g) to administer oath.
• said Pattison was granted
  administration on estate of James
  Watkins (SM). Appraisers: Gilbert
  Turberfeild, Thomas Spinke. Garrett
  Vansweringen (g) to administer oath.
Memorandum: on 6 November last,
exhibited will of Mark Cordea (SM).
Mr. James Pattison to prove said will.
Hester Cordea & James Cullins executors
were granted administration. Said
Pattison to administer oath.

Page 133

Memorandum: on 6 November 1685, said
Pattison was granted administration on
estates of said Ward & said Watkins.

13:266 14 December. Thomas Gerrard (SM) was
granted administration on estate of
Timothy Richardson (SM), as principle
creditor. Appraisers: Robert Toate,
John Wathen. Mr. Joseph Pile to
administer oath.

17 December. Christian Peterson widow
of Andrew Peterson (CE) was granted
administration on his estate.
Appraisers: William Ward, Henry
Eldersly. Nathaniel Garrett (CE) to
administer oath.

19 December. George Bussey (CV) was
granted administration on estate of John
King (CV), as chief creditor.
Appraisers: Francis Buckstone, William
Williams. Francis Hutchins to
administer oath.

Petition by Ann Doxey (SM) for a copy of
her husband's will.

William Treveale who married Mary
Luffman relict & executrix of William
Luffman (AA) exhibited accounts, proved
before Mr. Richard Hill.

21 December. William Elliott (mariner,
Dartmouth, ENG) exhibited that William
Inyce (merchant, Dartmouth) came to
Province in 1684. Said Inyce stayed in
Province & died last summer, making a
will constituting William Stevens
executor. Said Stevens has renounced
executorship.
13:267 Indenture: William Stevens executor of
William Inyce consigned to William
Elliott (mariner, Dartmouth) rights to
estate of said Inyce. Witnesses: John
Woodward, William Mannewry. Said
Elliott was granted administration.
Appraisers: George Robbins, James
Benson. Mr. William Combes to
administer oath.

Court Session: 1685

13:268   Edmond Stowe & his wife Jane were
granted renewal of administration on
estate of Edward Fletcher.

Exhibited will of John Dring (AA),
constituting Gabriel Parrott (AA)
executor. Richard Beard (AA) to prove
said will. Said Parrott cannot travel &
was granted administration. Appraisers:
Walter Phelps, Benjamine Williams. Said
Beard to administer oath.

William Wintersell who married widow of
Henry Dale (TA) was granted
administration on his estate.
Appraisers: Samuel Abbott, Joshua
Atkins. Mr. William Combes to
administer oath.

22 December. Richard Iles exhibited
that Maj. John Wheeler (CH) was granted
administration on estate of John Probart
(CH). Appraisers: Robert Middleton,
Phillip Hoskins. Mr. Ignatius Causeen
to administer oath.

Petition by Richard Johns for copy of
will of Thomas Binks. Delivered to
William Holland.

24 December. George Lingan petitioned
for appraisers for estate of Phillip
Jones: John Moffett, Gawen Hambleton.
William Lyles (CV) is executor.

13:269   Alice Smith (CV) widow of Thomas Smith
exhibited his will, constituting her
executrix. Said Alice was granted
administration. George Lingan to prove
said will & administer oath.

Gilbert Deavour (CV) who married widow
of John Johnson (CV) was granted
administration his estate. Appraisers:
Edward Harlick, John Leech. Francis
Hutchins to administer oath.

Exhibited inventory of Paul Bensy, by
appraisers John Whipps & William Lyle.

26 December. Mr. Robert Doyne (CH) to
prove will of Richard Henson (SM).

Page 135

Court Session: 1685

Exhibited inventory of Richard Garforth,
by appraisers Francis Harrison & John
Davis.

29 December. James Round (g, SO) was
granted administration on estate of John
Clarke (SO), as principle creditor.
Appraisers: John Emmett, Abraham Emmett.
Col. William Stevens to administer
oath.

William Combes (g, TA) to prove will of
William Richee (TA). Fees to be charged
to Alice Richee widow.

Exhibited will of William Mitchell (AA),
constituting his widow executrix.
George Yate (g) to prove said will, by
oaths of witnesses Henry Peirpoint &
Thomas Bowlas.

13:270 Exhibited will of Francis Watts (AA),
constituting his widow Sarah executrix.
Maj. Nicholas Gassaway to prove said
will. Said Sarah was granted
administration. Appraisers: Richard
Tydings, Robert Ward. Said Gassaway to
administer oath.

Exhibited will of William Welch (CE),
constituting Edward Beck, Walter Meck,
John Phillis, & Phillip Canadae
executors. Said executors were granted
administration. Appraisers: John
Jordaine, Robert Randall. Mr. Richard
Pullen to administer oath.

Col. William Stevens exhibited:
• will of John Wallas (Pocomoke River,
  late of IRE). Capt. David Browne
  to prove said will. Executor is
  dec'd; widow & executrix survives.
  Jane Wallis widow was granted
  administration. Appraisers: John
  Browne, William Lawes.
• Mr. James Round was granted
  administration on estate of John
  Clarke, a poor man who drowned
  leaving neither wife nor children,
  as principle creditor. Appraisers:
  John Emmett, Abraham Emmett.
Date: 17 November 1685 Pocomoke.

Page 136

Court Session: 1685

Exhibited will of Mark Cordea, proved by
Anthony Underwood, Garrat Vansweringen,
& Jane Barber before Mr. James
Pattison.

13:271 Said Pattison exhibited oath of James
Cullen & Hester Cordea executors. Also
exhibited oath of Thomas Courtney &
Thomas Grunwin, appraisers.

Mr. James Pattison exhibited oath of
Ann Doxey, Thomas Haddock, & Thomas Lees
executors of Thomas Doxey. Also
exhibited oath of Charles Edgerton &
Richard Attwood, appraisers.

30 December. Exhibited inventory of
Joseph Dawkins (CV), by appraisers
Christopher Bevin & Francis Higham.

Sheriff (SM) exhibited citation to
Richard Thompson & Robert Moorehouse
executors of Dr. James Bourne. They
are not found in his bailiwick.

2 January. Exhibited inventory of James
Magruther (CV), by appraisers Ninian
Beale & Thomas Ellis. Also exhibited
was bond; securities: James Magruther,
Ninian Beale.

Exhibited will of Thomas Trueman, Esq.
(CV), constituting widow Mary Trueman &
cousin Mary Trueman executrices (for
their parts), Thomas Greenfield on
behalf of Thomas Trueman Greenfield
executor & on behalf of his cousin
Elisabeth Trueman executrix (for their
parts). Mr. Thomas Brooke to prove
said will. Said executors were granted
administration. Appraisers: Mr.
Richard Marsham, Capt. Ninean Beale.
Said Brooke to administer oath.

13:272 Peter Oard (SM) exhibited that he is
security to Hannah Browne relict &
administratrix of Robert Browne (SM).
Other security is Timothy Richardson
since dec'd. Said Hannah has married
James Hall & they have wasted the
estate. Mentions: wife & children of
said Oard. Signed: Jos. Pile, Thomas
Mudd, Ja. Bowling, William Boarman, Jr.

Page 137

Court Session: 1685

Sheriff (SM) to summon said James Hall & his wife Sarah.

13:273　Miles Gibson (BA) was granted administration on estate of John Yeo (BA), whose wife is also dec'd & there are no children, as greatest creditor. Appraisers: Thomas Hedge, James Phillips. Mr. Edward Beedle to administer oath.

Marke Richardson (BA) guardian to George Uty petitioned that his uncle Nathaniel Utie (BA) died seized of considerable estate, leaving only 1 child John Utie who is since dec'd. Said George is next heir. Said estate is in possession of Capt. Henry Johnson who married widow & administratrix of said Nathaniel who refused to give my guardian my 2/3rds of "Persutia Island".

13:274　Mentions: Elisabeth wife Henry Johnson, said George (near 17 years) is son-in-law of said Richardson. Date: 19 November 1685. Sheriff (BA) to summon Henry Johnson & his wife Elisabeth.

Hon. William Diggs, Esq. exhibited oath of Justinian Gerrard & Thomas Jordaine, appraisers of John Butler. Also exhibited bond of Richard Cloud administrator. Securities: Justinian Gerrard, Thomas Jourdaine.

Ralfe Foster & John Hilton executors of (N) Maddox petitioned for copy of inventory of said estate. Delivered to Mr. Makin.

13:275　Exhibited inventory of John Darnall, Esq., by appraisers Mr. Henry Brent & Raphael Haywood.

5 January. John Skipper (SM) was granted administration on estate of John Snowden (SM). Appraisers: John Bullock, John Paler. Mr. Richard Gardiner to administer oath.

John Shanks (SM) exhibited will of George Yeeden (SM), constituting Elisabeth Shanks & said John executors.

Mr. Richard Gardiner to prove said will. Said Elisabeth & John were granted administration. Appraisers: MM Thomas Warren, Justinian Tennison. Said Gardiner to administer oath.

9 January. Exhibited will of Thomas Hawker (CE), constituting Dorothy Hawker executrix. Mr. Edward Inglish to prove said will. Said Dorothy was granted administration. Appraisers: Richard Pullen, George Higginbotham. Said Inglish to administer oath.

Mr. Ignatius Causeen exhibited oath of Maj. John Wheeler administrator of John Probart (CH), sworn 30 December 1685. **13:276** Securities: Robert Middleton, Thomas Wheeler.

11 January. Ann Hopewell widow of Francis Hopewell (CV) was granted administration on his estate. Appraisers: William Kerby, John Wiseman. Maj. Nicholas Sewall to administer oath.

22 January. Exhibited will of Thomas Gibson (CH), constituting George Newman & John Goouch executors. Mr. John Court to prove said will. Said Newman & John Crouch were granted administration. Appraisers: Anthony Neale, Rando. Brandt. Said Court to administer oath.

Ruth Gale widow of Edward Gale (CH) exhibited his will, constituting her executrix. Ignatius Causeen to prove said will. Said Ruth was granted administration. Said Causeen to administer oath.

Henry Darnall petitioned that William Marshall (CV) last Summer fraudulently obtained LoA on estate of William Jenkins (CV), which belongs to the bearer Oliver Richards. Date: 21 January 1685. Sheriff (CV) to summon said Marshall.

13:277 Henry Darnall exhibited accounts of John Powell & his wife Julian administratrix of Thomas Leedgett. Discharge was granted.

29 January. Exhibited will of Henry Kent (CV), constituting John Kent, Francis Freeman, Francis Mauldin, & George Young executors. Said executors were granted administration. Appraisers: James Macall, John Scott. Basill Waring to administer oath.

30 January. Capt. Richard Ladd (CV) exhibited will of Francis Swinfen (CV), constituting him executor. John Creycroft or Francis Hutchins to administer oath to said Ladd. Mr. Francis Collyer to administer oath to appraisers.

1 February. Gabriel Parrott (merchant, AA) exhibited renunciation of Dorothy Smith widow & administratrix of John Smith (p, AA), desiring said Parrott as administrator.

13:278 Date: 4 January 1685. Witnesses: Peter Parrott, Nicholas Nicholson. Said Gabriel was granted administration. Appraisers: Peter Barnett, Nicholas Nicholson. Mr. Richard Beard to administer oath.

Exhibited will of Thomas Smith (CV), proved before George Lingan (g, CV). "She being a Quaker would not swear to LoA." Date: 18 January 1685.

George Lingan exhibited oath of Susannah Bussy (CV) relict of Paul Bussy (CV), sworn 17 December 1685.

Paul Lingan exhibited oath of John Moffitt & Gawen Hambleton, appraisers of Phillip Jones (CV), sworn last December 1685. Also exhibited inventory.

13:279 Also exhibited bond of Susannah Bussey administratrix of Paul Bussey. Securities: William Selby, Richard Bowen.

Mr. George Lingan exhibited oath of Thomas Tamen & Thomas Tinsley,

Court Session: 1685

appraisers of Edward Fletcher, sworn 18
January 1685. Also exhibited inventory.
Also exhibited bond of Edmond Stow
administrator. Securities: William
Head, Richard Jackson.

2 February. Mr. Robert Carvile for
Henry Thomas (eldest son & heir of
Robert Thomas (SM)) vs. estate of his
father. Caveat exhibited.

Exhibited inventory of Thomas Binks
(CV), by appraisers John Hance & James
Cranford.

13:280 Exhibited will of George Yeeden, proved
before Richard Gardiner (g, SM). Also
exhibited oath of Thomas Warren &
Justinian Tennison, appraisers sworn 9
January 1685. Also exhibited oath of
Abigall Shanks & John Shanks executors,
sworn same day.

Richard Gardiner exhibited oath of John
Bullock & John Paten, appraisers of John
Snowden (SM), sworn 5 January 1685.
Also exhibited oath of John Skipper
administrator sworn same day.

Exhibited inventory of George Yeeden
(SM), by appraisers Thomas Warring &
Justinian Tennison.

John Skipper (SM) administrator of John
Snowden exhibited inventory, by
appraisers John Paten & John Bullock.
Also exhibited bond of said Skippers:
securities: John Shanks, John Paten.

4 February. Exhibited will of Maj.
Thomas Trueman (CV), proved before Col.
Henry Darnall.

13:281 Oliver Richards vs. William Marshall
Sheriff (CV) served summons. Said
Marshall did not appear.

5 February. Robert Carvile procurator
for said Richards vs. said Marshall.
Summons re-issued.

Sheriff (CV) to summon Susannah Keene to render accounts on estate of John Hunt (CV), at request of John Godscross (CV).

Sheriff (SO) to summon Arnold Elzy to render accounts on estate of Charles Ballard.

Robert Clarke vs. John Reswick & ux. Ruling: cause agreed.

13:282 Samuell Wheeler vs. Kenelme Cheseldyne procurator for Ralph Fishbourne executor of (N) Nash. Answer exhibited. Procurator for said Wheeler to exhibit his libel.

Sheriff (SM) to summon Nehemiah Blackiston attorney of Gerard Sly (g) administrator for Richard Chilman (SM) to answer exceptions by creditors.

Sheriff (SM) to summon John Addison attorney for Richard Thompson executor of Dr. James Bourne (SM) to render accounts.

6 February. Elisabeth Done (SM) widow exhibited will of Obadiah Donn (p, SM), constituting her executrix. Mr. Joshua Doyne to prove said will. Said Elisabeth was granted administration. Appraisers: Thomas Mattenly, Thomas Carvile. Said Doyen to administer oath.

13:283 William Richards (CV) petitioned that Lavina relict of was granted administration on his estate, which she did not fully administer. Said petitioner has married said Lavina, who is now dec'd. Said Richards was granted administration dbn. Appraisers: Timothy Gunter, Marke Smith. John Craycroft (CV) to administer oath.

8 February. Mrs. Barbera Rousby (CV) widow of John Rousby exhibited his will, constituting her executrix. Garrett Vansweringen (g) to prove said will & administer oath. Said will exhibited, proved.

Court Session: 1685

13:284 17 February. Mr. Robert Carvile exhibited letter of Mr. Hance Hanson. Sir Dr. John Porter (merchant, Bristoll) died in October 1684 at sea, coming to the Province. He had here at Chester River a plantation, with servants, stock, etc. Said Hanson has received orders from his wife in ENG. Said wife has miscarried. Mentions: children. Date: 20 January 1685 at Chester (KE). Said Hanson was granted administration on his estate.
13:285 Appraisers: Charles Hynson, William Harris. Mr. John Hynson (KE) to administer oath.

William Legg (KE) was granted administration on estate of John Dobbs (KE), as nearest of kin by marriage. Appraisers: Henry Williams, Thomas Davis. William Lawrence to administer oath.

William Thomas (KE) was granted administration on estate of James Lisson (KE), as principle creditor. Appraisers: John Beale, Henry Hozier. Daniel Norris (g) to administer oath.

20 February. Exhibited inventory of Marke Cordea (g, SM), by appraisers Thomas Courtney & Thomas Grunwin.

13:286 22 February. Christopher Foster (AA) exhibited will of Jone Hunter, constituting him executor. Richard Beard (g, AA) to prove said will. Said Foster was granted administration. Appraisers: Robert Ward, John Grey. Said Beard to administer oath.

Mr. Ignatius Causeen (CH) exhibited will of Edward Gaile, proved by John Lemaire, Thomas Lewis, & Elisabeth Goodwell. Also exhibited that Ruth Gaile refused to swear. Date: 1 February 1685.

Cato MackDaniel (CV) was granted administration on estate of Hugh Hanlen (CV), as nearest of kin. Appraisers: Mr. Thomas Greenfeild, William Selby.

Mr. Richard Marsham to administer oath.

23 February. Exhibited inventory of
John Fieckleton (KE), by appraisers John
Dobbs & John Butcher.

13:287   Sarah Jones widow of Thomas Jones (KE)
exhibited his will, constituting her
executrix. Cornelius Comegys to prove
said will. Said Sarah was granted
administration. Appraisers: John
Bowles, William True. Said Comegys to
administer oath.

24 February. Cuthbert Scott vs. John
Addison attorney for Richard Thompson
executor of James Bourne. Continuance
was granted.

George Uty heir to Nathaniell Uty vs.
Henry Johnson & wife administratrix of
said Uty. Sheriff (BA) issued summons.
Continuance was granted.

Sheriff (SM) exhibited summons to James
Hall & his wife Hannah administratrix of
Robert Browne. They did not appear.
Continuance was granted.

13:288   Oliver Richards vs. William Marshall
administrator of William Jenkins.
Attorney for both parties appeared.
Sheriff (CV) exhibited that said
Marshall could not be found.
Continuance was granted.

Michaell Taney (sheriff, CV) exhibited
summons to Susannah Keene administratrix
of (N) Hunt.

Sheriff (SO) exhibited summons to Arnold
Elzy (SO) administrator of Charles
Ballard.

Creditors of Richard Chilman vs.
Nehemiah Blackistone attorney for
Gerrard Slye administrator of said
Chilman. Sheriff (SM) returned "non
invent". Inventory due last Tuesday in
April.

Ralph Fishbourne executor of (N) Naish
vs. Samuell Wheeler. Continuance was
granted.

Samuel Wheeler vs. Ralph Fishbourne.
Continuance was granted.

Robert Davis (SM) who married Elisabeth
relict & administratrix of Hugh Baker
(SM) exhibited accounts. Estate is
overpaid. Discharge was granted.

Henry Hozier, Jr. son of Henry Hozier
(KE) exhibited his will, constituting
him executor. Cornelius Comegys (g) to
prove said will. Said Henry, Jr. was
granted administration. Appraisers:
Michaell Miller, John Bowles. Said
Comegys to administer oath.

13:289 Michaell Miller for John Baldwin (KE)
vs. estate of John Rycroft (CE). Caveat
exhibited.

Michaell Miller (KE) administrator of
James Bowly exhibited that one of the
appraisers was disposed of body.
Continuance was granted.

25 February. Ann Hargis (CH) widow of
William Hargis (CH) exhibited his will.
William Barton (g) to prove said will.
Said Ann was granted administration.
Appraisers: John Court, William
Hungerford. Said Barton to administer
oath.

Exhibited will of Thomas Price (TA),
proved before Mr. Edward Mann.

Exhibited inventory of Edward Ward (SM),
by appraisers Gilbert Turberfeild &
Thomas Spinke.

Exhibited inventory of James Watkins
(SM), by appraisers Gilbert Turberfeild
& Thomas Spinke.

13:290 Edict: that administrators have to show
sufficient grounds to administer an
estate.

Court Session: 1685

Richard Beard (AA) administrator of
Daniell Taylor was granted continuance.

Thomas Dixon (CH) who married relict &
administratrix of John Gwinn (CH)
exhibited accounts. Discharge was
granted.

Mr. Joseph Pile (g, SM) to prove will
of John Clarke (SM).

Mr. Robert Carvile procurator for
Oliver Richards vs. Mr. George Parker
for William Marshall. Libel exhibited.
Mentions: said Richards (p, CV) married
Ann (eldest sister of William Jenkins
(p, CV, dec'd);

13:291 Mary (another sister); Dorkis (another
sister); Elisabeth Jenkins (another
sister); said William died June last;
petitioner was then sick; said Marshall
is principle creditor & has embezzled
the estate; 100 a.;

13:292 4 sisters of said Jenkins. Ruling:
Marshall to pay Richards.

26 February. Arnold Elzey administrator
of Charles Ballard (SO) exhibited
accounts. Ruling: Col. William Stevens
to prove said accounts.

13:293 Cornelius Comegys (g, KE) for his son
William Comegys who married Elisabeth
Tiler sister of George Reed (d, SM) was
granted administration on his estate.
Appraisers: John Addison, Henry
Lawrence. Daniel Norris (KE) to
administer oath.

Ralph Fishbourne vs. Kenelme Cheseldyn
procurator for Samuel Wheeler. Said
Cheseldyn to exhibit answer to libel.

27 February. Jane Jones widow of
Richard Jones (CH) exhibited his will,
constituting her executrix. John Stone
(CH) to prove said will. Said Jane was
granted administration. Appraisers:
Thomas Craxton, Robert Benson. Said
Stone to administer oath.

Court Session: 1685

Ann Graves widow of William Graves (CV) exhibited his will, constituting her executrix. Col. Henry Jowles to prove said will. Said Ann was granted administration. Appraisers: John Dawsett, Jonathon Goosey. Said Jowles to administer oath.

Christopher Baynes (CV) was granted administration on estate of Richard Crackbourne (CV), as principle creditor. Appraisers: Francis Higham, John Bevene. Mr. Roger Brooke to administer oath.

13:294 Richard Beard (AA) administrator of Richard Beard exhibited accounts. Estate is overpaid. Discharge was granted.

John Heard (SM) administrator of Anthony Loughlin exhibited accounts.

Hannah Hungerford (DO) relict of John Hungerford (DO) exhibited that William Traverse, who was to administer oath, was out of the country. Appraisers: William Robinson, Richard Meekins. John Woodward (g) to administer oath.

George Ashman (BA) who married Elisabeth Cromwell exhibited will of William Ball (BA), constituting her executrix. Said Elisabeth was granted administration. Appraisers: James Jackson, William Slade. John Boring (g) to administer oath.

Exhibited inventory of John Offly (TA), by appraisers Robert Smith & William Sparke.

13:295 Mr. Joseph Pile (SM) exhibited oath of Thomas Gerrard administrator of Timothy Richardson. Securities: Joshua Doyne, Robert Toate. Also exhibited was oath of Robert Toate & John Hathan, appraisers.

Exhibited inventory of Joseph Serjeant (DO), by appraisers John Edwards & Richard Williams.

Court Session: 1685

Mr. David Browne (SO) exhibited oath of
Jane Wallace executrix of John Wallace,
Jr. (SO), sworn 19 January 1685. Also
exhibited will, proved by Robert King &
Aiton Rosse. Also exhibited oath of
John Browne & John Law, appraisers sworn
22 January 1685.

13:296 Francis Hutchins (g, CV) exhibited oath
of Gilbert Deavour administrator of John
Johnson. Securities: Richard Freeman,
Joseph Baker. Also exhibited oath of
Edward Hurlick & John Leech, appraisers.

Exhibited inventory of James Carrs (CV),
by appraisers John Chittham & William
Jones.

John Dossett & Jonathon Goosey executors
of Thomas Alwell exhibited accounts.

Exhibited bond of Thomas Wilson
administrator of James Carrs.
Securities: William Jones, Lawrence
Rouland.

Exhibited bond of James Godsgrace
administrator of Alice Goldson.
Securities: Samuell Goosey, William
Marks. Thomas Tasker (g, CV) exhibited
oath of William Turner & James Dassey,
appraisers of Alice Goldson.

2 March. William Hemsely (TA) exhibited
will of Robert Noble (TA), constituting
his widow Cornelia executrix, which is
long since proved. Said William Hemsley
& his wife Cornelia (widow of said
Noble) were granted administration.
Henry Coursey (g) to administer oath.

13:297 Edward Sweatnam (KE) exhibited that
Walter Jenkins (KE) made a will. Said
will was never exhibited & remains in
hands of Christopher Goodhand & his wife
Hannah. Sheriff (KE) to summon said
Christopher & Hannah.

Edward Sweatnam administrator of Edward
Rogers exhibited additional accounts.

Page 148

Court Session: 1685

SM Court   Newtowne, 5 January 1685.
Administrators & executors are allowed a
rate of 10%. Signed: John Blomfeild
(clerk).

George Robotham (g, TA) to prove will of
Robert Lambden. Fees to Ralph
Fishbourne.

Exhibited inventory of George Sealy
(DO), by appraisers John Davis & John
Prouse. Also exhibited oath of said
appraisers, sworn by Mr. John Alford
(DO).
13:298 Also exhibited will, proved before said
Alford.

Mr. William Combes (TA) exhibited oath
of Samuell Abbott & Joshua Atkins,
appraisers of Henry Dale (TA), sworn 26
December 1685. Also exhibited oath of
William Wintersell administrator, sworn
same day. Also exhibited inventory.

James Murphy (TA) exhibited will of
James Hall (TA), proved. Also exhibited
inventory, by appraisers Hugh Sherwood &
John Power.

Mr. George Robotham exhibited will of
James Earle (TA), proved before him.
Also exhibited oath of relict Rhoda
Earle executrix. Also exhibited oath of
Robert Bryan & John Earle, appraisers.
Also exhibited inventory.

13:299 Mr. George Parker (g, CV) exhibited
will of Henry Bennitt (AA), constituting
Col. Thomas Taillor executor. Maj.
Thomas Francis (g) to prove said will.
Said Taillor renounced administration on
25 February 1685, recommending Abraham
Clarke (p, CV). Mentions: George
Bennett brother of dec'd & father of
Henry Bennett (nephew of dec'd).
Witnesses: Robert Doyne, George Parker.
Said Clarke was granted administration.
Appraisers: Walter Carr, Charles Bevine.
Said Francis to administer oath.

13:300 Maj. Nicholas Sewall exhibited oath of
Richard Keene & Andrew Abbington,

Court Session: 1685

appraisers of John Rousby (CV).

Francis Chumley who married Barbara
relict & executrix of Charles Cullis
exhibited accounts.

Col. William Burges (AA) to examine
accounts of estate of John Welsh & to
administer oath to James Ellis & his
wife Mary executrix.

Joane Daniel (DO) widow of Thomas Daniel
exhibited his will, constituting her
executrix. Mr. Charles Hutchins to
prove said will. Said Joan was granted
administration. Appraisers: Thomas
Hicks, Thomas Harper. Said Hutchins to
administer oath.

Maj. Peter Sayer (g, TA) for Thomas
Emmerson (TA) was granted administration
on estate of William Cooke (TA), as
principle creditor. Appraisers: John
Aldridge, John Davis. George Robbins
(g) to administer oath.

13:301 Henry Coursey, Jr. (g, TA) to examine
accounts of estate of Robert Noble & to
administer oath to William Hemsley & his
wife Cornelia.

4 March. Mr. Henry Coursey to summon
William Hemsley & his wife Cornelia
administratrix of Charles Vaughan to
render accounts.

Clare Gary (DO) widow of Stephen Gary
exhibited his will, constituting her
executrix. Maj. Thomas Taylor to prove
said will. Said Clare was granted
administration. Appraisers: Edward
Pindar, Benjamin Priestly. Said Taylor
to administer oath.

Edmond Howard (SO) exhibited oath of
John Mackitt (alias John Mackitrick)
administrator of Henry Cole.
Securities: Samuel Cooper, William
Manlove. Also exhibited oath of
Jonathon Seaward & John Walton,
appraisers.

Court Session: 1685

Maj. John Wicke (g, KE) who married
Anna executrix of Benjamin Randall
exhibited that she is incapable of
travelling to Office to render accounts.
Col. Henry Coursey to examine accounts
& administer oath.

13:302 Jonathon Seaward & John Walton
appraisers of Henry Cole (SO) exhibited
his inventory.

Exhibited will of William Jones (TA),
proved before James Murphy (g).

Mary Harman widow of Henry Harman (DO)
was granted administration on his
estate. Appraisers: John Mackel, Jacob
Lookeman. Maj. Thomas Taylor (DO) to
administer oath.

Col. William Burges administrator of
Nicholas Painter was granted
continuance.

Col. William Burges administrator of
John Barker was granted continuance.

Leonard Greene (SM) administrator of
John Hawknett exhibited accounts.

Exhibited additional inventory of John
Darnall, Esq., by appraisers John Warner
& John Welsh.

Exhibited will of John Wheeler (AA),
proved before Col. William Burges.
Said Burges exhibited oath of Henry
Hanslap administrator. Securities:
Richard Beard, John Belt, Jr.
13:303 Also exhibited inventory, by appraisers
Murrain Duvall & Walter Phillips.

5 March. Edward Mann (g, TA) to prove
will of Thomas Green (TA).

Francis Hutchins (g, CV) exhibited oath
of Capt. Richard Ladd executor of
Francis Swinfen. Also exhibited was
will, proved.

Exhibited bond of John Lynand
administrator of (N) Heathcoate.

Court Session: 1685

7 March. Exhibited will of Stephen
Kaddy (KE), constituting relict
Katherine Kaddy & his daughter Rebeccah
executrices. Cornelius Comegys to prove
said will. Said Katherine has renounced
administration. Said Rebeccah is now
wife of Henry Hozier (KE). Said Henry &
Rebeccah were granted administration.
Appraisers: Michaell Miller, John
Bowles. Said Comegys to administer
oath.

13:304 John Kerke (SO) was granted
administration on estate of Edward
Furlong (SO), as principle creditor.
Appraisers: Thomas Jones, William Noble.
Col. William Stevens to administer
oath.

Henry Johnson petitioned that he & his
wife were unable to travel. Mary Beedle
was to take the accounts. Date: 16
February 1685. BA Court to organize
accounts of estate of Col. Nathaniell
Uty.

13:305 Col. William Stevens for Sarah White
executrix of John White (SO) was granted
continuous.

Mr. Robert Carvile petitioned that on
10 October 1685 before William Wightman
(Notary in London) appeared Mrs.
Elisabeth Scott widow of Samuell Scott
(citizen, haberdasher, London) & gave a
PoA to said Carvile to recover from MM
Thomas Hedge & Samuel Hedge (merchants,
MD).
13:306 Witnesses: Robert Lee, William Hill.
Said Carvile was granted administration.

11 March. Sarah Reynold (CV) exhibited
will of Henry West (CV), constituting
her executrix. Basil Wareing (g, CV) to
prove said will. Appraisers: John
Sunderland, Marke Clarke. Said Wareing
to administer oath.

13 March. Col. Vincent Lowe (TA) to
prove will of Col. Philemon Lloyd by
oath of Thomas Vaughan (TA).

Court Session: 1685

13:307 Mr. Edward Mann (TA) to prove will of
Thomas Long (TA). Mr. Edward Mann (TA)
to prove will of Mary Long (TA).

Ann Tiley widow of John Tiley (TA) &
widow of John Humberstone exhibited his
will. Edward Mann to prove said will.
Said Ann was granted administration on
said Humberstone. Appraisers: (N)
Winters, Richard White.

George Watts (TA) was granted
administration on estate of Mary Long
(TA). Said Watts is a legatee in her
will. Appraisers: William Winters,
Richard White. Mr. Edward Mann to
administer oath.

15 March. (N) Barkes widow of John
Barkes (TA) was granted administration
on his estate. Appraisers: John
Stanely, Thomas Robins. Mr. Edward
Mann to administer oath.

18 March. William Yorke & James Collyer
administrators of Capt. John Waterton
(BA) were granted continuance.

13:308 Capt. Richard Hill (AA) exhibited that
John Cross (AA) & John Rutter (AA) were
appraisers of estate of William Bateman,
& said Rutter is now dec'd. Said Hill
for Benjamin Bond administrator of said
Bateman petitioned for new appraisers:
Jacob Harnes, Lawrence Draper.

Exhibited inventory of Robert Graham
(SM), by appraisers John Adison & Robert
Mason.

Exhibited will of William Richee (TA),
proved before Mr. William Combes (TA).

Mr. Combes (TA) exhibited oath of George
Robins & James Benson, appraisers of
William Inyce (TA), sworn 1 February
1685. Also exhibited oath of William
Elliott administrator, sworn same day.
Security: William Stevens, William
Sharpe.

Mr. Joseph Hopkins (CE) exhibited oath of Ebenezar Blackistone administrator of John White.

3:309 20 March. Mr. William Combes exhibited oath of Samuel Abbott & Joshua Atkins, appraisers of Henry Dale (TA). Also exhibited was oath of William Wintersell administrator.

Exhibited bond of Ebenezar Blackistone administrator of John White. Securities: Michael Skidemore, Nathaniel Howell.

Mr. George Warner (CE) exhibited oath of John Hardin & his wife Elisabeth executrix of Morgan Penry. Also exhibited oath of John Brisco & Samuel Wheatherly, appraisers of said Morgan Penroy. Also exhibited will of said Penroy, proved by Samuel Wetherill, Joan Wetherill, & William Everd.

Daniel Longman (AA) exhibited will of Richard Arnold (AA), constituting his widow Martha executrix. Said Longman married said Martha, who is now also dec'd. Said Longman was granted administration. Appraisers: Nicholas Nicholson, Samuel Garland. Capt. Thomas Francis (g, AA) to administer oath.

13:310 22 March. Priscilla Taylor widow of John Taylor (DO) was granted administration on his estate. Appraisers: John Pollard, Phineas Blackwood. Maj. Thomas Taylor or Dr. Jacob Lookrman to administer oath. Said Priscilla also entered a caveat against said estate.

Exhibited inventory of Alice Goulson (CV), by appraisers William Turner & James Dossey.

George Lingan (CV) exhibited oath of MM Francis Maudlin & Francis Freeman, appraisers of Mr. Thomas Sterling (CV), sworn 15 August 1685. Also exhibited inventory.

13:311   Mr. Basill Wareing exhibited oath of
Sarah Renolds executrix of Henry West
(CV), sworn 15 March 1685. Also
exhibited oath of John Sunderland &
Marke Clare, appraisers, sworn same day.
Also exhibited will, proved before said
Wareing.

Mr. Basill Wareing exhibited oath of
John Kent, Francis Freeman, Francis
Mauldin, & John Young executors of Henry
Kent (CV), sworn 18 March 1685. Also
exhibited oath of James Macall & John
Scott, appraisers sworn same day. Also
exhibited will, proved before said
Wareing.

Elisabeth Forth widow of John Forth (AA)
was granted administration on his
estate. Capt. Richard Hill to
administer oath.

24 March. Exhibited inventory of
Nicholas Painter (CV).

Court Session: 1686

13:312   25 March. Col. Henry Jowles (CV)
exhibited oath of Ann relict & executrix
of William Graves (CV). Also exhibited
oath of John Dossett & Jonathon Goosey,
appraisers. Also exhibited will, proved
before said Jowles.

26 March. Col. Thomas Tailler (AA)
exhibited will of Abraham Birkhead,
proved.

29 March. Col. Henry Jowles (CV)
exhibited oath of Isaac Baker & Thomas
Purnell, appraisers of Thomas & Ann
Cleverly (CV). Also exhibited bond of
William Dunkin administrator. Security:
Henry Horton, Samuel Preston. Sheriff
(CV) to summon said Dunkin to render
inventory & to summon said Horton & said
Preston.

Sheriff (CV) to summon Capt. Samuell
Bourne (CV) administrator of Dorothy
King.

13:313   Exhibited bond of William Coursey
administrator of Henry Beedle.
Security: Trustrum Thomas.

Exhibited bond of Maj. William Coursey
administrator of Sophia Beedle.
Security: Trustrum Thomas.

Exhibited inventory of Henry Kent (CV),
by appraisers James Macall & John Scott.

30 March. Phillip Clarke (SM) who
married Hannah (now eldest daughter of
George Macall (dec'd)) exhibited that
said Macall made will, constituting his
widow Ann executrix. Said Ann married
Robert Graham & died before she fully
administered the estate. John Watson
(SM) & his wife Jane (then eldest
daughter of said Macall) were granted
administration dbn. Before she fully
administered the estate, she died. Said
Phillip & Hannah were granted
administration. Appraisers: John
Cheverall, Walter Woolverstone. Mr.
William Hatton to administer oath.

13:314   John Llewellin (g) exhibited will of
Thomas Darcy (alias Thomas Matchett,
CV), proved by James Grace. Charges to
Mr. Samuell Warcup (CV).

1 April. John Hales petitioned for John
Sewall on behalf of his sister Mary
Kellett widow of Christopher Kellett
(CV) for LoA. Said Mary was granted
administration. Appraisers: Dr. Symon
Wooton, John Scott. Mr. Thomas Tasker
to administer oath.

2 April. Exhibited will of William
Mitchell (AA), proved before George
Yate.

13:315   3 April. Daniel Longman (AA) exhibited
that Capt. Thomas Francis was to
administer oath to Richard Arnoll, but
said Francis died before it was
accomplished. Capt. Richard Hill to
administer oath.

Court Session: 1686

Richard Hill was granted administration
on estate of Joseph Norwood (KE, dec'd
for 12 months), as principle creditor.
His widow is alive, but refuses
administration. Appraisers (KI):
Phillip Conner, Allen Smith. Mr.
Christopher Goodhand (KE) to administer
oath. Mentions: no children.

Richard Gearing (inn holder, London) was
granted administration on estate of
Timothy Pearce (London, died at sea),
having children in ENG.
13:316 Maj. Nicholas Sewall (CV) to administer
oath to administrator. Appraisers:
Richard Keene, Heugh Hopewell. John
Llewellin (g) to administer oath to
appraisers.

7 April. Richard Hill petitioned for:
• Jacob Hallett administrator of
Jeremiah Hausliste (single man).
Appraisers: James Homewood, Patrick
Murphy.
• Thomas Pennington administrator of
Robert Tiler. Appraisers: Joseph
Connoway, Richard Moss.
• Benjamin Bond administrator of
William Bateman. Appraisers: John
Cross, John Rutter. Said Rutter
drowned this winter, & said Cross
refuses. New appraisers: Jacob
Harness, Lawrence Draper.
Date: 15 March 1685. Said Hallett was
granted administration. Said Hill to
administer oath.
13:317 Said Pennington was granted
administration. Said Hill to administer
oath. Said Hill to administer oath to
said Harniss & said Draper.

8 April. Mr. John Llewellin exhibited
oath of Richard Keene & Hugh Hopewell,
appraisers of Timothy Pearce.

Sheriff (CV) to summon Susannah Keene
administratrix of William Hunt (CV) to
render accounts.

Sheriff (CV) to summon Isaack Baker &
Thomas Purnell, appraisers of Thomas
Cleverly & his wife Ann to render their

inventory.

Elisabeth Coursey administratrix of
William Coursey was summoned to render
accounts. Sheriff (TA) to summon said
Elisabeth administratrix of said Coursey
who was administrator of Henry Beedle &
his wife Sophia to render accounts on
estate of said Sophia.

13:318 12 April. Mr. Edward Mann (TA) for
William Dale (TA) exhibited that said
Dale married the eldest daughter of
George Watts (dec'd), whose widow is
also dec'd. Said Dale was granted
administration.

Benjamin Parrott (TA) exhibited will of
Thomas Price (TA), proved but did not
name an executor. Said Parrott was
granted administration, as greatest
legatee. Appraisers: John Whittington,
John Baker. Mr. Edward Mann to
administer oath.

Exhibited inventory of Timothy Pearce
(London).

Sheriff (CV) to summon Henry Thomas to
contest his caveat vs. estate of Robert
Thomas (SM), at request of Abigall
Thomas.

17 April. Maj. Nicholas Sewall
exhibited oath of Richard Gearing
administrator of Timothy Pearce.
Securities: John Tanner, Richard Keene.

13:319 20 April. William Hatton (g, SM)
exhibited oath Hannah Clarke
administratrix of George Macall. Also
exhibited oath of John Cheverall &
Walter Woolverstone, appraisers. Also
exhibited bond of Phillip Clarke for
Hannah Clarke. Securities: Thomas
Waughob, Robert Mason. Also exhibited
inventory.

Exhibited will of James Bodkin (SM),
proved before Mr. Joseph Pile. Also
exhibited oath of MM Robert Carvile &
Clement Hill executors. Also exhibited

oath of Maj. William Boarman & Capt. James Bowling, appraisers.

Richard Gearing administrator of Timothy Pearce was issued LoA.

26 April. Capt. Samuel Bourne (CV) exhibited inventory of estate of Dorothy King. Continuance was granted.

13:320 Thomas Purnell (CV) & Isaack Baker (CV) appraisers of Thomas & Ann Cleverly exhibited inventory.

James Emson & his wife Elisabeth administratrix of John Daniel (CV) was granted continuance.

Sheriff (CV) exhibited that summons to Susanna Keene administratrix of William Hunt was delivered. Securities: Henry Orlon, James Preston. Also exhibited that summons to Isaack Baker & Thomas Purnell was delivered.

Sheriff (CV) exhibited that summons to Henry Thomas was delivered. Said Thomas did not appear. Ruling: regarding will of Robert Thomas, said will is valid & Abigall Thomas executrix was granted administration.

13:321 Appraisers: William Husbands, John Cambell.

26 April. Nathaniell Dare & his wife administratrix of Thomas Binks was granted administration dbn on estate of Thomas & Ann Cleverly. Appraisers: Henry Mitchell, Samuel Houldsworth. Capt. Richard Ladd to administer oath.

Exhibited inventory of Anthony Kingsland (CV), unadministered by his relict Lavina who is since dec'd.

Exhibited inventory of William Perfett (CH), by appraisers Thomas Gibson & John Butler.

Exhibited inventory of Robert Crackbourne (CV), by appraisers John Broome & Francis Higham.

Court Session: 1686

Exhibited will of Obadiah Donn (SM),
proved before Capt. Joshua Doyne.

13:322 Exhibited inventory of Mathew Reed (TA),
by appraisers Richard Jones & Nathaniel
Tucker.

Exhibited will of Thomas Jones (KE),
proved before Cornelius Comegys. Also
exhibited inventory, by appraisers John
Bowles & William True.

Exhibited inventory of Sybilla Broadrib
(KE), by appraisers Edward Fry & John
Piner. Also exhibited bond of Cornelius
Comegys administrator. Securities:
Daniel Norris, John Bowles.

Exhibited will of Patrick Sullivant
(KE), proved before Charles Tilden (g,
KE). Exhibited oath of Frances
Sullivant executrix. Also exhibited
oath of Henry Hozier & Hance Hanson,
appraisers.

13:323 Exhibited bond of William Thomas (KE)
administrator of James Lessong.
Securities: John Bowles, Daniel Norris.
Also exhibited inventory of said James
Lesson, by appraisers John Bowles &
Henry Hozier.

Exhibited inventory of Henry Herman
(DO), by appraisers Jacob Lookrman &
John Mackel.

Mr. Joseph Pile (SM) exhibited will of
John Clark (SM), proved.

Exhibited inventory of William Hargiss
(CH), by appraisers John Courts &
William Hungerford. William Barton (CH)
exhibited will, proved

13:324 Thomas Mattenly administrator of Robert
Curtis (SM) exhibited accounts.

Sarah Downes (TA) administratrix of
James Downes was granted continuance.

27 April. John Hodson (DO) who married
Rebeccah relict of James Agg (DO) was

granted administration on his estate.
Appraisers: Edward Pindar, Benjamin
Priestly. Maj. Thomas Taylor to
administer oath.

Exhibited inventory of Obadiah Donn
(SM), by appraisers Thomas Martingly &
Thomas Carvile.

Exhibited inventory of John King (CV),
by appraisers Francis Buckstone &
William Williams.

13:325   Richard Chambers (SO) & Stephen Costin
(SO) petitioned that they became
security to Honor Furnis relict &
administratrix of William Furnis (SO) on
8 September 1685. Said administratrix
is embezzling the estate. Sheriff (SO)
to summon said Honor.

13:326   Exhibited inventory of Jonathon Pearce
(CV), by appraisers Walter Evins &
Thomas Ellis.

Exhibited inventory of Joan Hunter (AA),
by appraisers John Gray & Robert Ward.

Exhibited will of Francis Watts (AA),
proved before Maj. Nicholas Gassaway
(g). Also exhibited inventory, by
appraisers Richard Tydings & Robert
Ward.

Exhibited will of Col. Philemon Lloyd,
proved before Col. Vincent Lowe.

28 April. Exhibited inventory of John
Smith (AA), by appraisers Peter Barnett
& Nicholas Nicholson.

13:327   Capt. Henry Hanslap (AA) for Mary
Everett exhibited will of John Everett
(AA), constituting James Chilcott &
James Manfeild executors in trust. Said
Mary was granted administration on his
estate. Appraisers: Thomas Knighton,
Samuel Rainger. Mr. Thomas Tench to
administer oath.

Jane Dunkin widow of Patrick Dunkin (AA)
was granted administration on his

estate. Appraisers: Henry Ridgley,
Lancelott Todd. Mr. Edward Burges (g,
AA) to administer oath.

Maj. Thomas Long (BA) to prove will of
David Johns.

Magrett James poor widow of Thomas James
petitioned that Mr. Ebenezar
Blackistone be granted administration on
her husband's estate, as greatest
creditor. Date: 20 February 1686. Said
Blackistone was granted administration.
Appraisers: George Sturton, Edward
Skidmore. Maj. Edward Inglish to
administer oath.

13:328   Maj. Peter Sayer (high sheriff, TA)
exhibited summons to Elisabeth Coursey
administratrix of William Coursey to
render accounts on estates of Henry &
Sophia Beedle. She did not appear.
Summons was renewed.

Mr. Thomas Tasker (CV) exhibited oath
of Mrs. Mary Kellett administratrix of
Christopher Kellett. Securities (CV):
Henry Fernely, James Sewall. Also
exhibited oath of Symon Wooton & John
Broome, appraisers.

Joseph Edloe (CV) executor of Dr.
Edward Mollens exhibited accounts.
Continuance was granted.

29 April. Abraham Clarke (AA) exhibited
that Maj. Thomas Francis was to prove
will of Henry Bennitt, but said Francis
died before it was accomplished. Capt.
Richard Hill to prove said will &
administer oath to appraisers: Walter
Carr, Robert Connant.

13:329   Col. William Stevens (SO) to examine
accounts of Honor Furnis administratrix
of William Furnis & administer oath.

Exhibited will of William Welch (CE),
proved before Maj. Edward Inglish.
Also exhibited inventory.

Court Session: 1686

Exhibited will of Thomas Hawker (CE),
proved before Maj. Edward Inglish.
Also exhibited inventory, by appraisers
Richard Pullen & George Higgenbotham.

Exhibited bond of Richard Edmonds (CE)
administrator of Francis Blangy.
Security: Ebenezar Blackiston.

Exhibited will of Thomas Greene (TA),
proved before Mr. James Murphy.

13:330 Exhibited inventory of John Dobbs (KE),
by appraisers Thomas Davis & Henry
Wilson.

Exhibited inventory of James Nuthall
(CV), by appraisers Robert Dove &
Richard Carleton.

Col. Henry Jowles (CV) exhibited oath
of James Bigger & his wife Margret
administratrix of James Nuthall.
Securities: John Bigger, Richard
Jenkins. Also exhibited oath of Robert
Dove & John Dossett, appraisers.

Capt. William Lawrence (KE) exhibited
will of Thomas Ferrabay (KE). Also
exhibited oath of Richard Kempstone &
William Temple, appraisers.

Sarah Collyer (BA) exhibited will of
Abraham Hollman (BA), but cited no
executor. Col. George Wells to prove
said will. Said Collyer was granted
administration, as greatest legatee.
Appraisers: John Hall, William Yorke.
Said Wells to administer oath.

13:331 John Chittham, Jr. (CV) who married
Dorothy relict of Joseph Williams (CV)
was granted administration on his
estate. Appraisers: John Willson,
William Andncah. Thomas Tasker (g) to
administer oath.

Exhibited inventory of Robert Castleton
(CH), by appraisers Phillip Hoskins &
John Lambeth.

Maj. Joseph Wicks (KE) for Anna Turner
widow of Charles Turner (d. 1 April
instant) petitioned for LoA on his
estate. Date: 19 April 1686.

13:332 30 April. Maj. Joseph Wicks (KE) as
father-in-law to said Anna was granted
administration on said Charles' estate,
as greatest creditor. Appraisers: Symon
Wilmore, William Thomas. Daniel Norris
to administer oath.

Elisabeth Calvert widow & administratrix
of William Calvert exhibited accounts.

William Dossett (DO) administrator of
John Dossey exhibited accounts.

Anthony Chilcott (DO) administrator of
James Harper exhibited accounts.

Exhibited will of Joseph Hopkins (CE),
constituting his widow Sarah executrix.
Said Sarah was granted administration.
Appraisers: Edward Beck, George
Higgenbotham. Richard Pullen (g) to
administer oath.

Exhibited will of John Harding (CE),
constituting Edward Coleman executor.
Said Coleman was granted administration.
Appraisers: Francis Childs, William
Jones. Edward Blay (g) to administer
oath.

13:333 Mr. Edward Mann (TA) to prove will of
Edward Gibbons (TA).

Thomasin Viney relict of Henry Kent was
granted administration on his estate.
Appraisers: Francis Freeman, Francis
Mauldin. Francis Hutchins (CV) to
administer oath.

Said Thomasin Viney was granted
administration on estate of Henry Viney
(CV). Appraisers: Francis Mauldin,
Francis Freeman. Francis Hutchins (g)
to administer oath.

Robert Connant (AA) was granted
administration on estate of Samuel

Court Session: 1686

Mitchell (AA). Appraisers: Richard
Thornebury, Leonard Coutes. Thomas
Tench (g, AA) to administer oath.

3 May. Exhibited will of Thomas Gibson
(CH), proved before Mr. John Courts.
Also exhibited oath of Anthony Noble &
Rando. Brandt, appraisers. Also
exhibited oath of John Newman & George
Gouge, executors.

13:334 Exhibited inventory of John Dring (AA),
by appraisers Walter Phelps & Benjamin
Williams.

Exhibited bond of Mathew Erreckson
administrator of Hance Rosmonson.
Securities (KE): Joseph Sadler, John
Coppedge. William Lewis exhibited oath
of the appraisers, sworn 12 November
1684.

Exhibited will of Richard Jones (CH),
proved before Mr. John Stone.

Exhibited bond of John Hinson (KE)
administrator of John Jackson.
Securities (KE): Edward Sweatnam,
Matthew Ereckson.

Exhibited bond of Robert Thompson
administrator of William Wright (CH).
Security (CH): John Hinderson.

Exhibited bond of Elisabeth Boyden
administratrix of William Boyden.
Securities: Mathew Saunders, Giles
Collom.

Exhibited bond of William Legg (KE)
administrator of John Dobbs.
Securities: Henry Williams, Thomas
Davis.

13:335 Exhibited bond of Mary Dike (CH)
administratrix of Thomas Alcock.
Securities: Edward Rookard, Richard
Clouder.

Exhibited bond of Thomas Mitchell (CH)
administrator of Edward Abbott.
Securities (CH): Michael Minock, John

Court Session: 1686

Bosswell.

Exhibited bond of George Bussey (CV)
administrator of John King. Securities
(CV): Hezekiah Bussey, Andrew Bradie.
Francis Hutchins (g, CV) exhibited oath
of Francis Buckstone & William Williams,
appraisers.

Mr. George Parker procurator for
Susanna Keen (CV) administratrix of
William Hunt was granted continuance.

13:336

Richard Hill for his daughter-in-law
Mary Francis widow of Maj. Thomas
Francis
was granted administration on his
estate. Appraisers: Ferdinando Battie,
James Sanders. Maj. Nicholas Gassaway
or said Hill to administer oath.

Said Hill for Elioner Macuben widow &
executrix of John Macuben was granted
administration on his estate. Said Hill
to prove said will of John Mackubin
(AA). Appraisers: Samuel Howard,
Lancelott Todd. Said Hill to administer
oath.

13:337

William Coursey (g, TA) was granted
administration on estate of George
Carrall.

4 May. Exhibited inventory of William
Inyce (TA), by appraisers George Robins
& James Benson.

Exhibited inventory of John Wilkinson
(TA), by appraisers John Chaires & John
Chafes.

5 May. Col. George Wells (BA) was
granted administration on estate of
Samuel Dockins (BA), as principle
creditor. Appraisers: Richard Edmonds,
Lawrence Taylor. Mr. Edward Beedle to
administer oath.

Susannah Bartlett widow of Ralph
Bartlett (CH) was granted administration
on his estate. Mr. Robert Doyne to
administer oath.

Court Session: 1686

Exhibited will of John Cammell (CE),
constituting his widow Rebecca
executrix. Edward Jones to prove said
will. Said Rebecca was granted
administration. Appraisers: John
Hyland, John Maddox. Said Jones to
administer oath.

13:338   Maj. Joseph Weeks & his wife Anna
administratrix of Benjamin Randall (KE)
exhibited accounts.

Thomas Jones (BA) was granted
administration on estate of Daniel Wine
(BA), as principle creditor.
Appraisers: William Yorke, Thomas
Preston. Col. George Wells (BA) to
administer oath.

James Maxfeild (AA) exhibited will of
Henry Everett (AA), constituting James
Chilcott & James Maxfeild executors.
Said Chilcott is since dec'd. Said
Maxfeild was granted administration.
Appraisers: Thomas Knighton, Thomas
Morgan. Thomas Tench (g, BA) to
administer oath.

6 May. Mr. Robert Doyne (CH) was
granted administration on estate of Owen
Newen (CH), as principle creditor. Mr.
John Stone to administer oath.

7 May. Exhibited will of Thomas
Robinson (CH), constituting Richard
Price executor. Robert Doyne (g) to
prove said Will. Said Price was granted
administration. Appraisers: Joseph
Gray, Phillip Hoskins. Said Doyne to
administer oath.

13:339   Col. Vincent Low (TA) to examine
accounts of John Hawkins & his wife
Elisabeth on estate of Dr. John Eustis.

James Collyer (BA) & William Yorke (BA)
administrators of John Wattertone
exhibited accounts.

8 May. Joseph Wicks & his wife Anna
administratrix of Benjamin Randall were
granted continuance.

Page 167

Court Session: 1686

Letter to Justices of BA Court: Miles
Gibson (g, BA) administrator of John Yeo
(BA) exhibited that said Yeo married
Sundea Garrate (now dec'd) relict &
administratrix of Rutherane Garratt
(BA), who died leaving an orphan (under
age). Said Justices are authorized to
summon Thomas Hedge &
13:340 James Phillips appraisers of estate of
said Yeo, to determine the orphan's
portion. Said estate is to be divided &
orphan's portion delivered to Mr.
Edward Beedle for use of said orphan.

At request of John Baker (g), sheriff
(TA) to summon Katharine Catterson widow
of Francis Catterson & to show cause why
she doesn't continue administration on
said estate.

Robert Doyne (g, CH) to administer oath
to Moses Harris & his wife Katherine
executrix of James Wheeler for their
accounts.

Exhibited will of Richard Morris (CH),
constituting Penellopea his executrix.
Said Penellopea was granted
administration. Appraisers: John Wood,
William Theobalds. Maj. John Wheeler
(g) to administer.

13:341 William Brereton (g, SO) attorney for
Thomas Brereton (g, VA) administrator of
Andrew Jones (SO) exhibited accounts.

10 May. Thomas Parslo (CV)
administrator of John Cooper was granted
continuance.

Col. William Burges (AA) executor of
Nicholas Painter was granted
continuance.

Exhibited will of Henry Hayman (SO),
constituting Elioner Hayman executrix.
Said Elioner was granted administration.
Appraisers: John Panther, Cornelius
Johnson. Mr. William Brereton to
administer oath.

Court Session: 1686

John Tarr husband to relict of Thomas
Profitt recommended that John Jones
(SO), brother to former wife of said
Profitt & uncle to surviving child,
administer said Profitt's estate. Date:
22 April 1686.

13:342 Said Jones was granted administration.
Appraisers: William Turvile, William
Browne. Col. William Stevens to
administer oath.

12 May. Commissioners of SO to examine
accounts of Honour Furnis administratrix
of William Furnis.

Col. William Stevens (SO) to examine
accounts of John Mackite (alias John
Mackatrick, SO) administrator of Henry
Cole.

Exhibited will of Walter Bonnsell (TA),
constituting John Lewis executor. Henry
Coursey, Jr. to prove said will. Said
Lewis was granted administration.
Appraisers: Robert Smith, Daniel Glover.
Said Coursey to administer oath.

Exhibited will of Symon West (TA),
constituting Charles Drury executor.
Mr. Henry Coursey to prove said will.
Said West was granted administration.

13:343 14 May. William Smith (CV) who married
Elisabeth widow of John Hunt petitioned
that said Elisabeth is also dec'd. Said
Smith was granted administration on
estate of said Elisabeth. Appraisers:
Capt. Richard Gardiner, Cornelius
Wilkinson. Col. Henry Jowles to
administer oath.

Exhibited will of Thomas Harris (p, CH),
constituting Mary executrix. Said Mary
married Richard Land, and is now dec'd.
Said Land was granted administration.
Humphrey Warren to administer oath.

15 May. Exhibited inventory of William
Graves (CV), by appraisers John Dossett
& Jonathon Goosey.

Exhibited inventory of John Lawrence
(London), by appraisers Hance Hanson &
Michael Miller. Also exhibited bond of
Robert Hearne (London) administrator.
Securities: William Harris, Michael
Miller.

Exhibited bond of Edward Day
administrator of Thomas Walker (SO).
Securities: George Wilson, William
Scott. Col. William Stevens (SO)
exhibited oath of said Day.

Sheriff (SM) to summon Richard Attwood &
Solomon Jones.

13:344   Exhibited will of Henry Parrott (TA),
proved before Mr. George Robotham.
Benjamin Furby (witness) would not
swear; other witness was not found.

Col. William Stevens (SO) exhibited
oath of William Brereton & Stephen
Luffe, appraisers of Thomas Walker (SO).

17 May. Col. William Colebourne (SO)
exhibited oath of Richard Lewis &
Richard Warren, appraisers of John White
(SO). Also exhibited will, proved
before Col. William Stevens.

19 May. Col. William Stevens (SO)
exhibited oath of Thomas Jones & William
Noble, appraisers of Edward Furlong.
Also exhibited bond of John Kerke (SO)
administrator. Securities (SO): William
Scott, Walter Lane.

13:345   20 May. Col. William Stevens (SO)
exhibited oath of James Round (SO)
administrator of John Clarke. Security:
John Farwell. Also exhibited oath of
John Emmett & Henry Emmett, appraisers.

26 May. Maj. Edward Inglish (CE)
exhibited oath of George Stinton &
Edward Skidemore, appraisers of Thomas
James (CE). Also exhibited inventory.
Also exhibited bond of Ebenezar
Blackiston administrator. Securities
(CE): George Stinton, Thomas Skidemore.

Court Session: 1686

Exhibited inventory of Robert Thomas
(SM), by appraisers John Cambell &
William Husbands.

Richard Attwood (SM) & Solomon Jones
(SM) appeared, per summons.

27 May. Exhibited inventory of Thomas
Bingham (TA), by appraisers John
Tillison & John Johnson.

13:346   William Shertcliffe (SM) administrator
of Joseph Harding exhibited accounts.
Estate is overpaid. Discharge was
granted.

28 May. Exhibited bond of Thomas Bayly
administrator of Thomas Bingham.
Securities (TA): Nicholas Cloud, Jeffery
Mattershaw.

Exhibited bond of Nicholas Cloud
administrator of Thomas Lewis.
Securities: Thomas Bayly, Jeffery
Mattershaw.

Exhibited bond of Nicholas Cloud
administrator of William Wood.
Securities: Thomas Bayly, Jeffery
Mattershaw.

29 May. Exhibited inventory of Hugh
Hanlen (CV), by appraisers William Selby
& Thomas Greenfeild. Exhibited bond of
Cato MackDaniel Securities: John Smith,
Phillip Larance. Mr. Richard Marsham
(CV) exhibited oath of said MackDaniel.
Also exhibited oath of appraisers.

13:347   Daniel Norris (g, KE) exhibited oath of
William Comegys (KE) administrator of
George Reed (SM), sworn 22 March 1685.

William Hatton (g, SM) exhibited oath of
Hanah Clarke administratrix of George
Macall, sworn 5 April 1686. Also
exhibited oath of John Cheverell &
Walter Woolverston, appraisers sworn 6
April 1686.

ultimate May. Maj. Thomas Taylor (DO)
exhibited oath of Jacob Lookrman & John

Makele, appraisers of Henry Herman.
Also exhibited bond of Mary Herman
administratrix. Securities (DO): John
Edwards, Benjamin Preistly.

1 June. Maj. Thomas Taylor (DO)
exhibited oath of Edward Pindar &
Benjamin Preistly, appraisers of Stephen
Gary. Also exhibited will, proved.
Also exhibited oath of Clare Gary
executrix.

13:348   2 May [sic]. Maj. John Wheeler (CH)
exhibited oath of John Wood & William
Theobalds, appraisers of Richard Morris
(CH). Also exhibited will, proved
before Maj. John Wheeler.

Exhibited inventory of John Probert
(CH), by appraisers Robert Middleton &
Phillip Hoskins.

5 June. Clement Hill for David Parson
(SM) who married widow of Humphrey Jones
was granted administration on his
estate. Mr. Hill to administer oath.

7 June. Exhibited will of Michael
Higgen (CV), proved before Col. Henry
Darnall. Mary Higgen executrix was
granted administration. Appraisers:
Francis Highman, John Smith. Thomas
Tasker (CV) to administer oath.

Edward Mann (TA) to prove will of
William Kircum. Fees to Alice Kircum.

13:349   9 June. Exhibited will of John Evans
(SO), constituting relict Mary Evans
executrix. John Dasheile (g, SO) to
prove said will. Said Mary was granted
administration. Appraisers: William
Brereton, Richard Crockett.

18 June [sic]. Exhibited will of John
Trueman (SO), constituting Richard
Stevens & John Booth executors. William
Brereton (g) to prove said will. Said
Stevens & Booth were granted
administration. Appraisers: Daniel
Hast, Phillip Ascue.

Court Session: 1686

Exhibited will of Edward Stevens (SO),
constituting Florence Tucker executrix.
Col. William Stevens to prove said
will. Said Tucker was granted
administration. Appraisers: William
Noble, Walter Lane. Said Stevens to
administer oath.

Edward Day (SO) was granted
administration on estate of William
Stevens (SO), as principle creditor.
Appraisers: Thomas Cox, Isaac Noble.
Col. William Stevens to administer
oath.

13:350   Exhibited inventory of Edward Furlong
(SO), by appraisers Thomas Jones &
William Noble.

12 June. Exhibited will of Mary Wenman
(CH), constituting John Godson (CH)
executor. Mr. Robert Doyne (CH) to
prove said will. Said Godson was
granted administration. Appraisers:
Phillip Hoskins, John Lambert. Said
Doyne to administer oath.

14 June. Exhibited inventory of Thomas
Gibson (CH), by appraisers Rando. Brandt
& Anthony Neale.

Clement Hill petitioned for Samuel
Chamberlaine for administration on
estate of Thomas Wright (SM), as
principle creditor. Date: 13 May 1686.
Appraisers: Thomas Mattenly, Thomas
Carvile. Joshua Doyne to administer
oath.

13:351   15 June. Exhibited inventory of John
Johnson (CV), by appraisers John Leech,
Sr., Edwan Hurlock.

Exhibited bond of Benjamin Bond (AA)
administrator of William Bateman.
Securities (AA): Lawrence Draper, Jacob
Harness. Capt. Richard Hill exhibited
oath of Benjamin Bond administrator.
Also exhibited inventory, by appraisers
Jacob Harness & Lawrence Draper.

Page 173

Court Session: 1686

Capt. Richard Hill exhibited oath of
Thomas Pennington administrator of
Robert Tiler. Securities (AA): William
Pennington, John Hurst. Also exhibited
oath of Joseph Connoway & Richard Moss,
appraisers.

16 June. Capt. Hill exhibited oath of
Daniel Longman administrator of Richard
Arnold. Securities: Samuel Garland,
Abell Browne. Also exhibited oath of
Nicholas Nicholson & Samuel Garland,
appraisers.

13:352 Mr. Francis Hutchins exhibited oath of
Thomas Viney administrator of Henry
Viney (CV), sworn 1 June 1686.
Securities (AA): John Kent, John Bounds.
Also exhibited oath of Francis Freeman &
Francis Mauldin, appraisers.

Mr. Francis Hutchins exhibited oath of
Thomas Viney administrator of Henry
Kent. Securities (CV): John Kent, John
Bounds. Also exhibited oath of Francis
Mauldin & Francis Freeman, appraisers.

Capt. Richard Hill (AA) exhibited oath
of Mary Francies administratrix of
Thomas Francies (AA). Securities (AA):
Nicholas Gassaway, Richard Hill. Also
exhibited oath of Fardinando Battee &
James Sanders, appraisers of said Thomas
Francis.

13:353 Capt. Richard Hill (AA) exhibited oath
of Jacob Hallet administrator of Henry
Hanslist (AA). Also exhibited oath of
William Pennington & John Clarke,
appraisers. Also exhibited inventory.

Exhibited inventory of Robert Clarkeson
(AA), by appraisers Nicholas Gassaway &
Fardinando Battee.

17 June. Richard Hill petitioned for
Joseph Connoway (p, AA) for
administration on estate of Joseph
Freene (AA), who died leaving neither
wife nor child nor other relations in
this Province except said Connaway, as
greatest creditor. Date: 28 May 1686.

Appraisers: William Pennington, Robert
Eagle. Capt. Richard Hill to
administer oath.

13:354 19 June. Exhibited inventory of John
Wallace (SO), by appraisers John Browne
& William Law.

Exhibited inventory of William Bishop
(TA), by appraisers Robert Jones &
Robert Smith.

Exhibited will of Joseph Hopkins (CE),
proved.

23 June. Henry Hooper (g, DO) to prove
will of John Taylor (DO).

Exhibited additional inventory of John
Munns (CH), by appraisers Robert
Middleton & Phillip Hoskins.

24 June. Mr. Phillip Hoskins (CH)
administrator of Richard Garforth was
granted continuance.

John Speak (CH) who married Winifred
executrix of John Munn (CH) was granted
continuance.

William Smith (CV) administrator of John
Hunt & his wife Elisabeth exhibited
inventory, by appraisers Cornelius
Wilkinson & Richard Gardiner.

13:355 26 June. Exhibited will of Augustine
Herman Bohemian (CE) constituting
Ephraim Herman, Casparus Herman, & John
Thompson executors. William Dare (g,
CE) to prove said will. Said executors
were granted administration. Said Dare
to administer oath.

William Dare (CE) was granted
administration on estate of Edward Fry
(CE). Appraisers: John Hiland, George
Oldfeild. Mr. Edward Jones to
administer oath.

29 June. Phillis White relict of
Gustavus White (CV) was granted
administration on his estate.

Appraisers: Thomas Parsloe, Jeremiah
Simpson. Mr. John Griggs to administer
oath.

Capt. Richard Hill exhibited that
Elisabeth Forth refused to take oath of
administratrix, alleging that her
husband left nothing to administer.
Date: 6 May 1686. [Note: Capt. Hanslapp
procured administration "I know not by
whose order."]

13:356   30 June. Exhibited inventory of
Elisabeth Heathcoate (widow of
Nathaniell Heathcoate (AA)), by
appraisers Walter Carr & Robert Connant.

3 July. Ignacius Causeen (CV) to prove
will of Henry Adams (CV), by oaths of
witnesses: Meverell Hulse, Robert
Thomas. Joseph Pile (SM) to prove said
will by oath of another witness: James
Turner.

5 July. Mr. Edward Jones (CE) to
administer oath to John Hiland & Samuell
Wheeler, new appraisers of John Cammell.
Former appraiser Jonas Maddox is dec'd.

Mr. Mathias Vanderheyden who married
Anna Margaretta administratrix of Capt.
Henry Ward (CE) exhibited accounts.
Continuance was granted.

13:357   8 July at SMC. Exhibited inventory of
Christopher Kellett (CV), by appraisers
Symon Wooten & John Brome.

Exhibited inventory of Francis Holland
(AA).

Exhibited inventory of Thomas Sted (CV),
by appraisers Thomas Bishop & Robert
Buntham.

Exhibited inventory of Henry Kent (CV),
by appraisers Francis Freeman & Francis
Mauldin.

Exhibited inventory of George Buckstone
(TA), by appraisers John Davis & James
Scott.

Exhibited inventory of Henry West (CV), by appraisers John Sunderland & Marke Clarke.

Exhibited inventory of John Aschcom (CV), by appraisers John Cooper (dec'd) & Gustavus White (dec'd).

Charles Tilden (KE) exhibited will of Samuel Pilesworth (CE), constituting Joseph Saunders (merchant, Bristoll) & said Tilden executors. Said Saunders is in ENG.

13:358 Said Tilden was granted administration. Mr. Edward Blay to administer oath. Said Blay to summon Richard Boyer & his wife Elisabeth regarding said estate.

William Combes (g, TA) to examine accounts of Sarah Hall executrix of James Hall (TA).

Exhibited inventory of James Bowley (CV), by appraisers Joseph Wickes & William Harris.

Hance Hanson (KE) exhibited that administration of estate of Dr. John Porter (Bristoll) was granted to him. Attorney for the widow is in the Province. Said attorney was granted administration on said estate.

Anthony Neale executor of James Neale
13:359 was granted continuance.

William Harris (KE) executor of Edward Toms exhibited accounts.

Said William Harris administrator of Thomas Boone (KE) exhibited accounts.

Meverell Hulse (CH) administrator of Thomas Hattrill petitioned for continuance, being "very ancient & not in a capacity to undertake such a journey."

13:360 Ruling: said Hulse summoned.

Sarah & Parthenia Burditt executrices of Ann Doubty petitioned to be excused. Ruling: said women were summoned.

Exhibited inventory, by appraisers James Littlepage & Edward Mines.

13:361 Henry Hardy & his wife Mary administratrix of William Ward were granted continuance.

Exhibited additional inventory of John Hamilton (CH). Richard Chandler (CH) & his wife Elisabeth relict of John Hamilton exhibited accounts.

Exhibited inventory of William Cocks (SM), by appraisers Marmaduke Semme & John Watson.

John Scott (CV) who married relict of Thomas Starling was granted continuance.

William Martin who married relict of George Abbott (CV) was granted continuance.

Hance Hanson (KE) administrator of Stephen Cuthbert exhibited accounts.

13:362 John Hinson (KE) administrator of John Jackson exhibited accounts.

Katharine Catterson widow of Francis Catterson (inn holder, TA) exhibited her renunciation & assigned her rights to John Baker (SMC). Witnesses: Ro. Carvile, Edward Boothby. Said Baker received a judgement against said Catterson on 3 March 1684. Said Baker was granted administration, as principle creditor.

13:363 Securities (SMC): John Llewellin, Thomas Grunwin. Mr. Edward Mann to administer oath. Said Mann to summon widow regarding the estate. Mr. William Combes (TA) to prove will of Francis Catterson (TA), per request of Katherine Catterson.

13:364 Petition of said Katherine for support for herself & child.

Michael Taney (g, CV) exhibited accounts on estate of Ambrose Vauder (?).

Court Session: 1686

Thomas Anderson (TA) administrator of
George Allumby exhibited accounts.
Continuance was granted.

Peter Anderton (TA) who married Elioner
relict & administratrix of John Morris
exhibited accounts.

Richard Roystone (TA) administrator of
daniel Taylor was granted continuance.

Exhibited bond of Thomas Seward
administrator of John Clark.
Securities: William Harris, Hance
Hanson.

13:365　William Harris (KE) petitioned that
Michael Miller (KE) attorney for Thomas
Thaxton be granted administration on his
estate as principle creditor.
Appraisers: William Burton, Josias
Wainewright. Mr. William Frisby (g,
KE) to administer oath.

John Hinson (g, KE) & Charles Tilden (g,
KE) were granted administration on
estate of Morgan Williams (KE), for
benefit of orphans. Hance Hanson (g) to
administer oath.

John Shelton & his wife Ann
administrators of Robert Crofts (SM)
were granted continuance.

Exhibited inventory of John Clarke (KE),
by appraisers John Hinson & William
Harris.

Thomas Danton (SM) administrator of
Peter Mills (SM) exhibited accounts.

Sheriff (DO) to summon Maj. Thomas
Taylor administrator of John Quigley to
render accounts.

Elioner Spicer (CV) administratrix of
Thomas Evenden exhibited accounts.
Continuance was granted.

13:366　William Meakin (SM) executor of Robert
Beard was granted continuance.

Court Session: 1686

Henry Greene (TA) administrator of
Albert Johnson exhibited accounts.
Continuance was granted.

Alice Butler (CV) administratrix of
Charles Butler exhibited accounts. Said
Alice & Daniel Phillips were granted
continuance.

Daniel Phillips (CV) administrator of
Richard Hewson was granted continuance.

Thomas Dillon (SM) executor of Peater
Wall exhibited additional accounts.
Continuance was granted.

Francis Higham (CV) & his wife Elisabeth
executrix of Francis Foukes were granted
continuance.

John Crooke (CV) & his wife Sarah
executrix of George Powell were granted
continuance.

Francis Hutchins (CV) to examine
accounts of Gilbert Deavour on estate of
John Johnson.

9 July. Robert Reed one of executors of
Robert Andrews (CV) was granted
continuance.

13:367 William Lyle (CV) administrator of
Phillip Jones was granted continuance.

Ralph Foster (SM) & John Hilton (SM)
administrators of Samuell Maddox
exhibited 1st accounts. Continuance was
granted.

Edward Smoot (SM) administrator of John
Gee was granted continuance.

James Turner (CH) administrator of
Arthur Turner was granted continuance.

Said Turner administrator of John
Bennitt was granted continuance.

Thomas Stone (CH) administrator of Giles
Tomkins was granted continuance.

Court Session: 1686

Benjamin Evans (CV) executor of George
Collins exhibited 1st accounts.
Continuance was granted.

Said Evans administrator of John Bowling
exhibited 1st accounts. Continuance was
granted.

Robert Arme & Richard Thornbury for
Abraham Thornebury administrator of
Mathew Axon & administrator of Richard
Bedworth
13:368 petitioned that said Abraham is "by
reason no way capacitate of himself for
want of understanding" to render
accounts. Continuance was granted.

Margarett Holland executrix of Francis
Holland petitioned that because of age
and inability of body, she is not able
to travel to Office. Justices (AA) to
examine her accounts.

Thomas Tench who married Margarett
executrix of Nathan Smith petitioned
13:369 that there are several debts in ENG.
Continuance was granted.

John Turner (AA) & his wife Elioner
executrix of Richard James were granted
continuance.

Henry Costin administrator of George
Buckstone (TA) petitioned that John
Aldridge, landlord for said Buckstone,
has disposed of the crop to his own use.
Suit pending. Continuance was granted.

George Newman (CH) administrator of
George Newman exhibited accounts.
Continuance was granted.

13:370 John Newman (CH) executor of Thomas
Gibson was granted continuance.

Thomas Braine (CV) who married Elisabeth
eldest daughter of Arthur Leadford (CV)
was granted administration on his
estate. Appraisers: Robert Dove,
Richard Clarke. Mr. Thomas Brooke (CV)
to administer oath.

Richard Pollard (CV) who married Mary
relict of William Gamball (CV) was
granted administration on his estate.
Appraisers: Michaell Dare, Isaac Baker.
Capt. Richard Ladd (g) to administer
oath.

James Emson (CV) administrator of John
Daniel exhibited final accounts.
Discharge was granted.

William Watts (SM) who married relict of
William Kennady exhibited 1st accounts.
Continuance was granted.

13:371   George Cocks (CV) administrator of
William Wright exhibited accounts.

Thomas Parslo (CV) administrator of John
Cooper exhibited 1st accounts.
Continuance was granted.

John Warren (SM) administrator of George
Henderson exhibited accounts.

Ignatius Warren (SM) administrator of
Augustine Warren exhibited accounts.

James Berry (CV) & his wife Ann
administratrix of James Milson were
granted continuance.

Samuel Bagby (CV) administrator of
Andrew Dickenson was granted
continuance.

Thomas Deakins (SM) administrator of
Daniell Hamond was granted continuance.

Walter Woolverstone administrator of
James Pagrace (SM) exhibited accounts.
Continuance was granted.

13:372   Samuel Warner & his wife Sarah
administratrix of Francis Dorrington
exhibited accounts.

John Gorly (CH) & his wife Barbara
relict & administratrix of Richard
Chapman exhibited accounts.

Court Session: 1686

Said John Gourly administrator of
William Hinsey (?) exhibited accounts.

Per request of Rebeccah Aisbiston orphan
of William Aisbiston, Richard Attwood
(SM) executor of said William was
ordered to pay her her legacy.

10 July. Edward Rookwood (CH) who
married Elisabeth relict &
administratrix of Henry Aspenaile
exhibited accounts. Said Elisabeth died
soon after her marriage to said
Rookwood. Continuance was granted.

13:373 Edward Rookwood (CH) administrator of
Nicholas Swinbourne exhibited accounts.
Discharge was granted.

Mathew Dike & his wife Mary
administratrix of Thomas Alcok were
granted continuance.

Mathew Bill (CV) & his wife Mary
executrix of Thomas Jessup were granted
continuance.

Clement Hill, Esq. executor of Stephen
Murty (SM) exhibited accounts.

Exhibited inventory of Henry Viney (CV),
by appraisers Francis Mauldin & Francis
Freeman.

Francis Meeke (CH) & his wife Mary
relict of Richard Pinner son & heir of
Ann Attkins executrix of William Pinner
were granted continuance on estate of
said William.

Christian Pethen relict of Thomas Pethen
(SM) was granted administration on his
estate. Appraisers: Edward Feild,
Thomas Dillon. Mr. Luke Gardiner (SM)
to administer oath.

Thomas Abbott (SM) administrator of John
Daniell exhibited that said Daniell
never had any estate. Ruling:
dismissed.

13:374 Rebeccah Simmons executrix of Bryan
Dayly (SM) administrator of Edward Size
exhibited accounts on estate of said
Size. Continuance was granted.

Rebeccah Simons executrix of Bryan Dayly
was granted continuance.

William Husbands (SM) administrator of
William Bowen exhibited final accounts.

Robert Carvile & Kenelme Cheseldyn
procurators petitioned that Col.
William Stevens return accounts on
estate of Charles Ballard.

Mr. Richard Gardiner administrator of
Collin Mackensie (SM) exhibited
accounts.

Adam Head administrator of Samuel
Burgess exhibited accounts.

Anthony Underwood procurator for John
Galwith (CV) administrator of Richard
Barton exhibited that said Galwith has
gone to ENG. Continuance was granted.

Thomas Spinke (SM) administrator of Jane
Paine was granted continuance.

13:375 Maj. Peter Sayer for Henrietta Maria
Lloyd (TA) administratrix of Phillimon
Lloyd, Esq. was granted continuance.

14 July. Per Capt. Bowling, Richard
Southerne & Richard Bright were granted
administration on estate of widow Mary
Trueman (CV), in right of their wives.
Appraisers: Maj. Ninian Beale, Mr.
Thomas Gant. Mr. Thomas Brooke to
administer oath.

13:376 16 July. John Pursell, Jr. (TA) who
married sister of Symon Stevens (TA) was
granted administration on his estate, on
behalf of her & the orphans. [She is
keeping them.] Appraisers: Richard
Sweatnam, Andrew Abington.

John Craycroft (g, CV) exhibited oath of
Timothy Gunter & Marke Smith, appraisers

Court Session: 1686

of Lavina Richards (alias Lavina
Kingsland).

Garrett Vansweringen (g, SM) exhibited
oath of James Pattison (SM)
administrator of Edward & James Watkins.
Also exhibited oath of Thomas Spinke &
Gilbert Turberfield, appraisers.

Maj. Thomas Taylor (g, DO) exhibited
oath of Benjamin Preistly & Phineous
Blackwood, appraisers of Hugh Abell.

Mr. William Boarman, Jr. exhibited oath
of Robert Greene & Thomas Simpson, Sr.,
appraisers of Edward Turner. Also
exhibited oath of Mr. Thomas Mudd
administrator.

13:377 Exhibited bond of Ann Hopewell
administratrix of Francis Hopewell.
Securities: Hugh Hopewell, Phillip Cox.

Exhibited bond of Thomas Mudd
administrator of Edward Turner.
Securities (SM): John Wathen, Abraham
Lemaister.

Exhibited bond of James Pattison
administrator of Edward (N). Securities
(SM): Gilbert Turberfeild, Thomas
Spinke.

Exhibited bond of James Pattison
administrator of James Watkins.
Securities (SM): Gilbert Turberfeild,
Thomas Spinke.

Exhibited bond of Henry Costin
administrator of George Buckstone.
Securities (TA): James Scott,
Christopher Sanclet.

Exhibited bond of Capt. Samuell Bourne
administrator of Dorothy King.
Securities (CV): Thomas Tasker, Thomas
Hughes.

Exhibited bond of William Dorsey
administrator of John Dossey.
Securities (DO): William Mishew,
Laurence Woodnutt.

Court Session: 1686

Exhibited bond of Abraham Blagg
administrator of Hugh Abell. Security
(DO): John Taylor,

John Griggs (g, CV) exhibited oath of
Samuel Bourne administrator of Dorothy
King. Also exhibited oath of Nathaniell
Ashcomb & Thomas Parslo, appraisers.

Mr. William Boarman exhibited LoA for
Mr. Gerrard administrator of Daniel
Johnson.

13:378   Richard Wellington (KE) who married
relict of Richard Gray (KE) was granted
administration on his estate. Cornelius
Comegys to administer oath.

Thomas Scudamore & James Phillips were
granted administration on estate of
Thomas Button (BA), as principle
creditors.

George Lingan (CV) petitioned for
Margery Mines (CV) widow of Robert Mines
(d. Spring 1686) to be granted
administration on his estate. Said
Margery cannot travel to Office. Date:
3 July 1686 Petuxent. Said Margery was
granted administration. Appraisers:
John Moffett, Gawen Hambleton. Said
Lingan to administer oath.

13:379   Thomas Waughob (SM) was granted
administration on estate of Edward Jones
(SM), as principle creditor. M.
William Hatton to administer oath.

Garrett Vansweringen (g, SM) exhibited
oath of Phillip Willen administrator of
Thomas Winn. Securities (SM): Samuel
Lee, John Cole. Also exhibited oath of
Abraham Rhoades & Thomas Price,
appraisers.

Exhibited bond of William Richards
administrator of Levina Richards (alias
Levina Kingsland). Securities (CV):
William Turner, Samuel Bagby.

22 July. Clement Hill petitioned for
Mr. James Keeth attorney for Mr.

Court Session: 1686

William Richards (merchant, London) to
be granted administration on estate of
Christopher Pinkny (CV). Date: 14 July
1686. Appraisers: Gabriell Burneham,
John Dossey. Col. Henry Jowles to
administer oath.

Exhibited will of Henry Adams (CH).

13:380 Exhibited inventory of James Agg (DO),
by appraisers Edward Pindar & Benjamin
Preistly.

Exhibited inventory of John Taylor (DO),
by appraisers John Pollard & Phineas
Blackwood.

Exhibited inventory of Stephen Gary
(DO), by appraisers Edward Pindar &
Benjamin Preistly.

Jacob Lookerman (g, DO) exhibited oath
of Priscilla Taylor administratrix of
John Taylor. Also exhibited oath of
John Pollard & Phineas Blackwood,
appraisers.

Exhibited inventory of William Hemsley
(TA), by appraisers Andrew Abbington &
Richard Sweatnam.

Exhibited bond of Jane Dunkins
administratrix of Patrick Dunkins.
Securities (AA): Walter Phillips,
William Fargason.

Exhibited bond of Priscilla Taylor (DO)
administratrix of John Taylor.
Securities: Thomas Pattison, James
Pattison.

24 July. Edward Man petitioned that he
had sent documents by Mr. Woodward.
Susan Evans executrix
13:381 is now Susan Richardson wife of John
Richardson. Date: 2 July 1686. John
Richardson & his wife Susan executrix of
Robert Evans were granted renewed
administration. Mr. Edward Mann to
administer oath.

Court Session: 1686

26 July. Leonard Greene (SM) for self &
Robert Greene & Francis Greene executors
of Henry Adams (CH) were granted
administration on his estate.
Appraisers: Robert Goodrick, Phillip
Jones. Capt. Ignatius Causeene to
administer oath.

Exhibited bond of John Chittam
administrator of Joseph Williams.
Securities (CV): Thomas Robinson, Thomas
Tucker. Thomas Tasker (g, CV) exhibited
oath of John Wilson & William Andmah
(?), appraisers of Joseph Williams.
Also exhibited inventory.

13:382 Mr. William Brereton (g, SO) exhibited
will of Henry Heyman (DO), proved.
However, none of the witnesses would
swear that the dec'd was of sound &
perfect mind. Said Brereton for
Ellioner Heyman executrix was granted
administration. Appraisers: Cornelius
Johnson, John Panter. Said Brereton to
administer oath.

Exhibited will of Richard Hill, Sr.
(SO), constituting his relict Willmett
Hill & Richard Hill executors. Mr.
James Round (SO) to prove said will.
Said Willmett & Richard were granted
administration. Appraisers: Thomas
Panther, John Smock. Said Round to
administer oath.

Col. William Stevens (SO) exhibited
oath of Florence Tucker (alias Florence
Melvile) executrix of Edward Stevens.
Also exhibited oath of Walter Lane &
William Noble, appraisers.

30 July. Mr. John Boring (g, BA)
exhibited oath of George Ashman & his
wife Elisabeth executrix of William
Ball. Also exhibited oath of James
Jackson & William Slade, appraisers.
Also exhibited inventory.
13:383 Also exhibited will, proved.

Capt. Richard Ladd (CV) exhibited oath
of Nathaniel Dare administrator of
Thomas & Ann Cleverly. Securities (CV):

Robert Dixon, John Watmore. Also
exhibited oath of Henry Mitchell &
Samuel Houldsworth, appraisers. Also
exhibited inventory.

4 August. Richard Southerne & Richard
Brightwell vs. executors of Maj. Thomas
Trueman. Libel exhibited. Mentions:
will of Thomas Trueman, Esq. bequeathed
to his wife Mary Trueman & residue to
cousins Mary Trueman, Elisabeth Trueman,
& Thomas Trueman Greenfeild &
constituted his wife & cousin Mary
Trueman executors & Thomas Greenfeild on
behalf of his son Thomas Trueman
Greenfeild & his cousin Elisabeth
Trueman executors.

13:384 Said Mary Trueman widow & Mary Trueman &
Thomas Greenfield were granted
administration. Appraisers: Mr.
Richard Marsham, Capt. Ninian Beale.
Said Mary Trueman widow is dec'd.
Richard Southerne & Richard Brightwell
(who married sisters of said Mary) were
granted administration on her estate.
Said Thomas Greenfeild & Mary Trueman
who married Thomas Holladay (g) conceal
the inventory.

Exhibited will of Francis Catterson
(TA), proved before Mr. William Combes.

Exhibited bond of Robert Carvile
administrator of Samuel Scott (London).
Security: Henry Denton (SM).

William Stevens petitioned that he
received by Capt. Whittington a letter
indicating LoA were not granted to Mr.
Traile on estate of (N) Batty because a
letter was received from Mr.

13:385 Archibald Ereskin who cited he was
principle creditor. Mentions: Mr. Batty
lived at Pocomoke. Said Stevens finds
no evidence that said Ereskin is a
creditor. Mentions: Mr. Jones, (N)
Ballard. Date: 30 July 1686 Rehoboth.
William Traile (SO) was granted
administration on estate of Hierome
Batty. Appraisers: Thomas Jones,
Samuell Cooper. Said Stevens to
administer oath.

Court Session: 1686

Anthony Underwood (g, SM) for Samuell
Warcup (g, CV) exhibited that Frances
now wife of said Warcup & relict of
Thomas Darcy (alias Thomas Matchett) was
granted administration.
13:386 LoA renewed. Col. Henry Jowles to
administer oath.

Exhibited inventory of Joseph Norwood
(KE), by appraisers Phillip Connor &
Alen Smith.

6 August. Capt. Richard Hill (AA)
exhibited oath of Ellioner Macubin
executrix of John Macubin. Also
exhibited oath of Samuel Howard &
Lancelott Todd, appraisers. Also
exhibited will, proved before said Hill.

Said Capt. Hill exhibited oath of Joseph
Connoway (AA) administrator of Joseph
Freene. Securities (AA): Richard Moss,
John Floyd. Also exhibited oath of
William Pennington & Robert Eagle,
appraisers.
13:387 Also exhibited inventory.

9 August   SMC. Exhibited will of
Edmond Webb (TA), proved before James
Murphy (g). Also exhibited inventory,
by appraisers John Newman & John Poore.

Exhibited letter from executors of (N)
Skipwith.

Henry Hanslap exhibited will of Robert
Phillips, constituting Francis Price
(infant) executor. Robert Lockwood who
married mother of said Price was granted
administration,
13:388 on behalf of said infant. Appraisers:
Samuel Garland, John Willowby.

Exhibited inventory of John Macubin
(AA), by appraisers Samuel Howard &
Lancelott Todd.

Exhibited bond of Daniel Longman
administrator of Richard Arnold (AA).
Securities (AA): Samuel Garland, Abell
Browne.

Page 190

Court Session: 1686

13:389 Petition of Ignatius Craycroft (CV) who married Sophia Beedle only daughter of Henry (dec'd) & Sophia Beedle (dec'd). Administration was originally granted to William Coursey (g, TA, now dec'd), & Elisabeth Coursey relict denies any account. Said Elisabeth summoned.

Thomas Whitchaly (CH) who married Jane Fanning executrix of John Fanning exhibited accounts.

Vertue Reader executrix of Symon Reader was granted continuance.

John Shankes (SM) who married Mary relict & administratrix of Robert Bridgin was granted continuance.

Sheriff (CH) exhibited summons to James Tyer executor of Peter Carr & that said Tyer "lies in such a languishing condition". Continuance was granted.

13:390 James Ellis who married relict of Maj. John Welch exhibited accounts, proved by Col. William Burges.

James Moore (CV) executor of Jonathon Pearce exhibited final accounts.

Exhibited were accounts of Lydia Quillaine on estate of Daniel Quillaine, examined by Col. William Stevens.

John Goudge one of executors of Thomas Gibson petitioned that John Newman the other executor be summoned.

Richard Hill petitioned that Blanch Burly now Blanch Stanton & Mary Bucknall now Mary Eager are exceedingly poor & incapable of coming down to SM. Date: 31 July 1686. Capt. Richard Hill to examine accounts of:
- George Eager & his wife Mary administratrix of Thomas Bucknall.
- William Stanton & his wife Blanch executrix of Stephen Burle.

13:391 Thomas Dryfeild administrator of William Fisher was granted continuance.

Richard Vowles (SM) who married relict & administratrix of William Cole exhibited accounts.

Richard Jenkins (CV) surviving executor of James Rumsey was granted continuance.

Commissioners (BA) exhibited accounts of estate of George Uty as inadequate.
13:392 Mentions bills of: John Turpin, John Ireland, John Davys.

William Meakin (SM) executor of Robert Beard exhibited accounts.

John Harrison who married relict & executrix of Thomas Baker (CH) exhibited accounts. Continuance was granted.

John Heard (SM) administrator of Daniel Louglin exhibited accounts.

James Veitch on behalf of his mother Mary Veitch was granted continuance on estate of James Veitch (CV).

John Reswick & his wife executrix of Abraham Combs were granted continuance.

13:393 Joseph Edlo (CV) administrator of Thomas Window was granted continuance.

John Crooke (CV) & his wife Sarah executrix of George Powell exhibited accounts. Continuance was granted.

William Jones (CV) exhibited accounts on estate of William Hitchcock. Continuance was granted.

John Skelton (SM) exhibited accounts on estate of Robert Croft. Continuance was granted.

Richard Bowen (CV) executor of Robert Stanely exhibited that several papers are in custody of Mr. Richard Marsham, who is gone to ENG. Continuance was granted.

John Reed (CV) administrator of Margaret Stagg was granted dismissal.

Court Session: 1686

Sarah Reynolds (CV) executrix of Henry Robinson was granted continuance.

13:394 Jeremiah Johnson (CV) & his wife Lucy administratrix of James Gilsterope exhibited accounts. Continuance was granted.

Margrett Dawkins (CV) executrix of Joseph Dawkins exhibited accounts. Continuance was granted.

Thomas George (SM) administrator of Benjamine George exhibited accounts.

William Medly administrator of Thomas Medly (SM) exhibited accounts.

Exhibited inventory of Maj. Thomas Trueman (CV), by appraisers Ninean Beale & Richard Marsham.

Joseph Cornell (CV) executor of John Pope exhibited accounts.

10 August. Martha Joy (CV) administratrix of Peter Joy exhibited accounts. Continuance was granted.

13:395 William Hatton (SM) exhibited accounts on estate of Richard Hatton.

James Barry (SM) exhibited accounts on estate of John Winn.

Capt. John Coode administrator of James Greene exhibited accounts.

Richard Newman (SM) exhibited accounts on estate of Michael Thompson.

John Cambell (g, SM) executor of Dorothy Homan exhibited accounts.

Lawrence Taylor (BA) administrator of Owen Williams was granted continuance.

Col. George Wells (BA) to summon Henry Johnson & his wife Elisabeth administratrix of Nathaniel Uty to render accounts. Said Wells to examine said accounts.

Court Session: 1686

13:396 Sheriff (BA) to summon Henry Johnson (BA) to be present at examination of accounts of Col. Nathaniell Uty.

Robert Carvile & other creditors of Richard Chillman (dec'd) vs. Gerard Slye administrator of said Chillman. Continuance was granted.

14 August. Robert Frazier (SM) who married Elisabeth widow of Dennis Hurley was granted administration on his estate. Appraisers: Phillip Briscoe, John Johnson. Capt. Joshua Doyne to administer oath.

13:397 **25 August.** Johannah Randall (AA) administratrix of Christopher Randall exhibited accounts.

Edward Fuller (AA) who married Sarah relict & administratrix of Thomas Tucker exhibited accounts.

Mary Eager (AA) executrix of Thomas Bucknall exhibited accounts.

Patrick Murphy (AA) exhibited accounts on estate of John Gray.

William Stanton (AA) exhibited accounts on estate of Stephen Burly.

John Griggs (g, CV) exhibited oath of Phillis White administratrix of Gustavus White, sworn 12 July 1686. Securities: John Evans, William King. Also exhibited oath of Thomas Parsloe & Jeremiah Simpson, appraisers sworn 13 July 1686. Also exhibited inventory.

13:398 Capt. Joshua Doyne (SM) exhibited oath of Samuel Chamberlaine administrator of Thomas Wright. Securities (SM): Thomas Carvile, Thomas Mattenly.

Capt. Joshua Doyne exhibited oath of appraisers of Dennis Hurley. Also exhibited bond of Robert Frazier administrator. Securities (SM): John Johnson, Thomas Barber.

Court Session: 1686

30 August. Exhibited inventory of
Edward Turner (SM), by appraisers Thomas
Simpson & Robert Greene.

Thomas Whitchaly (CH) who married
executrix of John Fanning exhibited
accounts.

2 September. John Ottidge (chirurgeon,
Bristoll, ENG) exhibited PoA from relict
of Dr. John Porter. Said Ottridge was
granted administration on estate of said
Porter. Appraisers: Charles Hinson,
William Harris. John Hinson (KE) to
administer oath.

Leonard Greene (SM) was granted
continuance on estate of Henry Adams.

13:399 Christopher Goodhand (KE) executor of
Sarah Harris was granted dismissal.

Allen Smith (KE) who married relict of
Lewis Blangey exhibited accounts.

6 September. Exhibited additional
inventory of Edward Connor (DO), by
appraisers Anthony Dawson & Richard
Willons. Bartholomew Ennalls executor
of said Connor exhibited accounts.

Richard Jenkins (CV) exhibited accounts
on estate of James Rumsey. Continuance
was granted.

13:400 Exhibited inventory of Dennis Hurley
(SM), by appraisers Phillip Briscoe &
John Johnson.

Richard Willons (DO) administrator of
Richard Dawson was granted continuance.

Richard Reed (CV) & Obadiah Evans (CV)
executors of Robert Andrews exhibited
accounts.

Elisabeth Higham (CV) executrix of
Francis Fooks exhibited accounts.

John Coates (CH) executor of Robert
Henly was granted continuance.

Per Miles Gibson (g, BA), new commission
was granted as per f. 339.

Sarah Collyer (BA) widow of John Collyer
was granted administration on his
estate. Appraisers: Arthur Taylor,
Robert Love. Miles Gibson (g) to
administer oath.

Sarah widow of John Tyllyard (BA)
exhibited his will, constituting her
executrix. Miles Gibson (g) to prove
said will. Said Sarah was granted
administration. Appraisers: Arthur
Taylor, Robert Love. Said Gibson to
administer oath.

13:401 7 September. Exhibited inventory of
Nathaniel Vening, by appraisers Randall
Brandt (CH) & John Cornell (CH).

Commissioners (AA) to summon Mary Shaw
orphan of John Shaw (AA) to choose a
guardian.

Exhibited oath of Mathias Matson &
Nicholas Allum executors of Thoes Rumsey
(CE). Also exhibited accounts.

Edward Laddamore (CE) exhibited accounts
on estate of Thomas Shelton.

Edward Laddimore son of Roger Laddimore
(CE) was granted administration on his
estate. Appraisers: James Robeson, John
Cox. Edward Jones (g, CE) to administer
oath.

John Hacker (TA) who married Bridgett
relict of David Johnson was granted
administration on his estate.
Appraisers: William Finney, John Damms.
Henry Coursey (g) to administer oath.

Gabriel Parrott (AA) exhibited accounts
on estate of John Dring.

13:402 George Uty next of kin & heir to Col.
Nathaniel Uty (BA) was granted
administration on his estate,
unadministered by Capt. Henry Johnson.
Appraisers: Edward Beedle, James

Phillips. Col. George Wells (g) to administer oath.

Capt. Henry Johnson (BA) exhibited accounts on estate of Col. Nathaniel Uty.

John Veitch (CV) on behalf of his mother Mary Veitch administratrix of James Veitch exhibited accounts.

John Goudge (CH) exhibited his renunciation, with consent of George Newman joint executor of Thomas Gibson. Witnesses: Samuel Cooper, W. Taylard.

Mathias Matson exhibited will of Henry Matson (CE), constituting him executor. Said Mathias was granted administration. Appraisers: Henry Riggs, William Ward. Nicholas Allum (g) to administer oath.

13:403 8 September. Phillip Holleager (CE) exhibited that he was a security to John Hagley (CE) administrator of Bartholomew Hendrickson & that said Hagley has failed in his administration of said estate. Said Holleager was granted administration on estate of said Hendrickson. Appraisers: Samuel Wheeler, Thomas Linsey. Nathaniel Garrett (g) to administer oath.

Katherine widow of Thomas Emmerson (TA) exhibited his will, constituting her executrix. George Robotham (g) to administer oath.

Henry Staples who married widow of Charles Turner (KE) was granted administration on his estate. Daniel Norris to administer oath.

John Browne (TA) exhibited will of Thomas Stevens (TA), constituting him executor. Said Browne was granted administration. George Robotham to prove said will & administer oath.

Thomas Deakins (SM) administrator of Daniel Hamond was granted continuance.

Court Session: 1686

13.404 John Lewis (TA) exhibited will of Walter
Bounsell (TA), constituting him
executor. Said Lewis was granted
administration. Appraisers: Daniel
Gl[?], Thomas Hinson.

John Thrift (TA) who married eldest
daughter of William Cooke (TA) was
granted administration on his estate.
George Robotham to administer oath.

Ebenezar Blackistone (CE) exhibited
accounts on estate of Sarah Blackistone.

Ebenezar Blackistone administrator of
Francis Herman exhibited inventory, by
appraisers Richard Pullen & Thomas
Hawkes. Administration was dismissed.

Elisabeth Ricaud (KE) executrix of
Benjamin Ricaud was granted continuance.

Cornelius Comegys (KE) was granted
administration on estate of William
Bunton (KE), as principle creditor.
Said estate is very inconsiderable.
Appraisers: John Bowles, Edward Fry.
Daniel Norris to administer oath.

13:405 Daniel Norris (KE) administrator of
Thomas Norris was granted continuance.

Exhibited bond of Samuel Luckett (CH)
who married administratrix of John
Gardiner. Securities (SM): Richard
Gardiner (g), Luke Gardiner (g).

Exhibited will of Samuel Pilesworth
(KE), proved before Mr. Edward Blay
(CE).

Thomas Mattenly (SM) administrator of
Robert Curtis was granted discharge.

Charles Tilden (KE) executor of Samuel
Pilesworth was granted continuance.

John Hawkins (TA) & his wife Elisabeth
exhibited accounts on estate of Dr.
James Eustis.

Court Session: 1686

Nicholas Cloud & Thomas Seaward
executors of William Bishop exhibited
accounts.

13:406 Nicholas Cloud & Thomas Seaward
executors of William Bishop exhibited
accounts on the following estates:
William Woods, Samuell Courcy, Thomas
Lewis, Hugh Johnson.

10 September. Robert Smith (TA)
administrator of Samuell Graves &
administrator of Henry Gill exhibited
accounts on both estates.

11 September. William Brereton (g, SO)
to administer oath to Thomas Cox & Isaac
Noble, appraisers of William Stevens.
Edward Day (SO) administrator of said
Stevens was granted continuance.

Theophilus Hackett executor of Henry
Howard was granted continuance.

Thomas Burford, Esq. on behalf of
Rebeccah Tyer (CH) exhibited the will of
James Tyre, constituting said Rebeckah
executrix. Said Burford to prove said
will & administer oath.

Richard Attwood (SM) exhibited accounts
on estate of William Aysbeston.

13:407 Robert Smith (g) petitioned for Henry
Coursey to examine accounts & administer
oath to the following, as they are
incapable of travelling as far as SM.
All are residents of TA.
• Margrett Peterson executrix of
  Mathias Peterson.
• William & Richard Powell executors
  of John Wilkinson.
• Thomas Bayly administrator of Thomas
  Bingham.

William Metcalfe (merchant, TA) as
nephew & attorney for Richard Metcalfe
(merchant, citizen, York, ENG, dec'd)
was granted administration on his
estate. Securities (TA): James Murphey
(g), Griffith Jones (g). Appraisers:
John Newman, Lawrence Knowles. James

Murphey to administer oath.

George Browne (KE) exhibited accounts on estate of Robert Newes.

John Godsgrace (CV) was granted administration on estate of James Godsgrace (CV). Appraisers: Edward Hurlong, John Leach.

13:408 14 September. Richard Lowder (KE) one of executors of William Hewson petitioned that the other executor Henry Hozier is dec'd. Said Lowder was summoned to render accounts.

Samuel Wheeler (CE) administrator of Alexander Naish exhibited accounts. New administration was granted to said Wheeler. Securities: Joseph Spernon, Michael Miller. Appraisers: Michael Miller, Allen Smith. Christopher Goodhand (g) to administer oath.

Michael Turbutt (TA) on behalf of Mrs. Elisabeth Coursey administratrix of William Coursey exhibited accounts on estate of Edward Beedle.

Col. Vincent Lowe to administer oath to Elisabeth Coursey administratrix of Maj. William Coursey on her accounts of his estate.

13:409 15 September. Nathaniel Cranford exhibited accounts on estate of John Gill (CV).

Joseph Spernon (CE) exhibited accounts on estate of Thomas Hinton.

16 September. William Harris (CV) brother of Henry Harris & his wife Ann was granted administration on estate of said Henry & Ann. Appraisers: William Taylor, Thomas Howe. Capt. Richard Ladd to administer oath.

Exhibited will of Maj. James Ringgold (KE), constituting his widow Mary executrix. John Hinson (g) to prove said will. Said Mary was granted

administration. Appraisers: Daniel
Norris, Phillip Davis. Said Hinson to
administer oath.

17 September. Edward Sweatnam (g, KE)
administrator of Edward Rogers exhibited
final accounts. Mentions: orphans
(under age).

13:410   Col. William Burges to administer oath
to Thomas Dryfeild administrator of Dr.
William Fisher for accounts. Mentions:
Mr. Neale.

Exhibited bond of David Parsons (SM)
administrator of Humphrey Jones.
Securities (SM): William Rosewell, John
Daish.

13:411   Exhibited inventory of Thomas Ferrabay
(KE), by appraisers Thomas Kemptone &
William Temple. Also exhibited will,
proved before William Lawrence (g).
Said Lawrence exhibited oath of Richard
Kempstone & William Temple, appraisers.

Nathaniel Garrett (g, CE) exhibited oath
of Christian Peterson administratrix of
Andrew Peterson (CE). Securities:
William Ward, Nicholas Dorrill. Also
exhibited oath of William Ward & Henry
Eldersly, appraisers. Also exhibited
inventory.

Exhibited inventory of Richard Arnold
(AA), by appraisers Samuel Garland &
Nicholas Nicholson.

Exhibited inventory of Capt. Joseph
Hopkins (CE), by appraisers Edward Beck
& George Higgenbotham.

Exhibited inventory of Nathaniell Reed
(TA), by appraisers Thomas Youl & Peter
Sides.

13:412   Exhibited will of Mary Wellman (CH),
proved before Robert Doyne (g).

Exhibited inventory of Richard & Rachell
Bayly (TA), by appraisers Thomas Robins
& Robert Bryant.

Court Session: 1686

Exhibited bond of William Young
administrator of Francis Parsons.
Securities (TA): William Dunderdell,
Edward Tomkins.

Exhibited inventory of Mary Long (TA),
by appraisers William Wintersell &
Richard White.

Mr. Henry Coursey (g, TA) exhibited
oath of:
- Mabell Offly administratrix of John
  Offly, sworn 30 October 1685.
- William Young administrator of
  Francis Parsons, sworn 27 October
  1685.
- Judith Hemsley executrix of William
  Hemsley, sworn 27 October 1685.
- Robert Smith administrator of Samuel
  Graves, Humphrey Davenport, & Henry
  Gill, sworn 24 January 1685.
- Margrett Peterson executrix of
  Mathias Peterson, sworn 5 April
  1686.
- Edward Thomlin administrator of
  Nathaniel Reed, sworn 6 January
  1685.
- Ursula Gould administratrix of
  Richard Gould, sworn 3 February
  1685.
- William Hemsley & his wife Cornelia
  executrix of Robert Noble, sworn 23
  March 1685.

13:413 Signed: Henry Coursey, Jr.
- will of Capt. Hemsley is not
  included.
- Ursula Gill cannot find security.
Further oaths:
- Robert Smith & William Sparkes,
  appraisers of John Offley, sworn 30
  October 1685.
- Thomas Ewell & William Clayton,
  appraisers of Francis Parsons, sworn
  27 October 1685.
- Richard Sweatnam & Andrew Abbington,
  appraisers of William Hemsley, sworn
  22 October 1685.
- Thomas Bruffe & Thomas Hinson,
  appraisers of Samuel Graves, Humphry
  Davenport, & Henry Gill, sworn 4
  January 1685/6.
- Robert Smith & Thomas Bruffe,

appraisers of Mathias Peterson,
sworn 4 January 1685/6.
• Peter Sides & Thomas Ewell,
appraisers of Nathaniell Reed, sworn
6 January 1685. Robert Smith & John
Whitting, appraisers of Richard
Gould, sworn 3 February 1685.

13:414 Exhibited will of Mary Long (TA), proved
before Mr. Edward Mann.

Exhibited will of Abraham Holman (BA),
proved before Col. George Wells. Also
exhibited oath of Sarah Collyer
administratrix. Also exhibited oath of
William Yorke & John Hall, appraisers.
Also exhibited inventory.

Exhibited inventory of Stephen Kaddy
(KE), by appraisers Michael Miller &
John Bowles.

20 September. Exhibited inventory of
John Cammell (CE), by appraisers John
Hiland & Samuel Wheeler.

Exhibited bond of Robert Smith
administrator of Henry Gill. Security:
Thomas Collins (TA).

Exhibited inventory of Robert Noble
(TA), by appraisers Richard Sweatnam &
Andrew Abbington.

Exhibited will of John Humberstone,
proved before Mr. Edward Mann (TA).

Exhibited will of Thomas Long, proved.

13:415 Exhibited bond of John Tiley
administrator of John Humberstone.
Securities (TA): John Eason, Francis
Chaplin.

Exhibited inventory of Humphry Davenport
(TA), by appraisers Thomas Hinson &
Thomas Bruffe.

Capt. Warren (CH) exhibited oath of
Richard Land administrator of Thomas &
Mary Harris. Securities (CH): Joseph
Cornell, William Hawton.

Exhibited inventory of Thomas Pellien
(SM), by appraisers Thomas Dillon &
Edward Feild.

Mr. Edward Mann exhibited oath of widow
Barks & certified that there is no
estate.

Exhibited inventory of Francis Parsons
(TA), by appraisers Thomas Ewell &
William Clayton.

Exhibited bond of Edward Thomlin
administrator of Nathaniel Reed (TA).
Securities: William Young, William
Dundedell.

Exhibited will of david Johnson (TA),
proved before Henry Coursey, Jr. (g).

Edward Beedle (g, BA) exhibited oath of
Col. George Wells administrator of
Samuel Dockins. Also exhibited oath of
Richard Edmonds & Lawrence Taylor,
appraisers.
13:416 Also exhibited bond of Col. George
Wells administrator of Symon Dockins
(BA). Securities (BA): Lawrence Taylor,
Peter Fugate. Also exhibited inventory.

Exhibited inventory of Humphrey Jones
(SM), by appraisers William Rosewell &
John Daish.

Exhibited inventory of Mathias Peterson
(TA), by appraisers Robert Smith &
Thomas Bonstel.

Exhibited bond of Robert Smith
administrator of Humphrey Davenport.
Security: Thomas Collins (TA).

Exhibited bond of John Godshall
administrator of Mary Wenman.
Securities (CH): Richard Clawler,
Christopher Breenes.

Exhibited will of Edward Gibbins, proved
before Mr. Edward Mann.

Exhibited will of Ann Doubty (CH),
proved before Robert Doyne (g).

Exhibited bond of Mabell Offly
administratrix of John Offly.
Securities (TA): Thomas Tench, John
Cealy. Also exhibited oath of Philip
Collins & Allen Smith, appraisers sworn
by Christopher Goodhand (KE).

13:417 21 September. Exhibited inventory of
Henry Everett (AA), by appraisers Thomas
Knighton & Thomas Morgan.

Exhibited inventory of John Gill (CV),
by appraisers William Williams & Joseph
Baker.

Exhibited will of Henry Everett (AA),
proved before Thomas Tench (g). Also
exhibited oath of James Maxfeild
executor. Also exhibited oath of Thomas
Knighton & Thomas Morgan, appraisers.

Thomas Tench (g) exhibited oath of
Robert Connant administrator of Samuel
Mitchell (CV). Also exhibited oath of
Richard Thornbury & Leonard Coates,
appraisers.

Exhibited will of Henry Bennett (AA),
proved before Mr. Thomas Tench. Also
exhibited oath of Samuel Clarke (CV)
administrator. Also exhibited oath of
Walter Carr & James Murphy, appraisers.

Exhibited will of Thomas Robinson (CH),
proved before Robert Doyne (g).
13:418 Exhibited inventory, by appraisers John
Cabell James Marling.

Exhibited inventory of Thomas Collins
(CV), by appraisers Robert Burle & (N).

Exhibited inventory of William Collins
(CV), by appraisers Robert Burle & John
Browne.

Henry Jowles (CV) exhibited oath of
James Keech administrator of Christopher
Pinkney. Security: Richard Gardiner (g,
CV). Also exhibited inventory, by
appraisers Gabriel Burnham & John
Dossett.

Exhibited inventory of Edward Stevens (SO), by appraisers William Noble & Walter Lane.

Exhibited inventory of Henry Hozier (KE), by appraisers Michael Miller & John Bowles.

Ignatius Causeene (g, CH) exhibited oath of Leonard Greene, Robert Greene, & Francis Greene executors of Henry Adams. Also exhibited oath of Robert Goodrick & Phillip (N), appraisers.

Exhibited bond of Robert Smith administrator of Samuel Graves. Security: Thomas Collins (TA).

13:419 Exhibited bond of Christian Pethens administratrix of Thomas Pethens. Securities (SM): Francis Knott, William Shercliffe.

Mary Shankes administratrix of Robert Bridgin exhibited accounts.

Exhibited inventory of Samuel Graves & inventory of John Gill, by appraisers Thomas Bruff & Thomas Hinson.

Thomas Burford, Esq. (CH) exhibited oath of Joseph Cornell & his wife Mary administratrix of Robert Worrall.

Exhibited will of Mathias Peterson (TA), proved before Henry Coursey, Jr. (g).

Exhibited inventory of John Humberstone (TA), by appraisers William Wintersell & Richard White.

Mr. Edward Mann (TA) exhibited oath of Richard Roystone & Thomas Vaughan, appraisers of Francis Catterson.

Exhibited bond of William Dale administrator of Mary Long. Securities (TA): John Yate, John Earos (?).

Exhibited will of Thomas Harris (CH), proved before Humphry Warren (g).

Court Session: 1686

William Brereton (g, SO) exhibited that
Richard Stevens & John Booth refused to
take oath as executors of John Trueman
(SO).
13:420 Exhibited inventory of said Trueman, by
appraisers Daniel Hast & Phillip Ascue.
Also exhibited will, proved before
William Brereton (g, SO).

Exhibited will of John Evans (SO),
proved before James Dashiel (g).
Exhibited inventory, by appraisers
William Brereton & Richard Crockett.

Exhibited will of Samuel Simms (SO),
constituting Benjamine Cottman executor.
Mr. William Brereton (g, SO) to prove
said will. Said Cottman was granted
administration. Appraisers: William
Robinson, Thomas Relph. Said Brereton
to administer oath.

Charles Tilden (g, KE) to administer
oath to Searah Jennings (alias Searah
Steward) administratrix of Charles
Steward (KE) on her accounts.

24 September. John Waters (AA) &
Richard Gottee (AA) exhibited will of
Thomas Pratt (AA), constituting them
executors. Said Waters & Gottee were
granted administration. Appraisers:
Walter Carr, Benjamine Capell. Capt.
Henry Hanslap to administer oath.

13:421 John Edwards (TA) was granted
administration on estate of James
Mitchell (TA). Appraisers: Walter
Phelps, Benjamin Evans. Capt. Henry
Hanslap to administer oath.

1 October. Exhibited inventory of
Arthur Leadford (CV), by appraisers
Robert Dow & Richard Clarke.

Thomas Tasker (g, CV) exhibited oath of
Francis Higham & John Smith, appraisers
of Michael Highgens, sworn 4 August
last. Also exhibited inventory of
Michael Higgens.

Court Session: 1686

Exhibited inventory of Thomas Wright
(SM), by appraisers Thomas Carvile &
Thomas Martingly.

6 September [sic]. Capt. Richard Hill
(g, AA) to administer oath to Lawrence
Draper administrator of Walter Smith.

Thomas Tench (g, AA) to administer oath
to Margrett Gill on accounts on estate
of Francis Holland.

Mr. Thomas Tench to administer oath to
Abraham Thornbury administrator of
Mathew Axon & administrator of Richard
Bedworth.

13:422   Exhibited inventory of Walter Smith, by
appraisers William Freeman & Thomas
Freebourne.

8 October. Mrs. Ann Gerrard (SM) widow
of Thomas Gerrard exhibited his will,
constituting her executrix. Mr. James
Bowling to prove said will. Said Ann
was granted administration. Appraisers:
Humphry Warren, Thomas Mudd. Said
Bowling to administer oath.

Mr. Ann Gerrard widow of Thomas Gerrard
exhibited that there never was any goods
or chattel possessed by estate of Daniel
Johnson (dec'd). Dismissal was granted.

Mrs. Ann Gerrard executrix of Thomas
Gerrard exhibited accounts on estate of
Robert Browne (SM). Continuance was
granted.

11 October. Ann Clarke (SM) executrix
of John Clarke exhibited his will. Said
Ann was granted administration.
Appraisers: Richard Edlen, John Compton.
Mr. Joseph Piles to administer oath.

12 September [sic]. Jane Buttram widow
of Nicholas Buttram (CV) was granted
administration on his estate.
Appraisers: Hezekiah Bussey, George
Bussey. Francis Hutchins to administer
oath.

13:423 20 October. Exhibited inventory of Francis Catterson (TA), by appraisers Richard Roystone & Thomas Vaughan.

23 October. Edward Seissons (SM) who married relict of John Morris (SM) was granted administration on his estate. Securities: Peter Carwardin, Phillip Jones. Appraisers: Peter Carwardin, Phillip Jones.

George Robotham (g) to examine accounts of John Lane & his wife Mary executrix of John Marks (TA).

29 October. Gilbert Hamilton (SO) exhibited that William Traile was granted administration on estate of Hierome Batty. But said Traile was not sworn & refuses administration. Said Hamilton was granted administration, as principle creditor. Appraisers: Archibald Arreskill, Richard Farewell. Col. William Stevens to administer oath.

George Robins (g, TA) to prove will of John Edmondson, Jr. (TA).

13:424 Capt. Richard Hill (AA) to prove will of John Sunderland, per request of Ann Sunderland (AA).

William Harris (g, KE) to prove will of Thomas Thorpe, per request of Robert Ereck (KE).

9 November. George Reed (TA) exhibited accounts on estate of William Beltore.

11 November. Exhibited inventory of John Maccubin (AA).

15 November. Col. George Wells (BA) was granted administration on estate of Nicholas Browne (BA), as principle creditor. Appraisers: George Gouldsmith, Richard Edmond. Edward Beedle (g, BA) to administer oath.

Michaell Miller was granted administration on estate of James Miller

(KE), as principle creditor.
Appraisers: George Greene, John Carter.
William Harris (g, KE) to administer
oath.

13:425 Rachell Willington, wife of Richard
Willington, relict of Richard Grey
(KE) renounced administration on his
estate, as estate is inconsiderable.
Date: 10 October 1686. Witnesses: M.
Miller, Thomas Keares. Cornelius
Comegys (KE) was granted administration
on said estate. Appraisers: Thomas
Piner, John Chaife. Daniel Norris (g)
to administer oath.

Mary Carpendar sister to William
Carpendar (TA) was granted
administration on his estate. Col.
Henry Coursey (g) to administer oath.

16 November. Ann widow of John Cocker
(CE) was granted administration on his
estate. Appraisers: William Mansfeild,
William Ball. William Dare (g) to
administer oath.

13:426 Phillip Barratt who married Ann relict
of William Sinckler (CE) was granted
administration on his estate. Edward
Jones (g, CE) to administer oath.

18 November. Exhibited will of Zachiah
Thomas (TA), constituting his widow
Priscilla executrix. Henry Coursey (g)
to prove said will. Said Priscilla was
granted administration. Appraisers:
Solomon Wright, Daniel Glover. Said
Coursey to administer oath.

20 November. Anthony Underwood
procurator for Stephen Luffe vs. Arnold
Elzy administrator of Charles Ballard.
Said Elzy has been cited numerous times
to render accounts but has not.
13:427 Ruling: Said Elzy to deliver to said
Luffe 1/3rd portion to be deducted from
the appraisal by David Browne & Roger
Woolford, due to said Luffe in right of
his wife Sarah widow of said Ballard.

Court Session: 1686

William Dare (g, CE) exhibited accounts
on estate of Francis Fry. Discharge was
granted.

William Dare (CE) for Martha Wamsly
administratrix of Thomas Wamsly
exhibited accounts.

23 November. Col. William Stevens (SO)
to prove will of Randall Revell (SO).
Appraisers: Robert King, John King.

13:428   Exhibited will of Henry Bishop (SO),
constituting his widow Ann Bishop
executrix. Col. William Stevens to
prove said will. Said Ann was granted
administration. Appraisers: Mathew
Scarborough, Samuell Hopkins. Said
Stevens to administer oath.

Magdalen widow of James Traine (SO) was
granted administration on his estate.
Appraisers: John Townsend, Henry Hudson.
Col. William Stevens to administer
oath.

Exhibited inventory of Garrett
Garrettson, which was deducted out of
estate of John Yeo, with receipt of
Edward Beedle.

Mr. Thomas Brooke (CV) to prove will of
Robert Skinner.

John Bayne (g, CH) exhibited
renunciation of executor of Robert
Browne, Jr. Thomas Gerrard (g, SM) is
the other executor. Date: 5 August
1686.

13:429   27 November. William Thomas (TA) who
married Ann Lanvin relict of Robert
Lanvin (TA) was granted administration
on his estate. Appraisers: (N), Thomas
Lurkey. James Murphy (g) to administer
oath.

Edward Jones (g, CE) exhibited oath of
John Hiland & George Oldfeild,
appraisers of Edward Fry (CE).

Court Session: 1686

Exhibited inventory of Mary Wenman (CH),
by appraisers John Lambert & Phillip
Hoskins.

Exhibited will of John Cammell (CE),
proved before Edward Jones. Also
exhibited inventory, by appraisers John
Hiland & Samuel Wheeler.

Mr. Henry Coursey (g, TA) exhibited:
• oath of John Hacker administrator of
  David Johnson, sworn 21 September.
  Also oath of William Finney,
  appraiser sworn same day. Also oath
  of John Dawson, appraiser sworn 19
  October.
• oath of John Lewis administrator of
  Walter Bounsell (TA), sworn 16
  October. Also oath of Thomas Bruffe
  & Thomas Hinson, appraisers sworn 18
  October.

13:430 Exhibited bond of John Hudson
administrator of James Agg (DO).
Securities (DO): John Woodward, William
Dossey.

Exhibited inventory of Thomas Robinson
(SM), by appraisers John Cabell & James
Marting.

George Robotham (g, TA) exhibited oath
of John Pursell (TA) administrator of
Symon Stevens. Securities (TA): Peter
Sydes, John Dames (or Davis). Also
exhibited oath of Richard Sweatnam &
Andrew Abbington, appraisers.

Exhibited will of Trustram Thomas (TA),
proved before George Robotham (g). Also
exhibited oath of Ann Thomas executrix.
Also exhibited oath of William Finney &
Peter Sides, appraisers. Also exhibited
inventory.

29 November. Col. George Wells (BA)
exhibited oath of Thomas Jones
administrator of Daniel Wine (BA).
Securities: William Osbourne, John
Wright. Also exhibited oath of William
Yorke & Thomas Preston, appraisers.
13:431 Also exhibited inventory.

Court Session: 1686

Francis Hutchins (g, CV) exhibited
accounts of Gilbert Deavour on estate of
John Johnson (CV).

Exhibited inventory of Thomas Harris &
Mary Harris (CH), by appraisers John
Courts (CH) & Ralph Smith (CH).

William Brereton (g, SO) exhibited oath
of Cornelius Johnson & John Poynter,
appraisers of Henry Hayman. Also
exhibited inventory. Also exhibited
bond ob Eleonor Hayman administratrix.
Securities: Cornelius Johnson, Henry
Maun.

Exhibited will of Walter Bounsell (TA),
proved before Henry Coursey (g).

George Lingan (g, CV) exhibited oath of
Margery Mines administratrix of Robert
Mines (CV). Securities (CV): Richard
Brooke, Obadiah Evans. Also exhibited
oath of John Muffett & Gawin Hamilton,
appraisers.

13:432 Also exhibited inventory.

Col. William Stevens (SO) exhibited
oath of John Macketrick administrator of
Henry Cole.

Exhibited inventory of Edward Abbott
(CH), by appraisers Michael Minock &
John Boswell.

Exhibited inventory of John White (SO),
by appraisers Richard Wood & Richard
Warren.

Exhibited inventory of Richard Morris
(CH), by appraisers John Wood & William
Theobalds.

Exhibited will of William Kercum (TA),
proved before George Robbins (g).

John Brooke (g, DO) exhibited oath of
Rebeccah Sergeant administratrix of
Joseph Sergeant. Securities (DO): James
Peterkin, John Salisbury. Also
exhibited oath of John Edwards & Richard
Willins, appraisers.

Court Session: 1686

Edward Jones (g, CE) exhibited oath of
John Hiland & George Oldfeild,
appraisers of Francis Fry. Also
exhibited inventory.

GENERAL INDEX

Archer
  Peter 21, 30, 31
Arden
  John 31
Ardesty
  George 10, 16
Ardis
  Robert 66, 70
Arfitt
  William 115
Arme
  Robert 181
Armstrong
  Anne 14, 25
  Eduard 25
Arnall
  Richard 52
Arnell
  Martha 24
Arnold
  Martha 154
  Richard 6, 154,
    174, 190, 201
Arnoll
  Richard 24, 156
Arreskill
  Archibald 209
Asbey
  William 3
Aschcom
  John 177
Ascomb
  Nathaniell 126
Ascue
  Phillip 172, 207
Ashcomb
  Nathaniell 186
Ashcombe
  John 70
Ashcome
  John 80
  Nathaniell 80
  Samuell 80
Ashford
  Michael 36, 132
Ashman
  Elisabeth 188
  George 147, 188
Aspeanwall
  Elisabeth 30
  Henry 29, 30
Aspenaile
  Henry 183
Atkins

Anne 114
Jos. 6
Joshua 135, 149,
  154
Atthow
  Thomas 92
Attkins
  Ann 183
Attwood
  Richard 123, 137,
    170, 171, 183,
    199
Atwood
  Richard 130
Awdery
  Simon 51
Axon
  Mathew 181, 208
  Matthew 91
Aysbeston
  William 199

Baall
  William 59
Bagby
  Samuel 10, 182, 186
  Samuell 16
Bagnall
  (N) 69, 77
  Robert 13
Bailey
  John 67
Bailly
  John 96
  Rachell 95
  Richard 95
Baily
  Rachell 54, 75
  Richard 75
Baker
  (N) 77
  Elisabeth 82, 84
  Hugh 82, 101, 145
  Isaac 127, 155, 182
  Isaack 157, 159
  John 12, 13, 77,
    158, 168, 178
  Joseph 13, 89, 113,
    148, 205
  Martha 78
  Thomas 78, 80, 85,
    192
  William 13

199
Bayne
    Christopher 108
    John 26, 85, 86,
        211
Baynes
    Christopher 122,
        147
Bayton
    George 84, 101
Beal
    Ninian 125
Beale
    John 143
    Matthew 58, 75
    Ninean 137, 193
    Ninian 137, 184,
        189
Beall
    Ninean 36
    Ninian 21, 30, 40
Beamont
    James 12, 77
Beand
    John 72
Beanes
    Christopher 118
Beard
    Richard 4, 29, 82,
        105, 135, 140,
        143, 146, 147,
        151
    Robert 97, 179, 192
Beauchamp
    Edm. 124
Beaumont
    John 78
Beck
    Eduard 21, 36, 62,
        64
    Edward 136, 164,
        201
Beckle
    Thomas 107
Bed
    John 93
Bedell
    Eduard 48
    Edward 31
Bedworth
    Richard 18, 28, 92,
        181, 208
    Sarah 18, 28
Beech

Elias 108
Beedle
    (N) 75
    Eduard 24
    Edward 138, 166,
        168, 196, 200,
        204, 209, 211
    Henry 156, 158,
        162, 191
    Mary 152
    Sophia 156, 158,
        162, 191
Beetonson
    Edmond 58
    Lydia 58
Bell
    Barbara 5
    Thomas 5
Belt
    John 82, 151
Beltore
    William 209
Bendger
    Robert 68
Benett
    John 40
Benfey
    Susanna 125
Benfy
    Paul 125
Bennett
    George 149
    Henry 149, 205
    John 41, 50, 65
    Margarett 83, 92
    Mary 83, 92
    William 83, 92, 97
Bennitt
    Henry 149, 162
    John 180
Benson
    James 126, 134,
        153, 166
    Robert 146
Bensy
    Paul 135
Berief
    William 3, 9, 29
Berry
    Ann 182
    James 182
Best
    John 107
Bevan

John 102
Bevans
Rowland 104
Bevene
John 147
Bevin
Christopher 137
John 126
Bevine
Charles 149
Bexley
William 99
Bigger
James 120, 123, 163
John 75, 163
Margarett 123
Margret 163
Biggs
John 58
Seth 29, 40
Bill
Mary 183
Mathew 183
Billingsly
George 98
Bingham
Rebeccah 122
Thomas 110, 114,
122, 171, 199
Binks
Elisabeth 121
Thomas 121, 132,
135, 141, 159
Bird
Elisabeth 9, 20,
23, 29, 51, 64
John 9, 20, 23, 29,
51, 64, 103
Birkett
Richard 88
Birkhead
Abraham 127, 155
Ann 127
Bisco
James 128
Bishop
Ann 211
Henry 211
Thomas 176
William 40, 43, 44,
63, 94, 107,
110, 113, 122,
175, 199
Blackburne

Eduard 14
Blackiston
Ebenezar 11, 45,
163, 170
John 11
Nehemiah 142
Sarah 11, 24
Blackistone
Ebenezar 154, 162,
198
Nehemiah 144
Sarah 198
Blackwood
Phineas 127, 154,
187
Phineous 185
Blagborne
Eduard 22
Blagburne
Eduard 25
Blagg
Abraham 127, 186
Blakiston
Ebenezar 100
Neh. 56
Nehemiah 61, 100
Blamford
Thomas 83
Blanckensteine
William 25
Bland
Thomas 29, 50, 60
Blandford
Thomas 21, 79
Blandfort
& 31
Thomas 30
Blang
Francis 43, 71, 82
Blangey
Lewis 66, 195
Blangy
Francis 163
Lewis 98, 105
Blankensteine
William 51, 65, 69,
77, 80
Blankenston
William 84
Blay
Edward 164, 177,
198
Blomfeild
John 61, 149

John 181
Bowls
    John 31
Bowly
    James 145
Boyce
    John 47
Boyden
    Elisabeth 109, 165
    William 109, 165
Boyer
    Elisabeth 177
    Richard 177
Bradie
    Andrew 166
Braine
    Elisabeth 181
    Thomas 181
Bramson
    Thomas 66
Bramstone
    Thomas 53, 63
Brandt
    Randall 196
    Rando. 139, 165,
       173
Breenes
    Christopher 204
Brent
    Henry 138
Brereton
    Thomas 168
    William 73, 93,
       126, 168, 170,
       172, 188, 199,
       207, 213
Brewer
    Charles 42
    Elisabeth 42
Bridgin
    Mary 112
    Robert 112, 191,
       206
Bright
    John 100
    Richard 184
Brightwell
    Richard 189
Brisco
    John 154
Briscoe
    John 113
    Phillip 81, 194,
       195

Broadrib
    Isabella 133
    Sybella 124
    Sybilla 160
Broadway
    Nicholas 61
Brome
    John 91, 176
Brook
    Thomas 88
Brooke
    Eduard 35
    Francis 103
    John 81, 126, 213
    Richard 213
    Roger 2, 5, 147
    Thomas 60, 77, 91,
       116, 117, 118,
       121, 137, 181,
       184, 211
Brookes
    John 75, 81
    Roger 46
    Thomas 51
Broome
    John 62, 71, 159,
       162
Brough
    Joseph 17, 69
    Thomas 100, 126
Broughton
    Richard 91
Brown
    John 95
    Robert 109
Browne
    Abell 1, 174, 190
    David 1, 2, 9, 116,
       136, 148, 210
    George 121, 200
    Hannah 109, 137
    John 13, 30, 67,
       71, 100, 123,
       136, 148, 175,
       197, 205
    Nicholas 209
    Peter 23, 25, 32,
       53, 72
    Robert 26, 32, 123,
       137, 144, 208,
       211
    Thomas 8, 73
    William 169
Bruff

Thomas 206
Bruffe
   Thomas 202, 203,
     212
Bryan
   Robert 96, 111, 149
Bryant
   Robert 201
Buckinall
   Mary 20
   Thomas 20
Bucknall
   Mary 30, 191
   Thomas 30, 191, 194
Buckston
   George 108
Buckstone
   Francis 134, 161,
     166
   George 176, 181,
     185
Bullett
   Joseph 14
Bullock
   John 1, 2, 11, 17,
     112, 138, 141
Buntham
   Robert 176
Bunton
   William 198
Buoges
   John 109
Burckhead
   Richard 41
Burcut
   Richard 114
Burdeck
   Parthenia 23
   Sarah 23
Burden
   William 57
Burditt
   Parthenia 47, 59,
     177
   Sarah 47, 59, 177
Burford
   Thomas 50, 199, 206
Burges
   Edward 162
   Samuell 87, 93, 104
   William 2, 44, 54,
     82, 87, 91, 102,
     150, 151, 168,
     191, 201

Burgess
   Edward 123
   Samuel 184
   William 39, 40, 55,
     63
Burgin
   Phillip 20
Burkett
   Richard 93
Burkhead
   Richard 56
Burle
   Blanch 44, 48
   Robert 205
   Stephen 44, 48, 53,
     191
Burly
   Blanch 191
   Stephen 194
Burman
   Robert 111
Burnam
   William 37, 41
Burne
   William 68
Burneham
   Gabriell 187
   William 116
Burnham
   Gabriel 205
   William 85
Burton
   Richard 23
   William 179
Bussey
   George 134, 166,
     208
   Hezekiah 166, 208
   Paul 140
   Susannah 140
Bussy
   Paul 140
   Susannah 140
Butcher
   John 33, 51, 121,
     144
Butler
   Alice 180
   Charles 180
   John 132, 133, 138,
     159
Button
   Thomas 186
Buttram

Mark 90
Clare
    Marke 50, 62, 89,
        94, 99, 155
Clark
    Daniell 82
    John 160, 179
Clarke
    Abraham 55, 149,
        162
    Ann 208
    Daniell 98, 104
    Eduard 13
    George 31, 53
    Hanah 171
    Hannah 156, 158
    James 126
    John 59, 79, 84,
        87, 94, 124,
        136, 146, 170,
        174, 179, 208
    Marke 152, 177
    Phillip 156, 158
    Richard 88, 91,
        181, 207
    Robert 118, 124,
        131, 142
    Samuel 205
    Samuell 101
    Sarah 118
    Susan 84, 93
    Susanna 90
    Thomas 17, 23, 87,
        88, 92, 97
Clarkeson
    Johanna 117
    Robert 117, 174
Clawler
    Richard 204
Clay
    Henry 43
Clayton
    William 202, 204
Clerk
    Eduard 13
Clerke
    Abraham 39
    John 48
Cleverly
    Ann 127, 155, 157,
        159, 188
    Thomas 121, 127,
        155, 157, 159,
        188

Climer
    Anne 74
    John 68, 74, 80
Clipsham
    Susanna 78, 85
    Thomas 14, 19, 41,
        49, 57, 78, 85
Clocker
    Daniell 24, 42
    Patience 24
Clothier
    Lewis 72
    Susanna 72
Cloud
    Nicholas 171, 199
    Richard 105, 132,
        133, 138
Clouder
    Richard 165
Clouds
    Nicholas 107, 110,
        113, 114
Clowder
    Richard 72
Coale
    Eduard 38
    Henery 38
    William 45, 48
Coates
    John 52, 195
    Leonard 205
Cobb
    James 7, 22, 25
Cobreadth
    John 50, 62
Cobreath
    John 39, 55, 98
Cock
    John 81
Cocke
    (N) 69
    William 51
Cocker
    Ann 210
    John 210
    Thomas 83, 92
Cockes
    Samuell 13
Cocks
    Audery 65, 69, 77,
        84
    George 84, 182
    William 53, 65, 69,
        77, 80, 84, 178

Coffin
Henry 108
Cole
Eduard 35
Edward 92, 94, 112
Henry 118, 150,
151, 169, 213
John 186
Margrett 37
Robert 77, 92, 129
William 37, 192
Colebourne
William 74, 118,
170
Coleman
Edward 164
Colland
James 6
Collfeild
George 41
Collings
George 36
Collins
George 40, 181
Philip 205
Thomas 203, 204,
205, 206
William 123, 205
Collom
Giles 165
Collyer
Francis 35, 125,
140
James 2, 16, 55,
153, 167
John 196
Sarah 163, 196, 203
Comb
Abraham 49
William 72
Combe
Abraham 70
Combes
Abraham 87, 118
Elisabeth 6
Margarett 87
Mr. 153
William 6, 16, 52,
75, 79, 83, 134,
135, 136, 149,
153, 154, 177,
178, 189
Combs
(N) 131

Abraham 192
Comegys
Cornelius 129, 130,
133, 144, 145,
146, 152, 160,
186, 198, 210
William 146, 171
Compton
John 208
Conant
Robert 18, 19, 28,
40, 44, 61
Connant
Robert 162, 164,
176, 205
Conner
Ednor 81
Phillip 85, 106,
108, 110, 157
Thomas 81
Connor
Edward 195
Philip 72, 74, 79
Phillip 3, 121,
125, 190
Connoway
Joseph 157, 174,
190
Constable
Henry 16, 31, 86,
90, 96, 97
William 35
Conybear
Samuell 63
Conykear
Samuell 43
Cood
John 27, 54
Coode
John 105, 106, 193
Cook
Samuell 109
Cooke
James 111
Thomas 57, 68
William 150, 198
Cooksey
Samuel 128
Coole
Peter 20
Coomb
Abraham 104
Margarett 93
Coombes

Robert 116
Craine
　Richard 2, 25
　Robert 11, 25, 29,
　　32
Craines
　Richard 1
Crane
　Robert 40, 43
Cranford
　James 55, 106, 121,
　　141
　Nathaniel 200
Cranson
　Thomas 83
Crawford
　James 50
Craxton
　Thomas 146
Craycroft
　Ignatius 191
　John 89, 142, 184
Crayker
　Samuel 131
Creycroft
　John 43, 60, 63,
　　71, 91, 110, 140
Crockett
　Richard 9, 23, 172,
　　207
Croft
　Robert 192
Crofts
　Robert 179
Cromwell
　Elisabeth 42, 59,
　　147
　William 42, 59
Crook
　John 117
Crooke
　John 122, 180, 192
　Sarah 122, 180, 192
Croshan
　William 34
Croshaw
　William 3, 57, 58,
　　69, 85
Croshow
　William 48, 65, 67
Cross
　John 128, 153, 157
Crouch
　John 139

Crow
　Gournay 10
Crowder
　Thomas 62
Crud
　William 7
Cullen
　Catherine 77
　James 37, 42, 58,
　　69, 77, 84, 87,
　　116, 128, 133,
　　137
　Mr. 93
Cullins
　James 133
Cullis
　Barbara 108
　Charles 108, 116,
　　150
Cuningham
　Alexander 72
Cunningham
　Alexander 94
Curer
　William 42
Currer
　William 57, 62
Curtis
　Robert 87, 94, 160,
　　198
Cusick
　Michael 128, 131
Custins
　Richard 7
Custis
　John 6
Cuthbert
　Stephen 83, 98, 178

Daborne
　Thomas 44, 54, 59,
　　63
Daish
　John 201, 204
Dakins
　Thomas 72
Dale
　Henry 135, 149, 154
　William 158, 206
Daley
　Brian 14
　Bryan 13, 14
　Bryant 65, 71

Rebecca 65
Dames
    John 212
Damms
    John 196
Daniel
    Joane 150
    John 159, 182
    Thomas 150
Daniell
    Elisabeth 89, 92
    Isaac 113
    John 89, 92, 183
Danton
    Thomas 179
Darcy
    Frances 120
    Thomas 120, 156,
        190
Dare
    Elisabeth 121, 132
    Michaell 182
    Nathaniel 121, 132,
        188
    Nathaniell 95, 159
    William 42, 78, 95,
        175, 210, 211
Darnall
    Col. 93, 94
    Henry 4, 6, 50, 58,
        65, 70, 80, 83,
        92, 100, 120,
        121, 131, 132,
        139, 141, 172
    John 32, 34, 46,
        59, 64, 80, 92,
        98, 121, 127,
        138, 151
    Susanna 92
Dash
    John 93
Dasheile
    John 172
Dashiel
    James 207
Dassey
    James 148
    John 98
Davenport
    Humphrey 202, 204
    Humphry 114, 129,
        202, 203
    Katherine 114
Davidg

Providence 16
    Robert 16
Davidge
    Robert 8, 50
Davies
    David 32, 34
    John 58, 75, 105
    William 58, 71
Davis
    Elisabeth 145
    John 115, 116, 132,
        136, 149, 150,
        176, 212
    Phillip 201
    Robert 145
    Thomas 91, 143,
        163, 165
Davys
    John 192
Dawkin
    William 127
Dawkins
    Joseph 118, 131,
        137, 193
    Margarett 118, 131
    Margrett 193
Dawsett
    John 117, 122, 147
Dawson
    Anthony 81, 195
    John 212
    Ralph 115
    Richard 18, 25, 81,
        195
Day
    Eduard 62
    Edward 124, 126,
        170, 173, 199
    Elisabeth 62
    John 128
    Thomas 39, 91
Dayly
    Bryan 184
Deacon
    George 13
Deakins
    Thomas 182, 197
Deane
    William 81, 101,
        121
Deavor
    Richard 18, 19, 28
Deavour
    Gilbert 135, 148,

180, 213
Delahay
  Thomas 54
DelaVallee
  Anne 65
Demondidier
  Anthony 31
Den 25
Denny
  Peter 32
  Phillip 100
  Rachell 100
Dent
  John 61
  Thomas 13
Denton
  Henry 189
  James 57, 68
Dermott
  Edmond 17, 23
Derumple
  James 126
Devine
  Anne 65
  Daniell 65, 71
Dickenson
  Andrew 16, 182
  Walter 6
Dickson
  Andrew 10
  Levina 10
Digges
  Col. 109
  William 4, 36, 59,
    65, 92, 94, 105
Diggs
  Col. 27
  William 50, 132,
    133, 138
Dike
  Mary 31, 38, 165,
    183
  Mathew 115, 183
  William 36
Dillon
  Thomas 112, 180,
    183, 204
Divine
  Daniell 85
Dix
  Elisabeth 10
  Robert 10
Dixon
  Robert 189

Thomas 2, 146
Dobbs
  John 121, 143, 144,
    163, 165
Dobson
  (N) 128
  Samuel 128
  Samuell 103
Dockins
  Samuel 166, 204
  Symon 204
Dolbery
  William 92
Dolebery
  William 97
Done
  Elisabeth 142
Donn
  Obadiah 142, 160,
    161
Donnavan
  Cornelius 15
  Darby 19
Donnovan
  Darby 78
  Derby 15, 22, 48,
    67
Dorington
  Francis 50, 62
  Sarah 50, 62
Dorrill
  Nicholas 201
Dorrington
  Francis 182
Dorsey
  Eduard 8, 16, 27,
    30, 34, 39, 60,
    70
  Edward 119, 131
  James 129
  William 185
Dosey
  James 92
Dossett
  John 88, 91, 148,
    155, 163, 169,
    205
  William 164
Dossey
  James 89, 154
  John 82, 104, 164,
    185, 187
  William 82, 212
Doubty

Ann 177, 204
Doughty
  Ann 58, 59
  Anne 23
  John 34
Dove
  Robert 116, 163,
    181
Dow
  Robert 207
Downes
  James 50, 62, 160
  Sarah 50, 62, 160
Doxey
  Ann 123, 134, 137
  John 13, 85
  Thomas 2, 14, 17,
    21, 65, 68, 69,
    70, 71, 85, 123,
    130, 132, 137
Doyne
  Joshua 17, 77, 115,
    142, 147, 160,
    173, 194
  Robert 4, 7, 13,
    23, 31, 46, 53,
    95, 112, 114,
    115, 116, 117,
    119, 124, 125,
    127, 128, 135,
    149, 166, 167,
    168, 173, 201,
    204, 205
Drake
  William 49
Draper
  Laurence 39, 63,
    131
  Lawrence 119, 153,
    157, 173, 208
Drifeld
  Thomas 53
Dring
  John 135, 165, 196
Driskeld
  Thomas 37
Drury
  Charles 169
  Robert 84, 101
Dryfeild
  Thomas 191, 201
Dudley
  Richard 52
Due

Patrick 120
Dundasse
  George 12
Dundedell
  William 204
Dunderdell
  William 202
Dundoet
  George 77
Dunkin
  Jane 161
  Patrick 161
  William 155
Dunkins
  Jane 187
  Patrick 187
Dunston
  John 3
Dunstone
  John 11
Durbin
  Thomas 44
Durbine
  Thomas 56
Duvall
  Maren 82, 87, 91
  Murrain 151

Eades
  Robert 7
Eager
  George 86, 97, 191
  Mary 191, 194
Eagle
  Robert 175, 190
Ealmes
  William 36
Eareckson
  Elisabeth 39, 54,
    76
  Mathew 39
  Matthew 51, 73
Earle
  James 111, 149
  John 111, 149
  Rhoda 111, 149
Earos
  John 206
Eason
  John 203
Eaton
  Samuell 47, 59
Edelen

Page 231

Robert 99, 187
Sarah 101
Susan 99, 187
Thomas 84, 101
Evenden
Ellinor 63
Thomas 63, 179
Evendon
Ellinor 43
Thomas 43
Evens
Mary 74, 79
Thomas 74
William 57
Everax
Richard 10
Everd
William 154
Everett
Francis 95
Henry 167, 205
John 161
Mary 161
Everitt
Henry 15
Evett
Nathaniell 86
Evins
Walter 161
Evitt
Nathaniell 32
Evitts
Ellin 32
Ellinor 45
Nathaniell 45
Ewell
Thomas 202, 203,
   204
Exon
Henry 78

Faghey
John 78
Falkner
John 112
Faning
John 74
Fanning
Jane 100, 191
John 41, 49, 52,
   57, 72, 78, 79,
   85, 86, 100,
   191, 195

Far
John 75
Farding
William 100
Farewell
Richard 209
Fargason
William 187
Farwell
John 170
Fawson
William 72, 79
Fearson
Grace 30, 38
John 30, 38
Feild
Eduard 67
Edward 183, 204
John 71
Ferckleton
John 121
Fernandis
Peter 47
Fernely
Henry 162
Ferrabay
Thomas 163, 201
Fieckleton
John 144
Fields
John 91
Filkes
James 38
Finley
Thomas 63
Finney
William 196, 212
Finny
William 8, 74
Fishbourne
(N) 124
Ralph 110, 112,
   117, 119, 130,
   142, 145, 146,
   149
Fisher
Alexander 10
John 44, 76
Nathaniell 13
Sarah 37
William 37, 53,
   191, 201
Fishwick
Eduard 33, 49

Page 233

Edward 28, 30
Margarett 28, 30
Fletcher
    Edward 133, 135,
        141
    Robert 115
    Sarah 8
Flow
    Thomas 101
Floyd
    John 190
Foard
    Robert 97
Fooke
    Elisabeth 7
    Francis 7
Fooks
    Francis 195
Foord
    Thomas 107
Ford
    Alice 107
    Thomas 19, 22, 29,
        100
Foreman
    William 131
Forrest
    Patrick 13
Forth
    Elisabeth 155, 176
    John 155
Fosse
    John 56
Foster
    Christopher 143
    Ralfe 138
    Ralph 89, 96, 115,
        180
Foukes
    Francis 180
Fouler
    Joseph 11
Fowke
    Anne 66
    Elisabeth 66
    Gerrard 66
    Mary 66
Fowkes
    Francis 22, 25
Fowler
    Joseph 1, 2, 11
Francies
    Mary 174
    Thomas 174

Francis
    Mary 166
    Thomas 6, 37, 52,
        53, 71, 149,
        154, 156, 162,
        166, 174
Francize
    Thomas 70
Francklin
    Robert 8
Franckum
    Henry 22
Francum
    Henry 22, 27, 28
Franklin
    Robert 102
Frazier
    Elisabeth 92, 194
    Robert 194
Freborne
    Thomas 131
Freeborne
    Thomas 119
Freebourne
    Thomas 208
Freeman
    Francis 35, 42,
        107, 109, 140,
        154, 155, 164,
        174, 176, 183
    Hendrick 114
    Joseph 102, 118
    Mary 102, 118
    Mathias 114
    Richard 148
    William 208
Freene
    Joseph 174, 190
French
    James 93
Frisby
    Mr. 35
    William 34, 101,
        179
Fry
    Edward 133, 160,
        175, 198, 211
    Francis 211, 214
Fugate
    Peter 204
Fuller
    Edward 194
    Sarah 194
Furbey

Thomas 110
Furby
    Benjamin 170
    Hannah 51
    Thomas 51, 130
Furlong
    Edward 152, 170,
        173
Furnis
    Honor 116, 161, 162
    Honour 169
    William 116, 161,
        162, 169

Gaile
    Edward 143
    Ruth 143
Gale
    Edward 139
    Ruth 139
Gallwith
    John 5, 46, 48
Galwith
    John 184
Gamball
    William 182
Gandry
    Benjamin 64
Gant
    Tho. 31
    Thomas 30, 58, 184
Gardiner
    Christopher 63
    Elisabeth 31
    John 2, 31, 198
    Luck 2
    Luke 35, 38, 87,
        94, 183, 198
    Richard 1, 25, 35,
        38, 80, 95, 100,
        117, 122, 138,
        139, 141, 169,
        175, 184, 198,
        205
Gardner
    Alexander 4, 14, 23
    Mary 14
Garett
    Nathaniell 60
Garforth
    Richard 26, 31, 53,
        136, 175
Garland

Samuel 154, 174,
    190, 201
Garnish
    John 78
Garrate
    Sundea 168
Garratt
    Nathaniell 42
    Rutherane 168
Garrett
    Nathaniel 134, 197,
        201
    Nathaniell 4, 20,
        33, 49, 51, 55,
        81, 112, 113,
        114
Garrettson
    Garrett 211
Garworth
    Richard 115
Gary
    Clare 150, 172
    John 121
    Laurence 4
    Stephen 150, 172,
        187
Gaskell
    John 3, 11
Gassaway
    Nicholas 1, 6, 39,
        70, 71, 117,
        136, 161, 166,
        174
Gassell
    William 43
Gaunt
    Richard 21
    Thomas 83
Gearing
    Richard 157, 158,
        159
Gee
    John 90, 96, 180
Gellut
    Ambrose 48
Gent
    Elisabeth 112
George
    Benjamin 86, 98,
        104
    Benjamine 193
    Thomas 86, 98, 193
Gerrard
    Ann 208

Greenfield
  Thomas 137, 189
  Thomas Trueman 137
Greenwood
  James 123
  Jonas 32
Grey
  John 27, 37, 48,
    55, 143
  Mary 27, 37
  Richard 210
  widow 44
Griffin
  Thomas 13
Griffith
  Robert 11
  Samuel 122
  Samuell 109, 119
Griggs
  John 60, 108, 109,
    114, 118, 120,
    121, 122, 123,
    126, 127, 131,
    176, 186, 194
Grille
  (N) 77
Grover
  John 46
Grunwin
  Thomas 2, 22, 111,
    116, 127, 128,
    133, 137, 143,
    178
Gudgeon
  Robert 8
Guest
  Elisabeth 125
  George 125
Guibert
  Joshua 87, 90
Gundry
  Benjamin 21, 55
  Gideon 43, 82, 127
Gunter
  Timothy 142, 184
Gurlin
  Richard 79
Guybert
  Joshua 12, 77, 93,
    104
Guyther
  Owen 14, 15, 26,
    65, 71
Gwibert

Joshua 116
Gwin
  Richard 16
Gwinn
  John 116, 146
  Richard 31
  Sarah 116

Hacker
  Bridgett 196
  John 196, 212
Hackett
  Nicholas 96
  Theophilus 40, 44,
    45, 199
Haddock
  Thomas 123, 132,
    137
Hagley
  John 20, 49, 81,
    197
  Margarett 20, 33,
    51, 60, 81
Hales
  John 156
Haley
  Clement 36, 63
  Daniell 92
Hall
  Hannah 123, 144
  James 83, 123, 137,
    138, 144, 149,
    177
  Jasper 130
  John 55, 163, 203
  Mary 10, 15
  Patrick 10, 15, 20
  Richard 16
  Samuell 12, 69, 77
  Sarah 83, 138, 177
  Thomas 117, 122
Hallet
  Jacob 174
Hallett
  Jacob 157
Halliman
  James 85
Hambleton
  Elisabeth 46, 47
  Gawen 135, 140, 186
  Gawin 109
  John 46, 47, 90
Hamer

John 95
Hamersly
  Francis 119
Hamilton
  Elisabeth 53, 58, 59
  Gawin 213
  Gilbert 209
  John 53, 58, 59, 73, 178
Hammersley
  Francis 119
Hammond
  Daniell 56, 62, 72
  Ellinor 67
  John 64
Hamond
  Daniel 197
  Daniell 41, 67, 78, 182
  Ellioner 62
  John 46
Hampstead
  Nicholas 83
Hamstead
  William 6
Hance
  John 34, 42, 92, 121, 141
Hanlen
  Hugh 143, 171
Hansen
  Hance 133
Hanslap
  Henry 8, 39, 82, 87, 91, 151, 161, 190, 207
Hanslapp
  Capt. 176
  Henry 125
Hanslist
  Henry 174
Hanson
  Hance 128, 143, 160, 170, 177, 178, 179
  Hans 83
  John 66
Hardgrave
  Edward 126, 131
Hardin
  Elisabeth 154
  John 154
Harding

Elisabeth 113
John 22, 113, 164
Joseph 90, 103, 171
Hardish
  George 110
Hardy
  Henry 116, 132, 178
  Mary 178
Hargis
  Ann 145
  William 145
Hargiss
  William 160
Harlick
  Edward 135
Harman
  Henry 151
  Mary 151
Harmer
  Francis 24, 45
Harnes
  Jacob 153
Harness
  Jacob 39, 157, 173
Harniss
  Jacob 56, 63
Harper
  Grace 123
  James 112, 164
  John 123
  Thomas 150
Harris
  Ann 200
  Elisabeth 27, 48, 57, 58, 65, 67, 68, 85
  Henry 200
  Katherine 168
  Mary 128, 203, 213
  Moses 168
  Moyses 8
  Samuell 27
  Sarah 72, 195
  Simon 126
  Thomas 128, 169, 203, 206, 213
  William 35, 36, 41, 57, 58, 62, 64, 65, 67, 69, 72, 79, 83, 85, 98, 111, 125, 143, 170, 177, 179, 195, 200, 209, 210

Harrison
    Francis 115, 124,
        136
    Henry 9
    John 192
    Richard 114
    Sarah 9
Hartley
    John 71, 94
Hartly
    John 131
Hartwell
    John 41, 56, 62, 78
Haseldyne
    Abigall 103
    Richard 103
Haslewood
    John 21
Hasse
    Daniell 24
Hast
    Daniel 172, 207
    Daniell 79, 93
Hatch
    William 38
Hatche
    William 30
Hateraill
    Thomas 28
Hatersill
    Thomas 24
Hathan
    John 147
Hatton
    Elisabeth 5
    John 19
    Richard 193
    Samuell 5, 54
    Thomas 13
    William 3, 25, 28,
        29, 32, 36, 43,
        56, 61, 66, 69,
        76, 77, 78, 80,
        82, 84, 86, 87,
        89, 94, 98, 102,
        103, 108, 122,
        156, 158, 171,
        186, 193
Hattrill
    Thomas 177
Hausliste
    Jeremiah 157
Hawker
    Dorothy 139

Thomas 24, 139, 163
Hawkes
    Thomas 198
Hawkins
    Elisabeth 20, 36,
        167, 198
    Henry 20, 28, 36
    John 97, 108, 167,
        198
Hawknett
    John 122, 151
Hawton
    William 203
Hayburne
    John 33
Hayman
    Eleonor 213
    Elioner 168
    Henry 168, 213
    John 124
Haywood
    Raphael 138
Head
    Adam 87, 90, 93,
        97, 104, 184
    William 141
Healey
    (N) 129
Heard
    John 13, 95, 100,
        147, 192
Hearne
    Robert 170
Heath
    John 118
    Thomas 24, 31, 57,
        85
Heathcoat
    John 45
    Joseph 45
Heathcoate
    (N) 129, 151
    Elisabeth 39, 44,
        57, 176
    John 57, 58
    Nathaniell 46, 57,
        58, 176
Heathcott
    Daniell 11
    Elisabeth 5
    John 5
    Nathaniell 5
    Samuel 5
Heavernam

Thomas 29
Heberne
    James 21
Hedge
    Samuel 152
    Thomas 33, 138,
        152, 168
Heifernam
    William 40
Heley
    Clement 20, 54, 66
Helger
    Philip 76
Hely
    Clement 20, 92
    Daniell 94
Hemsely
    William 148
Hemsley
    Capt. 202
    Cornelia 148, 150,
        202
    Judith 127, 202
    William 5, 44, 46,
        61, 64, 68, 75,
        80, 92, 98, 102,
        105, 127, 148,
        150, 187, 202
Henderson
    George 88, 93, 182
Hendrickson
    Bartholomew 81, 197
Henley
    Robert 14, 19, 41,
        49, 57
Henly
    Robert 195
Henrickson
    Bartholomew 20, 33,
        51, 60
    Hendrick 20
    Margarett 20
    Matthew 20
Hensey
    William 110
Henson
    Richard 135
Hepworth
    John 13
Herbert
    John 49
    Mary 49
    William 49, 51
Herman

Augustine 42, 55,
    175
Casparus 175
Ephraim 55, 175
Francis 198
Henry 160, 172
Mary 172
Herne
    Robert 133
Herron
    William 132
Hess
    Timothy 17, 24
Hewes
    William 10
Hewson
    Richard 109, 122,
        180
    William 200
Hext
    Joseph 13
Heyborne
    James 43
Heybourne
    James 82
Heyden
    Mr. 126
Heyley
    Clement 7
Heyman
    Ellioner 188
    Henry 188
Hicks
    Thomas 84, 150
Hickson
    Henry 116
Higgen
    Mary 172
    Michael 172
Higgenbotham
    George 163, 164,
        201
Higgens
    Joseph 106
    Michael 207
Higgimbotom
    George 64
Higginbotham
    George 139
Higham
    Elisabeth 180, 195
    Francis 7, 14, 22,
        137, 147, 159,
        180, 207

Hungherford
William 19
Hunt
(N) 144
Elisabeth 175
John 24, 39, 49,
  55, 88, 89, 91,
  124, 142, 169,
  175
William 157, 159,
  166
Wolfran 53
Woolfan 52
Woolfran 6, 7, 37,
  128, 131
Hunter
Joan 161
Jone 143
Hunton
Mordecai 9, 25
Mr. 9
Timothy 16
Hurley
Dennis 15, 48, 67,
  194, 195
Hurlick
Edward 148
Hurlock
Edwan 173
Edward 89
Hurlong
Edward 200
Hurlow
Dennis 78
Hurly
Dennis 92
Hurst
John 174
Husbands
Mary 80, 86
William 38, 159,
  171, 184
Hussey
Thomas 110, 115
Hutchens
Francis 89, 92
Hutchins
Charles 83, 84, 150
Francis 8, 16, 25,
  26, 60, 106,
  107, 109, 113,
  134, 135, 140,
  148, 151, 164,
  166, 174, 180,

  208, 213
William 114
Hutchison
William 122
Hykes
Peter 36
Hyland
John 95, 167
Hynson
Charles 83, 143
John 33, 79, 83,
  97, 111, 143
Randall 43
Thomas 57
Hypkis
Peter 20

Iles
Richard 129, 135
Immins
George 74
Hester 74
Inglish
Eduard 41, 65, 71,
  81
Edward 20, 35, 43,
  114, 121, 139,
  162, 163, 170
Innes
Patrick 88, 92
William 104
Innis
Patrick 87, 97, 104
William 74, 103
Inyce
William 134, 153,
  166
Ireland
John 192
Mary 18, 25
William 18, 25, 42

Jackson
Ezekiell 27
James 147, 188
John 33, 51, 165,
  178
Richard 11, 43, 63,
  110, 141
Thomas 46, 48, 49,
  51
Jaman

Kimball
  Robert 42
Kindall
  John 76
King
  Dorothy 125, 155,
    159, 185, 186
  Jane 110, 133
  John 43, 63, 110,
    116, 134, 161,
    166, 211
  Richard 14
  Robert 148, 211
  William 194
Kingsland
  Anthony 89, 91, 159
  Lavina 91, 142,
    159, 185
  Levina 186
Kircum
  Alice 172
  William 172
Kirkby
  Ed. 5
Knighton
  Thomas 161, 167,
    205
Knott
  Franc. 38
  Francis 31, 35, 45,
    87, 90, 94, 206
Knowles
  Lawrence 199

Ladamore
  Eduard 51, 60
Ladd
  Capt. 1
  Richard 9, 14, 18,
    23, 25, 26, 35,
    42, 45, 60, 107,
    140, 151, 159,
    182, 188, 200
Laddamore
  Edward 196
Laddimore
  Edward 196
  Roger 196
Lamb
  Anthony 25, 26, 29
Lambden
  Robert 149
Lambert

John 173, 212
Lambeth
  John 163
Land
  Richard 169, 203
Lane
  John 52, 209
  Mary 209
  Maurice 102
  Morris 126
  Walter 170, 173,
    188, 206
Langley
  Joseph 60
Langworth
  William 31
Lanham
  Barbara 34
  Josias 34
Lanvin
  Ann 211
  Robert 211
Larance
  Phillip 171
Lardge
  Robert 68
Lardger
  Robert 68
Laremore
  Alexander 49
Large
  Robert 17, 69, 70
Larkin
  John 113, 125
Larramore
  Alexander 24
Lascalles
  Gervais 57
Lascell
  Gervais 31
Lascells
  Gervais 24
Lassells
  Gervais 85
Laughlin
  Anthony 95
Laurence
  Benjamin 48
  Henry 89
  William 11, 19, 24,
    73
Law
  John 148
  William 175

Lawes
 William 136
Lawrence
 Abigall 133
 Benjamine 115
 Henry 89, 103, 146
 John 133, 170
 Mr. 33
 William 143, 163,
  201
Lawthorp
 William 127
Leach
 John 75, 200
Lead
 Dennis 23
Leadford
 Arthur 181, 207
Leake
 Henry 129
 Richard 3
LeCompte
 Anthony 37, 40, 43,
  58, 61, 69, 71,
  77
Ledgett
 Julian 93
 Thomas 93
Lee
 Eduard 49
 Robert 152
 Samuel 186
 Thomas 123
Leech
 John 58, 135, 148,
  173
Leedgett
 Thomas 140
Leeds
 William 43
Lees
 Thomas 137
Legg
 William 143, 165
LeMaire
 John 33, 37, 47,
  143
 Margarett 33
Lemaister
 Abraham 185
Lesson
 James 160
Lessong
 James 160

Letherland
 Robert 101
Lewis
 Elisabeth 9
 Henry 9, 20, 23,
  29, 51, 64
 John 169, 198, 212
 Richard 118, 170
 Thomas 110, 113,
  143, 171, 199
 William 9, 20, 23,
  29, 51, 165
Lile
 William 119
Lingam
 George 60
Lingan
 George 90, 99, 106,
  109, 119, 120,
  122, 125, 133,
  135, 140, 154,
  186, 213
 Paul 140
Lingham
 George 10, 16, 58,
  75
Linsey
 Katherine 4, 49, 66
 Thomas 66, 197
Lisson
 James 143
Little
 John 106
 Pheby 106
Littlepage
 James 23, 66, 178
Llewellin
 John 4, 128, 156,
  157, 178
Lloyd
 Col. 130
 Henrietta Maria
  116, 184
 Howell 42
 Phil. 6
 Philemon 5, 10, 52,
  53, 64, 74, 76,
  92, 103, 108,
  110, 111, 116,
  152, 161
 Phillimon 184
 Richard 2
Loade
 Dennes 17

Lockwood
  Richard 52
  Robert 44, 190
Loftis
  Phebe 54
Loggin
  Eleanor 123
  John 123
Loggins
  Elioner 131
  John 131
Loghlin
  Anthony 100
Lomax
  Cleborne 23, 47,
    49, 110, 115
Long
  Lucie 103
  Mary 153, 202, 203,
    206
  Thomas 2, 3, 42,
    48, 59, 103,
    153, 162, 203
Longman
  Daniel 154, 156,
    174, 190
Lookeman
  Jacob 151
Lookerman
  Jacob 187
Lookrman
  Jacob 154, 160, 171
Looton
  Jacob 38
Louday
  John 63
Loughlin
  Anthony 147
Louglin
  Daniel 192
Love
  Diana 117
  Robert 68, 196
  Thomas 117
  William 28
Lovelace
  Francis 44, 56
Low
  Robert 24, 31
  Vincent 167
Lowder
  Richard 10, 11, 24,
    81, 200
Lowe

  Vincent 32, 115,
    116, 152, 161,
    200
Luckett
  Samuel 198
Ludford
  Arthur 91
Luff
  Sarah 4
  Stephen 4
Luffe
  Sarah 14, 121, 210
  Stephen 1, 14, 20,
    23, 66, 73, 93,
    121, 124, 126,
    170, 210
Luffman
  Mary 134
  William 126, 134
Lun
  Thomas 22
Lunn
  Thomas 29
Lurkey
  Thomas 211
Lurky
  Thomas 76
Lyle
  William 109, 135,
    180
Lyles
  William 125, 135
Lynand
  John 151
Lyne
  Philip 39
Lynes
  Philip 22, 75, 76
  Phillip 85, 102,
    108, 111, 132
Lynham
  John 129

Macaal
  George 69
Macaall
  George 45, 77
  James 28
  Jane 77
Macall
  Ann 156
  George 156, 158,
    171

James 123, 131,
140, 155, 156
Maccubin
John 209
Mackaall
Anne 12
George 11, 12, 13,
18
Hanna 12
Jane 12, 13
Sarah 12
Mackatrick
John 169
MackDaniel
Cato 143, 171
Mackdowell
Henry 90
Mackeall
George 37
Mackel
John 151, 160
Mackensie
Collin 184
Colline 11, 61
Mackensye
Colline 1, 2
Macketrick
John 213
Mackewen
James 111
Mackglavin
James 14
Mackite
John 169
Mackitrick
John 150
Mackitt
John 150
Mackubin
John 166
Macuben
Elioner 166
John 166
Macubin
Ellioner 190
John 190
Maddock
Eduard 15, 22, 27,
38, 66, 81
Edward 28
Hanna 22
Maddocks
Samuell 19, 115
Maddox

(N) 138
John 167
Jonas 176
Samuel 89, 90
Samuell 22, 26, 96,
180
Maggison
Jane 106
John 106
Magruther
James 125, 137
John 125
Makele
John 172
Makin
Mr. 138
Makitrick
John 118
Makitt
John 118
Mallice
Richard 126
Man
Eduard 4, 6, 54,
75, 79
Edw. 83
Edward 96, 98, 99,
100, 101, 187
Manfeild
James 161
Manlove
William 150
Mann
Edward 115, 121,
130, 145, 151,
153, 158, 164,
172, 178, 187,
203, 204, 206
Mannewry
William 134
Manning
Cornelius 13, 15
Hugh 13, 14, 15
John 45, 109
Manroe
Parson 21
Mansell
Benjamin 54
Vincent 27
Mansfeild
Vincent 61
William 210
Mantle
John 106

Page 250

Newes
    Robert 200
Newfinger
    Judith 81
    William 81
Newhouse
    Gabriel 5
Newman
    George 15, 19, 30,
      139, 181, 197
    Henry 75
    John 115, 130, 165,
      181, 190, 191,
      199
    Lydia 15
    Richard 193
    Roger 97
Newton
    John 13
Nicholson
    Nicholas 52, 140,
      154, 161, 174,
      201
Noble
    Anthony 165
    Cornelia 53, 148
    Isaac 173, 199
    Robert 53, 64, 105,
      148, 150, 202,
      203
    William 152, 170,
      173, 188, 206
Norman
    Anne 35
    Daniell 122
Norris
    Daniel 143, 146,
      160, 164, 171,
      197, 198, 201,
      210
    Daniell 20
    Robert 122
    Thomas 20, 31, 198
Norwood
    Andrew 119
    Anne 72, 96
    Anthony 72
    Arthur 52, 96
    Joseph 157, 190
Notley
    Governor 101
Nottingham
    Thomas 56
Nowell

    William 27, 35
Nuthall
    James 116, 123, 163
    John 94, 116
    Margaret 116
    Margarett 116
Nuttwell
    (N) 120

O'Deary
    William 27
O'Maly
    Bryan 100
Oard
    Peter 137
Offley
    John 11, 44, 107,
      202
Offly
    John 123, 147, 202,
      205
    Mabell 123, 202,
      205
Oldfeild
    George 57, 62, 78,
      175, 211, 214
Oldfield
    George 95
Olivant
    William 25
Oliver
    John 61
Olwant
    William 18
Orlon
    Henry 159
Oroke
    James 52
Osborne
    John 61, 74, 103
    Thomas 54, 74, 106,
      125
    William 3
Osbourne
    Thomas 39
    William 212
Ottidge
    John 195
Owen
    John 42

Padley

Morgan 113
Pennington
    James 6
    Thomas 157, 174
    William 44, 48,
        174, 175, 190
Penroy
    Morgan 154
Penry
    Morgan 154
Perfett
    William 159
Person
    Thomas 45
Persons
    Thomas 54, 63
Persutia Island 138
Peterkin
    James 81, 213
Peters
    Amy 53, 63
    Margarett 129
    Mathias 129
Peterson
    Andrew 4, 50, 112,
        134, 201
    Christian 134, 201
    Margarett 99
    Margrett 199, 202
    Mathias 199, 202,
        203, 204, 206
    Mathyes 99
Pethen
    Christian 183
    Thomas 183
Pethens
    Christian 206
    Thomas 206
Pether
    Richard 3
Phelps
    Walter 29, 38, 82,
        123, 135, 165,
        207
Phenix
    (N) 18
    George 12, 13
Phidemon
    Richard 40
Phidemond
    Richard 63
Philemurphy
    Cornett 78
Philips

Henry 67, 71
James 24, 29, 31
Phillips
    Daniel 122, 180
    Daniell 109
    Henry 62
    James 2, 9, 11, 58,
        83, 113, 138,
        168, 186, 197
    Robert 190
    Walter 151, 187
Phillis
    John 136
Phipps
    Henry 13
Phoenix
    George 38
Piggott
    Bartholomew 87, 88,
        97, 98
Pile
    George 12
    Jos. 137
    Joseph 31, 35, 63,
        78, 87, 88, 92,
        97, 134, 146,
        147, 158, 160,
        176
Piles
    Joseph 7, 15, 54,
        61, 109, 208
    Joshua 81
Pilesworth
    Samuel 177, 198
Pindar
    Eduard 10
    Edward 84, 92, 97,
        150, 161, 172,
        187
Pine
    Charles 57, 68
Piner
    John 160
    Thomas 133, 210
Pinke
    Sarah 15
Pinkney
    Christopher 205
Pinkny
    Christopher 187
Pinner
    Mary 114
    Richard 114, 183
    William 183

Pitts
  William 13
Platt
  William 37
Play
  Eduard 33, 60
Plott
  Elisabeth 56
Poell
  Thomas 10
Pointer
  Thomas 74
Pollard
  John 154, 187
  Mary 182
  Richard 39, 55, 182
Poore
  John 190
Poosey
  John 111
Pope
  John 72, 85, 193
Poper
  John 86
Porter
  John 143, 177, 195
  William 3, 19
Pote
  John 86
Potter
  Elisabeth 2
Powell
  Charles 106
  George 105, 117,
    122, 180, 192
  John 139
  Julian 139
  Richard 99, 199
  Sarah 105, 117
  William 99, 199
Power
  John 40, 63, 83,
    130, 149
Powlter
  Henry 88
Poynter
  John 213
Pratt
  Thomas 7, 207
Preistly
  Benjamin 127, 172,
    185, 187
Preston
  James 159

Samuel 155
Thomas 167, 212
Price
  Andrew 102
  Francis 190
  John 26
  Judith 24, 49
  Richard 167
  Roger 24, 49
  Thomas 13, 101,
    111, 118, 145,
    158, 186
  William 49
Priest
  Charles 68, 84
  Sarah 68, 70, 84
Priestly
  Benjamin 82, 98,
    104, 112, 150,
    161
Probart
  John 135, 139
Probat
  John 129
Probert
  John 172
Proctor
  Elisabeth 131
Profitt
  Thomas 169
Prouse
  John 149
Puker
  William 42
Pullen
  Richard 21, 24, 36,
    64, 136, 139,
    163, 164, 198
Purnell
  John 126
  Thomas 127, 155,
    157, 159
Pursell
  John 184, 212
Pye
  Eduard 29
Pyle
  Joseph 20
Pyles
  Joseph 19
Pyne
  Charles 103

Page 257

Quigley
  John 179
Quillaine
  (N) 74
  Daniel 191
  Daniell 74, 103
  Lidia 103
  Lydia 191
Quinton
  Walter 6

Rackliffe
  Charles 74
Racliffe
  Charles 104
Rainger
  Samuel 161
Randall
  Anne 14
  Benjamin 14, 151,
    167
  Christopher 90, 96,
    194
  Johanna 96
  Johannah 90, 194
  Robert 136
  Samuell 124
Raspin
  Samuell 22, 36, 48,
    50
Ratcliffe
  Charles 104
Reade
  George 16
Reader
  Symon 112, 191
  Vertue 112, 191
Recant
  Joseph 2
Rede
  John 106
Redman
  John 98
Redmond
  John 84, 98
Reed
  George 146, 171,
    209
  John 192
  Mathew 160
  Matthew 98
  Nathaniel 129, 202,
    204

Nathaniell 201, 203
Richard 195
Robert 25, 180
Reede
  Abraham 66, 70
  Robert 14
Reeves
  Eduard 65, 67
  Thomas 90, 96
Relph
  Thomas 207
Rennolds
  Providence 8
Renolds
  Providence 50
  Sarah 94, 155
Reswick
  (N) 124
  John 118, 120, 123,
    131, 142, 192
  Margaret 118
Revell
  Randall 211
Reves
  Thomas 90
Reycroft
  John 49
Reynold
  Sarah 152
Reynolds
  Sarah 193
Rhoades
  Abraham 111, 186
Rhodes
  Abraham 86, 108,
    118, 122
Ricaud
  Benjamin 97, 198
  Elisabeth 97, 198
Richards
  Ann 146
  Lavina 185
  Levina 186
  Oliver 139, 141,
    144, 146
  William 46, 142,
    186, 187
Richardson
  John 187
  Marke 138
  Robert 11, 61
  Susan 187
  Susanna 11
  Thomas 68

Round
    James 136, 170, 188
Rousby
    Barbera 142
    Christopher 103
    John 11, 24, 66,
        142, 150
Rowland
    Grace 20
    Laurence 20
Royston
    Richard 40, 63, 104
Roystone
    Richard 119, 131,
        179, 206, 209
Rumball
    Anthony 104, 105
Rumsey
    James 78, 117, 121,
        122, 192, 195
    John 71
    Thoes 196
    Thomas 20, 33, 51,
        112
Russell
    Eduard 61
    Elisabeth 67
    John 89, 94
Rutter
    John 128, 153, 157
Rycroft
    John 13, 145
Ryder
    Henry 13

Saddler
    Henry 5, 10
Sadler 25
    Joseph 97, 165
    Robert 43, 63
Salisbury
    John 18, 27, 35,
        213
    Mary 64
    William 18, 19, 27
Samson
    Richard 44, 56
Samuell
    John 23
Sanclet
    Christopher 185
Sanders
    James 166, 174

Robert 60, 76
Sanderson
    Ambrose 1, 46
Saunders
    Joseph 177
    Mathew 165
Sawell
    John 5
Sawyer
    Peter 6, 61
Sayer
    Peter 46, 64, 75,
        116, 150, 162,
        184
Scarborough
    Mathew 211
    Matthew 74
Scarbrough
    Mathew 104
    Matt. 104
Scaroe
    George 21
Scarve
    George 8
    Mary 8
Scott
    Cuthbert 51, 55,
        56, 70, 87, 93,
        104, 132, 144
    Elisabeth 152
    James 176, 185
    John 3, 123, 131,
        140, 155, 156,
        178
    Samuel 189
    Samuell 152
    William 170
Scudamore
    Anne 17
    Nicholas 17
    Thomas 186
Sealy
    George 121, 149
    Mary 121
Searles
    John 81
Seath
    Jacob 71
Seaward
    Jonathon 150, 151
    Josias 118
    Thomas 107, 110,
        113, 114, 199
Sedwick

James 80
Seeme
    Marmaduck 77
Seems
    Marmaduck 12
    Marmaduke 86
Seissons
    Edward 209
Selby
    William 52, 71,
      140, 143, 171
Semm
    Marmaduke 122
Semme
    Marmaduke 77, 178
Semms
    Marmaduck 80
Sergeant
    Joseph 213
    Rebeccah 213
    Seth 102, 111
Serjeant
    John 64
    Joseph 126, 147
    Rebecca 126
Seth
    Jacob 94, 131
Sewall
    James 162
    John 156
    Nicholas 66, 70,
      94, 97, 118,
      131, 139, 149,
      157, 158
Seward
    Thomas 79, 179
Sewell
    Nicholas 4
Sewick
    William 91, 92, 106
Shanke
    Abigall 94
    John 94
Shankes
    John 61, 75, 87,
      191
    Mary 191, 206
Shanks
    Abigall 141
    Elisabeth 138
    John 88, 89, 138,
      141
Sharpe
    William 75, 153

Shaw
    John 196
    Mary 196
Shearly
    William 112
Shelton
    Ann 179
    John 179
    Thomas 51, 60, 196
Shepard
    Nicholas 70
Sheppard
    Francis 40, 44
Shercliffe
    William 30, 38, 206
Shertcliffe
    William 28, 32, 33,
      37, 45, 48, 103,
      171
Sherwood
    Hugh 83, 149
Shipley
    Adam 8, 60, 70
Shirtcliffe
    William 90
Shortley
    William 37
Shrigley
    John 5, 26
Sickes
    John 82
Sides
    Peter 201, 203, 212
Sigsworth
    Thomas 100
Sike
    Eduard 26
Sikes
    John 94
Silly
    Mathew 7
Simmons
    Rebeccah 184
Simms
    Samuel 207
Simonds
    Thomas 13
Simons
    Henry 9
    Rebeccah 184
    Robert 13
Simpers
    Thomas 7
Simpson

Jeremiah 107, 176,
194
Thomas 78, 128,
185, 195
Sims
Marmaduke 108
Richard 83
Sinckler
William 210
Size
Eduard 13, 14, 15
Edward 184
Skelton
Israell 57, 113,
126
John 192
Thomas 3, 4, 19
Skidemore
Edward 170
Michael 154
Thomas 170
Skidmore
Anne 68, 69, 70
Edward 100, 162
Nicholas 68, 69, 70
Skinner
Robert 211
Skipper
John 107, 138, 141
Skippers
John 90
Skipwith
(N) 190
Elisabeth 41
George 41, 62
Skudamore
(N) 21
Slade
William 147, 188
Sloper
Thomas 95
Sly
Gerard 142
Slye
Gerard 21, 194
Gerrard 13, 17, 22,
61, 69, 144
Smith
Abraham 34, 35, 64
Alen 190
Alexander 21
Alice 135
Allen 127, 157,
195, 200, 205

Capt. 13
Charles 85
Daniel 89
Daniell 13, 102
Dorothy 140
Elisabeth 169
Ellinor 86
Henry 1, 9, 14, 17,
21, 68, 69, 70,
79, 108
James 100
John 41, 71, 85,
89, 96, 105,
140, 161, 171,
172, 207
Margarett 70, 71
Marke 142, 184
Mary 35, 98
Nathan 70, 71, 181
Ralph 15, 19, 30,
213
Richard 2, 9, 22
Robert 46, 64, 99,
107, 110, 111,
113, 114, 124,
126, 129, 147,
169, 175, 199,
202, 203, 204,
206
Thomas 86, 98, 130,
135, 140
Walter 119, 131,
208
William 29, 30, 46,
53, 169, 175
Smithson
Thomas 97, 115, 116
William 39, 75, 132
Smock
John 188
Smoot
Edward 180
Smoote
Edward 90, 96, 115
Smoothe
Eduard 19
Snowden
John 138, 141
Sollars
John 5, 26
Soller
John 106
Sollers
John 91, 92

Sone
  Joseph 101
Soulsby
  Eduard 5
Southarne
  Valentine 54
Southerne
  Richard 184, 189
Sowerton
  Francis 13
Sparke
  William 124, 147
Sparkes
  William 124, 202
Sparnon
  Alice 41, 57
  Joseph 41, 42
Speak
  John 175
  Winifred 175
Speake
  (N) 117
Spencer
  John 10, 15, 20
Spernon
  Joseph 3, 57, 200
Spicer
  Elioner 179
Spickernell
  Robert 18, 42
Spink
  Henry 89
Spinke
  Henry 55, 90, 103
  Thomas 13, 69, 77,
    82, 101, 133,
    145, 184, 185
Sprigg
  Nathaniell 94
Squire
  Jonathon 87
Squires
  Jonathon 13, 102,
    107
St. George
  Anne 14
Stacey
  Symon 60
Stacy
  Simon 46
  Symon 64, 77
Stagg
  Margaret 192
  Margarett 93

Staires
  Bennett 11
Standley
  Robert 52
  Robt. 68
Standlye
  Robert 71
Stanely
  John 153
  Robert 192
Stanesby
  (N) 53
  John 16, 33
  Mary 16, 33, 55
  widow 33, 53
Stanley
  (N) 77
  John 54
Stannaway
  Joseph 80
Stansby
  John 2, 55
  Mary 2
Stanton
  Blanch 191
  William 191, 194
Stapells
  Henry 34
Stapleford
  Mr. 21
Staples
  Henry 197
Starling
  Thomas 41, 62, 94,
    178
Sted
  Thomas 176
Steed
  Thomas 125
Steevens
  Giles 4
  Richard 50
  William 74
Stephens
  Charles 8
  John 126
Stephenson
  William 32
Sterling
  Christian 109
  Thomas 89, 109, 154
Stevens
  Edward 102, 118,
    124, 173, 188,

William 189, 209
Traine
James 211
Magdalen 211
Traverse
William 86, 147
Treaveale
William 14
Treveale
William 134
Treveil
William 23
Trevele
William 126
Trevile
William 5
Triggs
Richard 114
Tripp
Henry 75
True
Richard 116
William 144, 160
Trueman
Elisabeth 137, 189
Henry 71, 122
John 172, 207
Mary 137, 184, 189
Thomas 79, 83, 117,
122, 137, 141,
189, 193
Truman
Henry 91, 108
Thomas 83, 93, 105,
106
William 83
Tucker
Florence 102, 118,
173, 188
Nathaniel 160
Nathaniell 99
Sarah 58, 76
Thomas 58, 76, 188,
194
Turberfeild
Gilbert 133, 145,
185
Turberfield
Gilbert 185
Turberville
Gilbert 82, 101
Turbutt
Michael 200
Turin

East. 63
Eust. 50, 62
Eustachius 3, 50
Turke
William 105
Turner
Abraham 30
Anna 164
Arthur 38, 41, 180
Charles 164, 197
Edward 26, 90, 96,
128, 185, 195
Elioner 181
James 30, 38, 41,
50, 176, 180
John 114, 181
William 89, 92,
129, 148, 154,
186
Turpin
John 192
Turvile
William 13, 169
Twiney
John 81
Mary 81
Tydings
Richard 136, 161
Tyer
James 14, 19, 36,
37, 41, 60, 85,
105, 127, 132,
191
Rebeccah 199
Tylden
Charles 112
Tyllyard
John 196
Sarah 196
Tyre
James 48, 49, 199

Underwood
(N) 127
Anthony 57, 58, 61,
69, 77, 84, 95,
124, 137, 184,
190, 210
Utie
John 138
Nathaniel 138
Uty
George 138, 144,

Page 267

Walton
    John 118, 150, 151
    William 61
Waman
    Leonard 38
Wamsley
    Martha 95
    Thomas 95
Wamsly
    Martha 211
    Thomas 211
Wansey
    Shary 101
Warcup
    Frances 190
    Samuell 156, 190
Ward
    Anna Margaretta 42,
        55
    Edward 133, 145
    Henry 3, 4, 19, 36,
        42, 55, 126, 176
    John 29, 30, 38, 81
    Katherine 133
    Mary 111
    Mathew 13
    Mr. 13
    Robert 136, 143,
        161
    William 20, 22, 33,
        51, 111, 134,
        178, 197, 201
Warder
    William 85
Wareing
    Basil 152
    Basill 155
Warford
    Simon 11, 19, 24
Waring
    Basill 42, 140
    Thomas 26
Warner
    George 60, 76, 113,
        127, 154
    John 151
    Samuel 182
    Sarah 182
Warren
    Augustine 88, 93,
        182
    Basill 7, 121
    Capt. 203
    Elisabeth 101

Hum. 74
Humphrey 14, 15,
    19, 30, 38, 41,
    52, 59, 68, 72,
    78, 85, 169
Humphry 50, 206,
    208
Ignatius 67, 93,
    182
John 13, 93, 182
Richard 118, 170,
    213
Thomas 33, 81, 86,
    101, 139, 141
Warrin
    Thomas 14
Warring
    Bazil 107
    Thomas 141
Waters
    Alexander 106, 125
    Edward 83
    John 43, 45, 207
Waterton
    John 111, 153
Wathen
    John 134, 185
Watkins
    Edward 185
    Francis 48
    James 133, 145, 185
    John 6
    Thomas 58, 96
Watmore
    John 189
Watson
    Jane 12, 77, 156
    John 11, 12, 13,
        77, 156, 178
Wattertone
    John 167
Wattkins
    John 52
Watts
    Alice 108, 120
    Charles 61
    Eduard 61
    Emma 61
    Francis 136, 161
    George 153, 158
    Peter 28, 37, 66
    Sarah 136
    William 61, 75,
        108, 120, 122,

182

Wattson
  Jane 18
  John 18, 28, 46,
    69, 77, 80
Waughob
  Archibald 47, 59
  Thomas 158, 186
Waughop
  Thomas 69, 76, 77
Way
  Richard 112
Wayman
  Leonard 29
  Rice 124
Weatherly
  Samuell 113
Webb
  Edmond 130, 190
  Jane 39, 55
  Robert 39, 55
  William 130
Weeks
  Anna 167
  Joseph 14, 125, 167
Welch
  (N) 77
  John 34, 191
  William 136, 162
Wellington
  Richard 186
Wellman
  Mary 201
Wells
  George 2, 16, 17,
    26, 44, 62, 76,
    84, 95, 163,
    166, 167, 193,
    197, 203, 204,
    209, 212
Welsh
  John 5, 6, 7, 18,
    24, 26, 28, 29,
    39, 48, 72, 150,
    151
  Mary 39, 72
Wenman
  Mary 173, 204, 212
West
  Henry 152, 155, 177
  Joana 53
  Joane 33, 60, 76
  John 20, 33, 53,
    60, 76

Symon 169
  William 128
Wetherill
  Joan 154
  Samuel 154
Whahob
  John 12
Whealas
  Da. 5
Wheatherly
  Samuel 154
Wheeler
  (N) 124
  James 87, 168
  John 82, 113, 119,
    124, 135, 139,
    151, 168, 172
  Katherine 87
  Samuel 145, 146,
    197, 200, 203,
    212
  Samuell 3, 42, 55,
    108, 112, 117,
    119, 120, 142,
    145, 176
  Thomas 139
Whipps
  John 135
Whitchaly
  Thomas 191, 195
White
  Gustavus 80, 175,
    177, 194
  John 100, 118, 152,
    154, 170, 213
  Mary 8, 21
  Phillis 175, 194
  Richard 153, 202,
    206
  Sarah 118, 152
  William 113
Whitting
  John 203
Whittington
  Andrew 116
  Capt. 189
  John 131, 158
  William 89, 91
Whitton
  Richard 95
Whitty
  Richard 9, 23
Wicke
  Anna 151

Wiseman
    John 118, 130, 131,
       139
Witchcott
    Benjamin 22
Wolfe
    Mary 124
Wood
    Frances 122
    John 83, 95, 108,
      116, 168, 172,
      213
    Richard 213
    Robert 120
    William 111, 114,
      122, 171
Woodcocke
    William 35, 38, 45
Woodnutt
    Laurence 185
Woods
    William 199
Woodward
    John 83, 134, 147,
      212
    Mr. 187
Woolfe
    Joseph 124
Woolford
    Roger 1, 2, 9, 210
Woolverston
    Walter 171
Woolverstone
    Walter 89, 103,
      156, 158, 182
Wooten
    Symon 106, 176
Wooton
    Symon 156, 162
Worall
    Margarett 41
    Robert 41
Workman
    Anthony 72, 74, 127
Worland
    John 85
Worrall
    John 78
    Robert 206
Worrell
    Margarett 37
    Robert 37
Wrath
    James 127

Wright
    Arthur 21
    John 4, 112, 212
    Mary 84
    Solomon 122, 210
    Thomas 173, 194,
      208
    William 7, 82, 83,
      84, 98, 104,
      165, 182
Wyatt
    Thomas 95
Wyne
    Francis 20, 36
    John 77
Wynn
    John 89
Wynne
    Anne 102
    John 82, 94, 102
    Thomas 111, 118
Wyseman
    John 97

Yanton
    Timothy 26
Yate
    George 136, 156
    John 206
Yeare
    James 65
Yeeden
    George 138, 141
Yeo
    John 48, 65, 67,
      138, 168, 211
Yieldhall
    Jane 70
    Katherine 60
    William 60, 70
Yore
    James 71
Yorke
    William 2, 16, 33,
      153, 163, 167,
      203, 212
Youl
    Thomas 201
Young
    Anne 38
    Elisabeth 117
    George 140
    John 155

Laurence 85
Theodorus 117
William 126, 202,
  204

Index to Equity Cases

Phillips vs. Harris 58
Pye vs. estate of Hodgeson 29

Rice vs. Maddock 22
Richards vs. Marshall 141, 144, 146
Rosewell vs. estate of Bourne 79

Scott vs. Thompson 144
Sheppard vs. estate of Johnson 40
Skidmore vs. Smith & Doxey 68, 69, 70
Slye vs. Carvile 22
Southerne & Brightwell vs. estate of Trueman 189

Thomas vs. estate of Thomas 141

Uty vs. Johnson 144

Wattson vs. Graham 18, 69
Wheeler vs. Fishbourne 124, 142, 145
Williams vs. Maddock 28

www.ingramcontent.com/pod-product-compliance
Lightning Source LLC
Chambersburg PA
CBHW061005280326
41935CB00009B/838